The Tillamook
A Created Forest Comes of Age

Second Edition

The Tillamook
A Created Forest Comes of Age

SECOND EDITION

by Gail Wells

Oregon State University Press
Corvallis

For Daddy, who would be proud

The paper in this book meets the guidelines for permanence and durability of the Committee on Production Guidelines for Book Longevity of the Council on Library Resources and the minimum requirements of the American National Standard for Permanence of Paper for Printed Library Materials Z39.48-1984.

Library of Congress Cataloging-in-Publication Data
Wells, Gail, 1952-
   The Tillamook : a created forest comes of age / by Gail Wells.
     p. cm. — (Culture and environment in the Pacific West)
   Includes bibliographic references (p.) and index.
ISBN 0-87071-006-0 (alk. paper)
1. Tillamook State Forest (Or.)—History. 2. Tillamook State Forest (Or.)—Management—History. 3. Forest fires—Oregon—Tillamook State Forest—History. 4. Reforestation—Oregon—Tillamook State Forest—History. I. Title. II. Series.
SD428.A2075 1999
333.75'15'097954—dc21   98-31993
                                                  CIP

Oregon State University Press
101 Waldo Hall
Corvallis OR 97331-6407
541-737-3166 •fax 541-737-3170
http://oregonstate.edu/dept/press

OREGON STATE
UNIVERSITY

Contents

Acknowledgements vi
Series Editor's Preface vii
Art acknowledgements viii

Introduction 1

1. The Legend 7

2. Timber Forever 19

3. Tillamook Legend and Frontier Culture 37

4. The Legend-spinners 56

5. Field Trip: Mark Labhart
"I just call it a win-win" 69

6. Field Trip: Bill Emmingham
Creating Biodiversity 94

7. The Search for Sustainability 109

8. Field Trip: Sybil Ackerman
Saving the Tillamook Forest 125

9. Field Trip: Ric Balfour
Taming the Wild West 144

10. A Walk Up Gales Creek Canyon 154

Epilogue to the Second Edition 175
References 180
Index 186

Acknowledgements

I am grateful, first of all, to the many scholars who took the time to share their work with me in lay person's terms. I knew I was approaching this task as a non-biologist, non-ecologist, non-forester, and non-historian who needed to draw heavily on these disciplines to provide a credible intellectual foundation for this book. I am particularly grateful to those here at the Oregon State University College of Forestry who have served as teachers, mentors, idea-bouncers, and friendly critics. I will single out George Brown, Steve Daniels, Bill Emmingham, John Hayes, Dave Hibbs, Steve Hobbs, Royal Jackson, Mike Newton, Steve Radosevich, Bruce Shindler, and John Tappeiner for special mention, but there are many others who have also edified me.

Thanks to Paul Farber and Bill Robbins of the OSU Department of History, and Chris Anderson and Simon Johnson of the Department of English, for their cogent comments on early drafts of the manuscript and their ongoing encouragement. I am very grateful to Bill Lang, of the Portland State University Department of History, who steered me toward sources I didn't know about and helped me strengthen the historical context of the Tillamook's story.

My deepest appreciation to those in the Oregon Department of Forestry who answered my many questions in courteous and thoughtful detail, especially Ric Balfour, Doug Decker, Ross Holloway, Mark Labhart, Mike Schnee, and Lou Torres. Thanks also to Larry Fick, Peg Foster, and George Martin for helping me track down some of the department's historic photos. Also, I owe a debt of gratitude to members of the environmentalist/conservation community, especially Sybil Ackerman, Rick Brown, and Jenny Holmes, for articulating their vision so clearly for me.

Needless to say, none of these people is to be blamed for any errors of fact, logic, or interpretation that may have crept in—these are on my shoulders alone.

I owe an enormous debt to members of my writing group. They stuck with me through my early struggles with this idea, listening patiently to my fuzzy and contradictory notions about what I was trying to do, and they helped me think it through, develop the themes, strengthen the logic, and lighten my customary pedantry. Thank you, my friends: Marion McNamara, Kathy Moore, David Platt, and Steve Radosevich.

Finally, to John, Gavin, and Mary, who now know more about the Tillamook Forest than they ever bargained for, my heartfelt thanks and my best love. You know all the reasons why.

Gail Wells, August 1998

Series Editor's Preface

DISCUSSIONS ABOUT THE FATE of five-hundred-year-old trees have been commonplace in the political arena for more than two decades in the forested regions of the Pacific West. Since the listing of the Northern Spotted Owl as an endangered species, many concerned citizens have demanded preservation of the ancient forests because of the biological resource they represent and the incalculable value they hold for humans. Environmentalists have rarely argued as passionately or intelligently for younger forests—those that have been harvested and harvested again. Old-growth trees that are four or more feet across make second-growth trees look spindly and the environments the smaller trees inhabit look nothing like our image of forest primeval. Some question whether a planted, tended, sprayed, thinned, and largely managed stand of trees can be called a forest at all.

In *The Tillamook*, Gail Wells takes up the question and cause of a younger forest. She takes us deeply into one of the Pacific West's most famous managed forests. Ravaged by twentieth-century wildfires that came every six years between 1933 and 1951, the Tillamook forest endured a devastating ecological shock and timber-dependent communities suffered crippling economic blows. Some six decades after the first of the infernos struck, a new stand of trees covers the hills of the Tillamook, the work of small armies of tree-planters and the nurture of professional foresters. This new forest is a manipulated place, what some environmental scholars call "second nature," as contrasted to a nature that is little disturbed by humans.

In this personal exploration of the meeting ground of ecological science, environmental protection, and timber economy, Wells asks the vexing question: what should be done with the new Tillamook forest? Should it be cut for merchantable timber? Should it be preserved as a memorial to the horrendous conflagrations and the phoenix-like renewal? What is the highest social use of this new forest?

The Tillamook explores these questions through analysis of the roles forests play in our imaginations and our economics. The author begins by reminding readers that nature is both ecological reality and social construct, that humans make decisions about how nature is used according to myths and even legends about what nature means. Wells penetrates the official statements and policies of land managers and environmental commentators to uncover the relationships between forested places and the construction of our own communities. The realities of the Tillamook come from her probing questions directed at people on the ground in the new forest, and the answers are often surprising and more complicated than expected.

Each of the people Wells cameos as emblematic of the range of viewpoints about the potential fate of the Tillamook is portrayed in proximate and personal terms. These are people who believe strongly in their vision of the Tillamook's future and their articulate explanations expose the vacuity of simplistic proposals about a complex problem. This investigation of a forested place is an example of modern environmental inquiry that avoids stereotyped and predictably political descriptions about what humans desire from their environments.

In many respects, this book epitomizes what the Culture and Environment in the Pacific West series is about. The series publishes books that highlight the intersections between environment and culture in the region west of the Rockies. The books are meant for general readership and classroom use, and the editor and publisher hope that they will stimulate discussion about the relationships between human communities and the non-human environment. With the knowledge that there is much more unknown than known about this general subject, *The Tillamook* opens readers' eyes to what forest can mean and does mean to people who live, work, play, and study in a manipulated and revitalized landscape. Coming to terms with what should be done on the Tillamook forest is an inquiry into the meaning of nature at the end of the twentieth century.

William L. Lang

Art acknowledgements

Photos courtesy of Oregon Historical Society:
    page 8 (OrHi49536); page 13 and cover (OrHi 63466); page 17
    (OrHi 63465); page 24 (OrHi Gi7199); page 35 (OrHi 98686)
Photos courtesy of Oregon Department of Forestry:
    pages 9, 10, 12, 15, 20, 30, 61, 66, and tree border on cover
Maps on pages 14 and 15 by Dave Myhrum
Diagrams on page 81 courtesy of Oregon Department of Forestry
Maps on pages 84 and 85 courtesy of Oregon Department of Forestry

Introduction

WHEN I SET OUT TO WRITE THIS BOOK, I WANTED TO tell the story of a forest in a broad way, a way that would include the stories of the people who knew it and still know it, the people who were and still are influenced by it, and the people who hold its fate in their hands. I chose the Tillamook because all the right ingredients were there. The story of the Tillamook Burn has fascinated me ever since I was a child growing up in Coos Bay, the heart of Oregon's timber country ("lumber shipping capital of the world," as the town's boosters bragged in those days). I was the daughter of a sawmill owner and dealer in logs and lumber. The postwar economy was at its height then, and early in life I breathed an atmosphere thick with phrases like "board feet" and "saw kerf" and the promise of a timber boom that never seemed to stop. "The trees will grow *back*," my father would say with exasperated patience whenever anyone expressed distaste at the sight of a clear-cut.

We grew up together, the Tillamook Forest and I. Out between Tillamook and Forest Grove, the trees were growing back, just as my dad said they would. He and my mother told me about the Burn—the several burns, actually. They remembered the smoke columns and the two-inch headlines in *The Oregonian,* and the bizarre regularity of the fires, six years apart, one right after the other. They told me about the school children who went out from Portland and planted the trees that now cloaked the ashy earth. My father, especially, stressed the millions of board feet of timber those trees would provide to me and to my children some day.

When I got a little older, I learned that timber booms don't last and that trees don't always grow back. The first Earth Day was observed the year I entered college. I could see that not everybody held the same ideas about forests that I grew up taking for granted. Many people I encountered had different opinions about what forests were, what they meant, what they were *for.* I began to understand that forestry was not a simple process of harvest-and-replant-the-tree, but a complex set of issues that encompassed science, economics, politics, and human hungers and drives.

During those years and afterward, people were battling over whether to log the small amount of old-growth forest left in the Northwest. This conflict became the defining issue for the emerging environmental movement here, and the issue that I think has polarized regional opinion more than any other. It seemed to me, however, that there was less interest generally in young, second-growth forests, of which there were many, the legacy of the heavy logging of the 1940s, '50s, and '60s. I began to wonder what would happen to these forests as their trees grew big enough to log. Would there be the same bitter conflict? Or would some consensus emerge?

And so my attention was drawn once again to the Tillamook. Here was a landscape that seemed to force a rethinking of what the word "forest" means. Burned by wildfire four times over, the steep hillsides had been stripped of their cloak of ancient Douglas firs, cedars, and hemlocks, and stood naked and ash-covered. Had it ceased to be a forest then? But the hillsides had been planted like a garden with seedlings, and sowed like a wheatfield with seeds scattered from airplanes and helicopters. And the trees took root and grew and became another forest—a created forest. Not a forest in the sense of "ancient forest," the term now used by many to refer to a tree-covered landscape that has been standing undisturbed for a while. And yet not a tree farm, either, in the sense of a landscape covered with corn-straight rows of identical conifers and nothing else. Because it didn't take long for other plants to spring up alongside the new trees, sprouting from seeds that had blown in, or dropped in the feces of birds, or emerged from the soil, where after a long imprisonment the fires had set them free. Some of these opportunistic invaders erupted from underground rhizomes that had survived the fires or crept in from unburned remnants of the forest. Within a couple of decades the new conifers were joined by red alder and bigleaf maple, and the ground beneath them was tangled with salmonberry, vine maple, red elderberry, wild currant, bracken, sword fern, sorrel, Oregon grape. A new forest community was thriving. What else to call it but a forest?

What's more to the point, perhaps, is that the Tillamook *feels* like a forest when you walk through it. The sunlight cast down through the trees' canopy feels like a green cloak on your shoulders. The ground, if you stoop and lay your palm down, feels like the rough pelt of some woolly animal, and if you stamp your booted foot the earth gives off a faint hollow report that I have heard only among trees. (Try it sometime.) A forest, then, seems the most logical and straightforward thing to call this landscape.

With the birth of the new forest, the story of the Tillamook Burn seemed to be entering a new chapter, and the logical next question was, "What happens now? We've had the beginning and the middle; now what's the end of the story?" I didn't know, so I set out to tell the story myself. Telling a forest's story, I found, is a complicated business. It doesn't exactly lend itself to an opening like, "Once there was a king who had three beautiful daughters; and one day there came into the castle a mysterious knight all in black . . . " This sort of opening sets up an expectation of a beginning, a middle, and an end, with cause-effect relationships drawn for all to see, and all the loose facts neatly woven back in. A forest, in contrast, is not a story; there's no beginning and middle and end. A forest is processes—a complex dynamic of events that precede and follow other events; layers of cause and effect with multiple feedbacks and short circuits and, sometimes, catastrophic interruptions. The event that begins one process may end another, or it may function as some midpoint in the working-out of a third process; and all these processes may be linked in a host of other ways.

People describe these processes in terms of stories all the time—it's the way our minds work—but the fit is not always neat. For example, consider the idea of a "climax" forest. In the dominant conceptual model of the development of Douglas fir forests west of the Cascades, the forest is assumed to begin after a catastrophic fire—a "stand-replacing" fire, in the vocabulary of silviculturists. First to appear on the burned land are soil organisms: fungi, bacteria, and yeasts. Next are the low-growing plants, the grasses and the leafy, soft-stemmed forbs: hawksbeard, dandelion, fireweed, thistle. Then come the hardwood shrubs and trees: salmonberry, vine maple, blackcap, ceanothus, alder, bigleaf maple. All this time Douglas fir and hemlock seeds are being blown into the burn by the wind, or carried by birds from nearby trees. The seeds (Douglas fir seeds look like little brown dots with goldfish tails) drop, sprout, and take root, eventually elbowing out the grasses, forbs, and shrubs. After a long time, centuries, the Douglas fir come to dominate, and the hemlock retires to the shadows. After more centuries, the biggest, oldest Douglas firs ("ancient" or "decadent," depending on your perspective) topple and fall. In the raw new patches of sunlight, hemlock stretch upward and drop their seeds, which germinate in their turn. Eventually the hemlocks rise above the sunken, moss-covered bodies of the old Douglas firs, and the forest enters its climax.

Who says it's a climax? We do, because stories are such a comfortable way for us to convey and receive information, to absorb wisdom. The progression (that word, too, begs the question of story) from naked land to clothed, from small living things to large, from empty landscape to full, makes casting it as a story seem natural and unremarkable, but the assumption is arbitrary just the same. For all the forest cares, the climax might as easily come in what we call the middle, when the salmonberry and vine maple grow eye-to-eye with the Douglas firs. In fact, the notion of "climax" has become problematic in the world of plant ecology, as theories based on assumptions of orderly processes and steady states in nature are giving way to theories based on assumptions of fundamental dynamism and even chaos.

Who says what's the beginning and what's the end? Who says what's the cause and what's the effect? The forest won't tell us, so it's the storyteller's task. Thus, even if the story starts with, "Once there was a forest with many acres of beautiful and valuable trees; and one day there came a big fire . . . ," the storyteller is faced with decisions about cause and effect, where the beginning begins and where the ending ends, as well as a lot of loose facts that can't be neatly woven back in. The complexity grows by orders of magnitude when the story takes in the actions of human beings.

And so, in struggling with this task, I came to see that the notion of "story" is far richer and more complex than I had initially understood it to be. In his excellent essay, "A Place for Stories: Nature, History, and Narrative," the historian William Cronon draws on literary theory to show that stories are human inventions that help us make sense of our experience, "a peculiarly human way of organizing reality" (Cronon 1992, 1367). Stories are crucial in the fundamental human task of understanding—that is, distilling meaning from—the events of our lives. Stories, Cronon writes, are "our best and most compelling tool for searching out meaning in a conflicted and contradictory world" (1374).

However, stories have a big disadvantage: they can never tell the-whole-truth-and-nothing-but-the-truth, and we should be suspicious of a historical narrative that purports to do just that. The very authority that stories have in organizing our reality is gained by leaving out or distorting the chunks of that reality that don't fit the story. A good story has a coherent plot—it makes what happened seem like an inevitable unfolding of events according to plan or destiny. But it achieves this coherency by leaving out the pieces that reveal the parts played by accident, contingency, and pure dumb luck.

Cronon illustrates his point by showing us two radically different readings of the causes of the Dust Bowl in North America's Great Plains in the mid-1930s. He presents two historians who look at the exact same set of events, and by arranging the relationships among these events in different ways draw very different conclusions.

My aim in this book is to take a similar approach by looking at the Tillamook through the lenses of two different stories. I have chosen two big stories out of the many that the Tillamook offers. I call them the "arcadian" story and the "frontier" story. My job will be to explore how each of these stories shapes a different understanding of, and argues a different meaning for, the Tillamook's history, its current circumstances, and its various potential futures.

Lest anyone think I should have dumped the stories and tried instead for a storyless neutral objectivity, let me say that first, I didn't want to do that. Stories are far more interesting than a mere chronicle of events. Secondly, and more to the point, I don't think it's possible. Once you start reciting your chronicle, you find yourself telling a story in spite of all your good objective intentions. You find yourself glossing over extraneous or awkward detail, tracing cause-effect relationships, drawing conclusions. There is no escaping story. We can't understand our lives without it.

The best a responsible storyteller can do when tackling historical narrative is to tell stories "consciously, responsibly, self-critically" (Cronon, 1376). That means, first, realizing that you are telling a story. It ought to be as truthful a story as you can make it, but it can never be, objectively and neutrally, "the truth." Secondly, responsible storytelling means grounding your story in things that really happened, and not making up things that didn't happen. And finally, it means submitting your story to the critical judgment of others, and being willing to let it be shaped and enriched by their versions of what happened.

This is what I have tried to do in telling this story of how a created forest is coming of age. Some perhaps may fault me for oversimplifying complex issues—neatening the landscape, sweeping out the nourishing debris, tidying up the site the way enlightened loggers used to do until quite recently. All I can say is that I've tried to be as thorough and as honest as I can be. Where the story demands condensation or summarizing, I do my best to condense or summarize fairly, honoring the complexity of a real forest and real human beings. To see the Tillamook face to face, in its full throb and color, I urge readers to make further explorations into the literature listed in the back, and into the Tillamook itself.

In telling this story, I know I am sending it out into a world that is in painful conflict about the right human relationship to nature. Forests seem today to be both an actual and a symbolic venue for this conflict. They seem to stand in for every brutality and every betrayal we have perpetrated on our natural surroundings, and for every shred of guilt and remorse we have felt as a result. Forests are charged with emotion, enmeshed in meaning; we carry them around in our heads. It's hard to tell a story that begins, "Once there was a forest . . . " without tapping into deep currents of feeling in the audience—currents that may take a reader far from the destination I hope to reach.

Nevertheless, I would like to try to tell this story in a way that moves past easy answers and false dilemmas, past the oversimplified discourse that has already worn grooves in people's thinking—the "owls-or-jobs" groove, or the "cut-it-down-or-lock-it-up" groove. I grew up in forested country, and forests live in my soul. I am dismayed at our sorry past—the heedless exploitation, the waste and the greed—and I'm disturbed when this history is discounted or dismissed. I'm also disturbed that some people seem ready to declare humans the enemy and banish them from the forest altogether.

And so the hypothesis that informs this whole effort—the proposed answer to the question, "What happens now on the Tillamook?"—is: "Here we finally have a chance to form a truly stable, sustainable, and humane relationship with our forests." To find out whether this might be true, I knew I had to explore the territory between the grooves. Although I draw on a lot of literature in the forestry and historical disciplines, I do not approach this task as a professional historian or a professional forester, for I'm neither. What I hope to achieve here is a work of good solid journalism, by which I mean a well-researched, responsibly reported, and interesting story, broad rather than deep, concrete rather than theoretical, a synthesis rather than an analysis. My intended audience is not scholars (although I hope they will be interested, too), but ordinary citizens who live in Oregon and other places where natural-resource issues have caused social and political turmoil.

I enter the task with both hope and skepticism. Skepticism because our history suggests we aren't capable of a long-term partnership with our forests, one that sustains both the forests and ourselves. And hope, because the Tillamook, with its redemptive past and the enlightened intentions of its current managers, seems to show us a lesson partly mastered.

1

The Legend

SIXTY-FIVE YEARS AGO, A GREAT FIRE BURNED MANY ACRES OF A virgin forest in northwestern Oregon. The forest was composed of Douglas fir, western red cedar, and white fir on the higher elevations and western hemlock and Sitka spruce on the lower slopes. The trees were 150 to 400 years old, and they were immense—from three to seven feet thick. There were about five million of them. The forest was "truly the best virgin stand of timber in the state of Oregon" (Beh 1951). That first fire, in 1933, was followed by three more fires at six-year intervals. The fires burned 355,000 acres of forest land in all.

The events surrounding the great Tillamook fires and the planting of young trees on the Burn have been told and retold over three generations. The story that has come down to the present day is a story of heroism and sacrifice, of human ingenuity and pluck, of people laying aside their differences to make common cause against a common enemy. It is a legend that still lives in the minds of people born and raised in the Pacific Northwest, even those too young to remember the fires. This is the legend.[1]

The Fires

The story begins on August 14, 1933, a hot, dry day at the end of a hot, dry summer. A suffocating east wind had sucked the moisture from the needles of the trees. Humidity in the air was 20 percent. The duff on the forest floor was so dry it powdered the loggers' boots. At noon, a sweating runner arrived at the Gales Creek Logging Company. Panting and dripping, he delivered the message from the fire-watching authorities: Shut down or you'll have a fire on your hands. The crew paused. The boss glanced at the huge Douglas fir log just now ready to drag to the landing. "One more," he said. The whistle punk blew the signal. The mainline snapped taut. The big log reared and thrashed. With a rasp of steel cable against dry bark,

Fire across the hillsides, Tillamook Burn, 1930s.

the log began to move toward the landing, grinding its way over a downed cedar. There was a trickle of smoke, a flame. Loggers ran to the fire with shovels and axes, but it had already climbed a tall snag. The snag became a torch. The wind carried flaming bits of moss and rotting wood into a logged-over patch of woods half a mile across the canyon. The slash blazed up and the fire raced on.

Smoke billowed out of the canyon. The watchmen at Hoffman lookout, ten miles to the northeast, and at Saddle Mountain lookout to the south saw the smoke and sounded the alarm: "Fire on Gales Creek!" All available men from the nearby mills and logging camps were dispatched to the scene. They fought all night long, digging miles of firebreaks, but the fire quickly crowned—climbed into the treetops—and raced away into the adjoining trees.

More men were called in, farmers and loggers and men from the city, as well as a thousand enrollees from the Civilian Conservation Corps. The town of Forest Grove, a few miles southeast of Gales Creek canyon, became the staging area for the firefighting. The town took on the earnest, hurried feeling of an Army camp in wartime. In fact the Army was there, distributing food and equipment to the firefighters, directing the trucks that rolled in from the cities with supplies.

Two firefighters, Tillamook Burn, 1930s.

The men fought the fire for ten days, digging firebreaks and watching the fire gobble them up, backing up and digging more firebreaks. The fire climbed up the west side of Saddle Mountain and destroyed the lookout station only moments before the watchman fled down the east side. By the tenth day, Wednesday, August 23, the fire had spread to 40,000 acres, big enough to engulf Mount Rainier. The tenth day brought a sprinkle of rain, and the fire slowed. Hopes were buoyed. But the eleventh day, Thursday, August 24, was again hot and dry. A new east wind surged in, and the humidity dived. And suddenly the fire blew up. A wall of flame blasted into a stand of old growth 250 feet tall, slowing only an instant as it climbed to the crowns, and then it roared off across the treetops. It consumed 166 acres every minute, almost three acres every second. Its terrific heat cracked the ground and caused the air to explode upward. The resulting vacuum sucked in a sudden gale that uprooted trees, twisting them out of the ground as easily as a gardener pulls weeds. Frank Palmer, a CCC firefighter from Illinois, died when a burning snag fell on him. Another firefighter who was with him was badly hurt.

On that Thursday, employees of the Oregon-American Lumber Company had to flee the company's logging camp, Camp McGregor, when the wind shifted. The logging train full of people careered down the mountain. Half an hour after they abandoned the camp, the fire overtook it. Also on that Thursday, an arsonist set fire to a mass of logging slash outside the fire line, up on Wolf Creek, six miles to the north. By the end of the day the Wolf Creek fire had traveled eighteen miles. It burned 60,000 acres before it was finally stopped.

Smoke from the fires rose to eight miles high. People in Yellowstone Park could see it. It darkened the skies and rained ashes and charred fir needles on towns, farms, and beaches. Ash fell onto the decks of ships 500 miles at sea. Cars turned on their headlights in midmorning. Chickens roosted at noon. The fire spread to 240,000 acres, an area a third the size of Rhode Island. That night the east wind calmed and a fog rolled in from the ocean. On Friday, August 25, the fire began to die down; the change in the weather and the firebreaks dug by 3,000 firefighters had finally broken its back. The woods continued to smolder for another two weeks until the fall rains came. Finally, on September 5, the fire fizzled, steamed, and died.

The Tillamook country looked like the end of the world. It was a 400-square-mile moonscape of cinders and ash. On a map, the burned area looked roughly like your left fist, closed fingers up. About where your two last fingernails would bite into your palm,

Wilson River stage road in the aftermath of the 1933 fire.

there was a small, teardrop-shaped patch of unburned forest—spared thanks to the capricious mercy of wind and terrain. Standing at the western edge of that patch, a viewer could look north and south and see nothing but blackened earth and ghostly snags. It was a grievous sight.

Accounts of the time describe the loss, completely without irony, as the "killing" of billions of board feet of timber—as if a board foot of timber were a living thing. Which it was, in a sense, for the people of the time, because timber was their life's blood. Just about everybody worked in the woods or the mills, or was married to someone who did, or worked for businesses that depended on timber dollars. Thus, even more grievous than the ugliness of the landscape was the twelve and a half billion board feet of clear, fine-grained, premium-quality timber that lay on the ground, a feast for the bugs and a temptation for the next fire. A shameful, heartbreaking waste, was how people saw it. That timber would have kept every sawmill, shingle mill, and pulp mill in the United States busy for a year, at the rate timber was being processed in 1932. It would have kept all the Portland sawmills going for thirty years. If the Tillamook timber had not burned but had instead been logged over the twenty-year period between 1933 and 1953, it would have been worth $442.4 million.[2] Loggers and mill workers would have earned $350 million in wages. Forest landowners would have paid $2.4 million in property taxes. The massive timber salvage operation, begun almost before the embers were cold, was hailed as a bright spot in a otherwise dismal picture. The salvage logging eventually recovered $100 million, less than a quarter of what the unburned timber would have been worth.

Fire revisited the Burn country at eerily regular intervals, six years from fire to fire. The 1939 fire, also allegedly touched off by a logging operation, burned 190,000 acres. Much of it was within the original Burn, but there was no containing it once it grabbed hold of the dead, dry snags and sticks. The 1945 fire burned 180,000 acres. The 1951 fire was mercifully smaller: only 32,700 acres, and it was confined within already-burned areas.

The 1945 fire was the one that made the biggest headlines. It was the third visitation of a monstrous event; that and the freakishness of the timing stirred something in people's hearts. The Burn was close to Portland, Oregon's largest city, into which the wartime economy had recently drawn another quarter-million people. City dwellers traveling to the coast had to drive through the Burn and see its ugliness up close. People started saying that something had

Burned equipment after the 1951 fire.

to be done to renew the Burn, to reclaim the lost empire of timber that the fires had stolen from the people of Oregon and to keep such fires from happening ever again.

Governor Earl Snell appointed a citizens' committee to find a solution. The committee came back with a challenge: Oregon needed to undertake a huge forest rehabilitation project, the biggest tree-planting job ever attempted anywhere. The purpose was to restore the area to its "natural, wealth-producing status" by transforming "the non-producing burn land into a 300,000-acre growing tree farm," in the words of a contemporary newspaper account.

The Restoration

Timber forever was the promise that rose from the ashes of the Tillamook Burn. But replanting the Burn was a bigger job than any state or federal agency had ever attempted. Nobody knew how to do such a thing. The Forest Service declined to help—not only was it financially risky, they said; it was humanly impossible. Many people agreed. The Burn was too rugged, too huge; it had been scorched too badly. There was talk of letting the grass take over and turning the Burn into rangeland. But a few people clung to the vision of restoring the Tillamook's former green richness, its wealth of timber. One of them was Nelson S. Rogers, the Oregon state forester. Rogers had grown up around Gales Creek, and he knew good tree-growing land when he saw it. He devised a plan and took it to Governor Snell: Fireproof the Burn by felling the snags and punching through a network of fire roads and trails. Build lookout stations and beef up firefighting crews. Then create a vast patchwork of tree plantations on land that once lay under virgin forest. With Oregon's people behind him, Rogers was convinced, his state forestry department could do it.

The idea of state ownership of forest lands was a controversial one. Back in the depressed 1920s and 1930s, when taxes were high and profits were low, many lumbermen advocated the idea. Let the state bear the trouble and expense of reforesting the lands, they said, and we'll be happy to come back in and cut the timber when it's ready (Levesque 1985, 1:379). But by the mid-1930s, with tax relief, better reforestation methods, and rising stumpage prices making reforestation more feasible, these lumbermen began to view such ideas with alarm, even as more cut-over forest lands were coming into state ownership (Levesque, 1:380).

High school boys from Hillsboro, Forest Grove, and Timber heading out to plant trees on Tillamook Burn. Photo taken March 5, 1945.

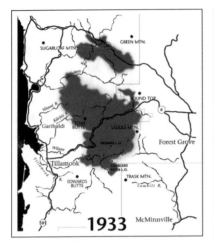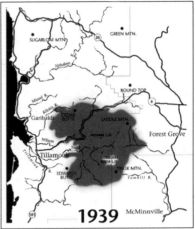

The boundaries of the four Tillamook Burn fires

Even assuming the state of Oregon could or should take on a project of this magnitude, there were other problems, big problems. First of all, who would pay for such a massive project? A Clatsop County judge named Guy Boyington came up with an intriguing idea: Float a statewide bond issue to finance the reforestation, a scheme that would require a constitutional amendment. The legislature wrestled with the idea and then submitted a proposal to the voters, who narrowly approved it in 1948. At a ceremony at Owl Camp, at the top of the Coast Range divide, sitting on a wide stump, Governor Douglas McKay signed the bond papers in July of 1949. Nelson Rogers, gravely ill, did not attend. Three months later he was dead, but his dream of restoring the Tillamook Burn had received the official blessing of the people.

Before any firebreaks could be plowed or trees planted, the state had to acquire title to the burned lands. Many acres of the Burn belonged to the counties of Tillamook, Yamhill, and Washington. The counties had acquired this land through property tax foreclosures on private landowners, mostly timber companies, during the Depression. The counties agreed to turn the land over to the state to be replanted. In exchange, they would get to keep most of any future timber revenue. The state, in other words, would hold the land and manage its timber, in a trust-type arrangement for the counties, forever.

There was another complication. The counties had previously sold salvage rights to the fire-killed trees on much of the land. When

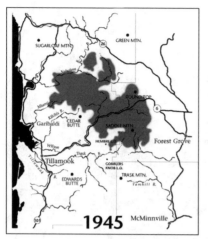
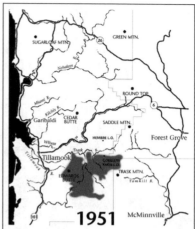

the state acquired the land, those salvage contracts were still in effect. Loggers continued to salvage timber from the Burn through the 1940s and 1950s, a time when timber prices were rising rapidly. They were reluctant to let go of their salvage contracts until they had removed every saleable stick of wood. These logging operations seriously hampered the reforestation efforts of the early 1950s.

The New Forest

The state foresters started by surveying the vast Burn to see what had to be done. They reestablished property corners and ran boundary lines. They laid out access roads and cleared firebreaks, dividing the Burn into compartments so that firefighters could more easily contain and suppress future fires. They established lookout stations. They mapped the remnants of living forest, studied the conditions of soils and sites, and determined how to get young trees growing.

They had little knowledge go to on. The Tillamook was the site of a lot of trial-and-error research in the course of the reforestation. Foresters learned much about the relationship of soil, climate, and elevation to the successful growing of trees; about planting techniques; about nursery tree culture; about controlling brush and animal pests. They tried dropping Douglas fir seeds from airplanes and helicopters—eventually scattering thirty-six tons of Douglas fir

Tree-planting crew using short-handled hoes.

seed over 98,000 acres. But planting by hand, they discovered, was the more reliable method. Beginning in November of 1949, forestry crews planted more than 108,000 acres of the Burn with seventy-two million two-year-old Douglas fir seedlings. Inmates of the South Fork minimum security prison camp planted some of the trees. Volunteers, many of them children, planted trees. Each spring for twenty years, fleets of yellow school buses and chartered Greyhounds from Portland and the smaller towns nearby would bring grade-school and high-school students out to the Burn. The children would carry hoedads—a tree-planting tool—and lunch buckets. Special tracts were set aside for these plantings; most of them lie next to the Wilson River Highway just west of Forest Grove.

The new trees had to fight for their survival. Wood rats ate many of the seeds as soon as they hit the ground. Deer nibbled on the tender new seedlings. Mountain beavers clipped the smaller seedlings off right at the ground, and they stripped the bark off the bigger ones. Foresters sprayed the brush that competed with the young trees, and they killed some of the rodents with poisoned bait—a controversial tactic. The seedlings that survived were nurtured by the rich soil and moist climate of the Tillamook country. Gradually, the feathery tips of Douglas fir started showing above the bracken fern. By the early 1960s, the Burn was cloaking itself in green.

State Forester Nelson Rogers (left) plants a Port Orford cedar on the spot near the Wilson River highway where the Tillamook fire started in August 1933. Looking on are Cecil Kyle, Northwest District fire warden, Arthur Priaulx, public relations head of the West Coast Lumbermen's Association, and Lynn Cronemiller, assistant state forester.

On July 18, 1973, twenty-four years to the day after Governor McKay had signed the reforestation bond into law, Governor Tom McCall dedicated the Burn as the new Tillamook State Forest. That ceremony too took place at Owl Camp, which had become the main staging area for the reforestation. By then it had been renamed Rogers Camp, after the visionary state forester who did not live to see his plan become reality. McCall had to stand on a podium; the stump on which Governor McKay had sat twenty-four years earlier was gone, removed along with the rest of the dead wood from the Burn.

In his remarks, Governor McCall said, "Around us now we see the result of our lending a helping hand to the natural process. More than a million snags are gone, . . . and in their place is a new stand of Oregon's economic life blood. The trees will grow, and suffer our harvest, and grow again. The forest . . . again will feed us." The promise of the Tillamook, *timber forever*, seemed to be coming true.

Notes

1. Taken from accounts in Beh 1951, Fick and Martin 1992, "From Ruin to Rejuvenation" (videocassette) 1978, Holbrook 1941, Levesque 1985, Lucia 1983, Oregon Department of Forestry 1993, and Pyne 1982.

2. Calculated in 1993 dollars.

2

Timber Forever

THE FIRES WERE A LONG TIME AGO, AND THE NAME "TILLAMOOK" means a lot of other things now. Tillamook is a town of 4,245 (Oregon Employment Department, Region 1 Update, December 1996) on Oregon's north coast. It is a lush-meadowed dairy-farming county with more cows than people. It is a stocking-shaped bay into which the Miami, Kilchis, Wilson, Trask, and Tillamook Rivers flow. It is the tribe of Indians (rendered in Lewis and Clark's journals as "Kilamox" and "Killamuck") after whom city, county, river, and bay are named (Tillamook Pioneer Association 1972). It is the home of the world's largest cheese factory, and the birthplace of the famous Tillamook Cheese. It is also a wide stretch of young Douglas-fir forest out west of Portland, along the Wilson River highway, a place where Portland citizens go to hike, where dirt bikers go to tear through the woods, where high-school kids go to drink and party and skinny-dip, where elk hunters pitch their tents and park their RVs on frosty November days.

But among the people who live in the small towns adjacent to the Tillamook, especially those who came of age in Oregon between the Great Depression and the Vietnam War, the name "Tillamook" will always mean, first, the Tillamook Burn. The memory is especially vivid among those raised in the towns ringing the Burn—Forest Grove, Gales Creek, Glenwood, Timber, Vernonia, Mist, Jewell, Elsie, Nehalem—but anyone who lived here between 1933 and 1973 will know what the Tillamook Burn was, and they will likely be able to tell you how it changed the face of Oregon.

The real old-timers remember the snapping-dry August day in 1933 when the woods caught fire and didn't stop burning until the September rains came, soaking 380 square miles (Levesque 1985, 1:213) of dead, blackened Douglas fir trees. They remember the second fire, and the third, and the fourth, all at six-year intervals, visitations of a malevolent genie that seemed to be able to read a human calendar. They remember the strenuous salvage logging; the railroad flatcars and log trucks rolling out of the Burn loaded with

Old-growth Douglas fir forest before the 1933 fire. Photo taken in 1926.

charred, barkless logs. They remember the men who felled the brittle snags, raising clouds of soot, coming back to camp looking like chimney sweeps.

The World War II generation remembers the sea of snags, miles and miles of them bleached silver from the sun, rising from the burned landscape like the masts of ghost ships. They remember the sense of widespread dismay that followed the 1945 fire, the feeling that something had to be done to bring back the timbered wealth that the fires had stolen. They remember, if they were old enough to vote, the 1948 constitutional amendment to finance the most massive reforestation project ever attempted any time, anywhere. They remember the army of workers who bulldozed roads, felled snags, planted trees, and scattered Douglas fir seeds from airplanes and helicopters. Some of them remember going out to the Burn with their school classmates and planting trees alongside the highway.

Their children are my generation. We remember driving out to the coast with our parents and watching the thickets of green flash by the car windows. We noticed the pattern of the silvery foliage on the hillsides and the occasional bleached snag sticking up from the high steep slopes and the carpet of bracken fern that turned gold in the fall, and we couldn't quite picture it when our parents told us what this place used to look like. By that time the scar was healing over. A new forest had been created out of a burned void by human minds, hearts, and hands, and the promise of this new forest was *timber forever.*

It is important to remember that *timber forever* had a clear meaning in the minds of the people of the Tillamook. It wasn't just a beautiful green hillside they wanted—although the new forest was and is beautiful, a herringbone stippling of silver-on-green across deep canyons—and people invariably express delight in its rugged vistas. No, the forest was to be a source of prosperity for the future, a never-to-be-emptied cornucopia of wood that would provide for the people of Tillamook and Yamhill counties down through the generations. When the people voted to tax themselves to reforest the burned lands, it was with the promise that most of the future revenues from the land—money that would be derived from the logging of the timber when it was ready—would be theirs. This was viewed as a firm contract, a solemn trust.

The Tillamook Frontier

After the Burn, there was a consensus that the forest's main job is to produce wealth for the people. That idea made perfect sense in the context of the time and place. It was just the way people saw things. You could pick that up from newspaper editorials, from sitting in a fourth-grade classroom listening to a lesson on "our natural resources," from everyday conversation. A 1945 editorial in the Tillamook *Headlight Herald* raised the question of whether the county should reforest and reseed the Burn or turn the job over to the state or federal government. It is plain from the tone and terminology of the editorial that the writer believed the principal goal of any arrangement would be to restore the flow of timber revenue to the county: "What will the Tillamook citizen do to help the county . . . develop and make the forest lands profitable again to the county?" (Levesque 2:548). Governor Earl Snell, in appointing a special forestry committee in 1945 with the "responsibility of exploring methods, policies and laws and action affecting the forestry program in our state" (836), made it clear that timber revenues and jobs were foremost on his mind:

The lumbering industry is an industry that has consistently occupied first or second place in the commercial activities of the state's economy. In normal times it is a resource that represents around a quarter of a billion dollars to our state and an industry that employs a quarter of a million men (Levesque 2:833-4).

A *Headlight Herald* editorial in November of 1945, offering "the opinion of a majority of our citizens" on fire protection, shows a similar priority in referring to the three fires that "have consumed the wealth of Tillamook County." Timber, in short, was still king in the Tillamook country, just as in the frontier days. And that was understandable, for it had been less than a hundred years since European-American settlers had first arrived on Tillamook Bay.

At that time, in the mid-nineteenth century, the United States was in an expansionist mood. The development of what was called Manifest Destiny, and its many impacts on the culture and geography of the American West, have been extensively and enlighteningly laid out by many historians (for example Limerick 1987, Meinig 1993, Schwantes 1989, and White 1991). They are too complex to go into here, but what is most pertinent to my story is that from the expansionism of the nineteenth century came an ideology of the frontier as a place of opportunity and haven, a place where you could transform your fortunes and your destiny through your own efforts, and a place where the taming of Nature to human ends was the main task. The experience of "penetrating the wilderness, breaking the land, creating farms, founding towns, and forming civil societies in this great 'frontier,'" says the historian Donald Meinig, "has long provided the basis for the most famous—and endlessly controversial—generalizations about the emergence of a distinctly American civilization" (Meinig, 223).

We will talk more later about how early and contemporary historians regard the notion of the frontier as not only the chronicle but the crucible of American social evolution. What is important here is that the West became a fabled place for people who had never seen it. It became associated with freedom and independence in a country "that regarded freedom and independence as its peculiar hallmark" (White, 620). It became a place where violence (white male violence, says the historian Richard White) against the inhabitants of nature (particularly Indians but also uncultivated natural landscapes) was made to seem "natural, timeless, and inescapable" (620).

This frontier fascination produced a high popular enthusiasm in the East for all things pertaining to the Oregon country (Schwantes, 78). Glowing descriptions of the mild climate and natural riches of "the Eden at the end of the trail" (White, 190) appeared both in Eastern and Western newspapers and in handbills and prospectuses intended to lure settlers westward. One of the best known was an 1830 booklet of eighty pages called "A Geographical Sketch of that Part of North America Called Oregon." Its author was Hall J. Kelley, a Massachusetts textbook writer who had never been to Oregon, but who had read Lewis and Clark's journals in 1818 "and underwent a change of life" (Meinig, 104).

"It is the concurrent testimony of the many, who have explored the country," wrote Kelley, ". . . that the top soil is a deep black mould; that the forests are heavy and extensive; and the trees are of vast dimensions; and vegetation generally is luxuriant to a degree unknown in any other part of America; and we can add, that there are physical causes to render the climate the most healthful in the world" (Kelley 1830, quoted in Liberty 1997). Kelley eventually did pay a visit to Fort Vancouver, after an unsuccessful attempt to round up would-be colonists and a lengthy journey to Oregon by way of New Orleans. He arrived sick and evidently a bit unhinged, and the people at Fort Vancouver shipped him home after four strained months (Meinig, 108). In any event, Kelley's obsession and that of other Western boosters made convenient propaganda for an American government that was increasingly vexed by the British presence in the Oregon territory.

Early descriptions of the Tillamook country play a rhapsody of frontier themes and imagery. In prose dripping with sensuality, they portray it as a land of Edenic vegetation, perfect climate, friendly natives, and abundant natural wealth ripe for the picking. "Tillamook valley is the choicest nook of the whole Oregon coast so far as the mildness of climate, productiveness of soil, wealth of timber abundance and variety of fish and game can make it," said the *Yamhill Reporter* in 1883 (Tillamook Pioneer Association 1972, 185). "The labor of making a living is certainly lighter there than in any other corner of Oregon, for the woods, rivers and ocean supply so much that man so content has little to do but gather and eat."

Traders, entrepreneurs, and missionaries had been coming to the Oregon country since the late 1700s, and the first settlers started arriving in the 1840s. The first white men to settle on Tillamook

Tillamook County homestead in the woods, before the fires.

Bay were Joe E. Champion, Samuel Howard, and W. Taylor. "On the first day of April A.D. 1851, I left the Columbia in a whale boat with provisions for six months," wrote Champion in his journal. The men entered Tillamook Bay the next morning. "The Indians generally seemed pleased with the prospect of having the Whites to settle among them (Poor Fools), they showed me a large hollow dead Spruce Tree, into which we conveyed all my property. I christened it my Castle, . . . " (Tillamook Pioneer Association 1972, 6). On December 15, 1853, the territorial legislature created Tillamook County.

Because it was so remote, ringed by rugged mountains and accessible only by sea and primitive wagon roads (the first railroad did not penetrate the mountains until 1911), the Tillamook country was slower to develop than the interior parts of the region. For most of the earliest settlers—there were 408 in the county in 1870—the magnificent old trees were just a nuisance. These pioneers came there to fish, farm, and raise milk cows on the rich coastal plains. "A fine growth of indigenous clover grew spontaneously," says Paul Levesque (1985, 1:1). "The lush pasture grasses were the best butter producers known. Moreover, there were no weeds to plague settlers." The trees, however, were considered large weeds by many. Forest fires, if they didn't threaten settlements, were welcomed because they cleared the land for farming. As elsewhere on the frontier, the settlers felled the trees, laboriously, with single-bitted axes and crosscut saws, and used them to build homes, barns, and fences, and to keep themselves warm. Three pioneer sawmills were running by 1870, filling local building needs.

Land Giveaways and Grabs

To encourage colonization and development of the West, the federal government was giving away, or selling for a pittance, millions of acres of Western land. The Donation Land Claim Act of 1850 allowed a married couple to claim as a homestead 640 acres of Oregon land—a whole section, amounting to a square mile—in exchange for living on the land and cultivating it for four years. The Donation Land Act brought in about 30,000 settlers into Tillamook County by 1855 and conveyed about two and a half million acres into private hands (Levesque 1:53-56). The Homestead Act of 1862 allowed 320-acre claims for a $16 filing fee and five years of residence and cultivation.

These laws and others were based on the assumption that the West's new settlers would all be farmers. For a long time Western land law embodied the Jeffersonian vision of a nation of small, independent farmers as a bulwark of democracy, and it also reflected the inability of an Eastern Congress to grasp how unlike the East this frontier really was. Much of the land in the West was unsuitable for farming, or at least for the kind of self-sufficient, smallholder farming that the Congressmen had in mind. On the other hand, the West had millions of acres of lands valuable to timbermen, graziers, and miners, but no laws covered the sale or lease of these lands. For a long time there was no guidance from Washington on how the Land Office was supposed to dispose of lands containing precious metals, or lands best suited for grazing, or lands that grew magnificent timber but pitiful farm crops (White, 147-8). Extralegal arrangements sprang up to take care of local needs. These fixes were widely tolerated; federal officials colluded so as to increase the public revenues. Says Richard White:

> *Initially, loggers simply stole logs off the public domain, but in Washington the federal attorney for the territory moved to control the practice. He, and the officials who followed, however, were not unreasonable men. They were overworked and overextended, and*

*they had no desire to spend their days in damp woods searching
for timber thieves. They were willing to work out a modus vivendi
with the lumbermen. If the timbermen agreed to report how much
lumber they had stolen, the agents agreed to fine them at a
prearranged rate. In effect, the government treated lumbermen
the way most western cities treated prostitutes. They tolerated
crimes they could not prevent in order to fine the criminals and
gain public revenues* (148).

With the Mining Act of 1872, Congress finally provided for the
sale of mineral lands in the West. The Timber and Stone Act of 1878
allowed settlers to claim up to 160 acres for $2.50 an acre, but they
could use the timber and stone on the land only for their own fuel
or building needs—they were not supposed to sell it or the land
(White, 150). There were no residency or improvement
requirements—all a claimant had to do was swear that he would
occupy or use the land for himself alone and that he was not acting
for anyone else.

This law, like the Homestead Act, turned out to be a gilt-edged
invitation to fraud—a story that has been well told elsewhere (Puter
1908). Some operators were caught and tried, but most escaped with
their land holdings intact (Robbins 1988, 28). Timber companies
hired "dummy entrymen" to file claims—the practice was so
widespread that some companies recruited warm bodies with ads
in the Seattle newspapers. The false claimants were then paid to
transfer title to the company. "We hired two Swedes at $1.50 per
day, each, and furnished them with a tent, provisions and tools, and
set them to work constructing the shacks . . . " wrote Stephen Puter
in his 1908 expose. Puter was a professional land locator who got
caught, went to jail, and wrote a book naming names (Levesque
1:69). Much of Tillamook County's public land was transferred to
private ownership (by fair means as well as foul) under this law.

Some of Oregon's best timber lay on its school grant lands, almost
seven million acres at statehood in 1859. By 1910 the state had
disposed of most of its best forest lands (Office of the Attorney
General 1997, 2). And government land grants proved a windfall
for railroad companies, which accumulated more grant land than
all the homesteaders combined (Levesque 1:47). The Northern
Pacific Railroad Company was chartered in 1864; President Lincoln
signed the bill that gave the new company a grant of sixty million
acres of public land—the largest grant ever offered to an American

railroad, a swath six times the size of New England (Schwantes 1989, 143-4). In exchange, the railroad was to build a rail link from the Great Lakes to Pacific tidewater (Long 1993). In 1866, the Oregon and California Railroad Company received a grant of 3.7 million acres to build a railroad between Oregon and California. Eventually the Northern Pacific, the O&C, and fifty-nine other railroad companies were granted a total of 131 billion acres before Congress terminated the land-grant program in 1871 (Schwantes, 143). The land came with strings attached, of course. Among other things, the railroads were supposed to sell their lands to settlers at low cost. But much of the timber land ended up in the hands of Eastern timber companies (Beuter 1994, 10). Some of the railroad grant land was ultimately taken back by the federal government when the railroads did not comply with this and other terms of the grants.

The presence of millions of acres of undervalued land in an atmosphere of untrammeled development created a frenzied speculation in timber land during the last decades of the nineteenth century (Robbins, 26). By 1900, virtually all the good farmland and most of the prime timber land in Oregon was in private hands (Office of the Attorney General 1997, 3). Large Eastern-based companies owned most of Tillamook County's timber land, and held it mostly in large tracts, until the 1933 fire (Levesque, 1:49). Says Thomas Cox in his well-researched history of Pacific Coast lumbering, ". . . during the eighties huge amounts of capital accumulated in the Lake States were being reinvested not in the declining lumber industry of that area, but in the Far West" (Cox 1974). Rumors of impending corporate moves appeared frequently in newspapers, and enough new mills sprang up to lend these rumors credence. Says Cox:

> A group of lumbermen from Michigan established the Michigan Mill Company and erected a plant in Vancouver, Washington. J.W. McDonnell and others from the same state built a mill at Ballard, only to sell it to another millman from Michigan, Charles Stimson. Chauncey and Everett Griggs arrived from Minnesota and established the St. Paul and Tacoma Lumber Company. They had behind them one and one-half million dollars of paid-up capital (239).

By the mid-nineties, officials in Washington, D.C. were beginning to get suspicious about the high volume of timber land claims in Oregon and Washington, but local residents, eager for economic development, were not so fussy about the rules. One Jerry Buckley, in an interview quoted in the Tillamook *Headlight* in 1891, said, somewhat defensively:

> Now I will give you the names of the parties who bought about all the lands purchased here: They are Whitney, Stinchfield & Remmick, A.L. Stebbins, W.W. Curtis and Mr. Bowen, all of Detroit; Tillotsen, Rust & Burrows, Ezra Rust, ex congressman Bliss, Chas. Green, E.G. King, Thomas Merrill, Isaac Stevens and J.D. Fordney, all of Saginaw; D.A. Blodgett of Grand Rapids; Stimson & Co. of Muskegon; Thomas Devine of Deluth, Minnesota and Lacy & Co. These gentlemen are as honest as other responsible businessmen, and are no more likely to be engaged in stealing lands, than a lot of bankers in plundering the United States Treasury (Levesque 1:67).

The Promise of the Frontier

Part of the lure of the frontier has always been the promise that with shrewdness, grit, and hard work any man could make himself rich. "New comers can do worse in this country than go to the Tillamook valley," said the Yamhill *Reporter* in 1883 (Tillamook Pioneer Association 1972, 185), with surprising understatement. "The future development of the country is as certain to make the owners of 160 acres of land unincumbered a comparatively rich man. The government gives the land to whoever will take it."

Echoing this glowing prospectus language, Ellis Lucia wrote much later, "Millions could be made here by those who had the know-how and the stamina" (1975, 12). But in fact, the wealth of the Northwest coast was the wealth of a colony, requiring capital and technology to exploit to its fullest. As with all colonial economies, the capital and technology that developed the Northwest came from outside, first from San Francisco, which financed the early maritime lumber trade, then mostly from Eastern banks, with European investors also contributing (Schwantes, 145).

Anyone could catch a fish, but it took money and infrastructure to build a cannery and transport the product to market. Anyone could trap a beaver, but turning beaver pelts into gold required manufacturing capability, a transportation network, knowledge of distant markets, and a keen eye for fashion trends. Lumbering in particular was and remains a capital- and technology-intensive enterprise. The opportunity to amass wealth, in the early days of the West, was confined largely to those who already had it. "Historians have found," writes Richard White (285-87), "that opportunity in both the nineteenth- and the twentieth-century West was not as great as popularly believed . . . in most places and in most occupations, rags to riches stories were as rare in the West as in the East."

To be sure, there were some locally grown entrepreneurs, and their stories embodied and reinforced the frontier ideal. In 1883 one Joseph Smith and his two husky sons arrived in Hobsonville, a rocky point jutting into Tillamook Bay between Bay City and Garibaldi. The Tillamook country was still almost a wilderness—the overland route to Astoria consisted of an Indian trail along the coastline—but there were two fish canneries, both owned by Astoria companies, on the waterfront. As a sideline, the canneries sawed spruce into barrel staves which they shipped to Astoria and thence to San Francisco, where the staves were used to make kegs for pickles and syrup (Levesque 1:9-10). Joseph Smith figured there must be a market for milled lumber, and he figured he could find a way to ship it directly to San Francisco, bypassing the Astoria leg. The Smiths bought a piece of rocky beach from Charles Robson, the pioneer who held the original land claim, for $325. Smith and his boys blasted a sawmill site out of solid rock. Then they ordered a steam boiler, circular saws, and other machinery.

The mill machinery was sitting in an Astoria warehouse, waiting for shipment to Tillamook, when a great fire burned Astoria in July of 1883. Scorched but not destroyed, the equipment was transported to Tillamook Bay, where the boat carrying it was wrecked. Undaunted, Smith salvaged the machinery, installed it, and began sawing lumber in the fall of 1883 (Levesque 1:10-11). Wrote Charles Oluf Olson in 1937:

> *Their enterprise was more than a venture—it was adventure. It was built on faith that Tillamook County was a coming Country. As yet the population of the whole region was only about 2,500. . . . The city of Tillamook had but a few hundred inhabitants; . . .*
> (Tillamook Pioneer Association 1972, 142)

For millworkers, Smith employed homesteaders "who divided their time between their claims and their mill jobs, and worked the customary eleven or twelve hours a day without murmur; or Indians who knew nothing of the value of time and had only a primitive idea of wages." There were bunkhouses for "Indian bucks and single

This large fir log was characteristic of those growing in the Coast Range before the Tillamook fires. This log was cut in Polk County.

white men." Family men built shanties on the rocky shelves above the mill (Levesque 1:11). The workers' meager life and uncomplaining hard work gives a truer idea of what it took to make a life on the frontier than all the glowing descriptions in the newspapers.

Buying cheap logs ("settlers in many instances burned them, to rid their land of them"), Smith turned out lumber that was "rough, sound and serviceable, but not fancy," and sold it to his pioneer neighbors (Tillamook Pioneer Association 1972, 142). He also began negotiating for cargo space on San Francisco-bound ships. But California shippers, fearful of the Tillamook bar crossing, were reluctant to call at Hobsonville. Smith sent his son Buck to San Francisco with orders to come back with a ship. Buck leased the steamer *Santa Maria* and returned on her in 1886, with himself as pilot.

The Tillamook bar's reputation for treachery was deserved. Buck Smith, probably familiar with its hazards, evidently guided the *Santa Maria* into the bay without mishap. But when the time came for the loaded steamer to depart, her captain revealed that he feared the bar crossing and probably wouldn't be back. The elder Smith tried to reassure him; after he had crossed a few times he would think nothing of it, he told the captain. But the captain was still dubious.

So Smith talked him into waiting till he had made the outward crossing before making up his mind. He was to blow one long whistle if he was not coming back; three blasts if he had decided to return.

Paul Levesque recounts what happened next:

> Operations at the mill ceased while the Santa Maria proceeded with the outward bar crossing. Everyone climbed the cliffs to watch. When at last she was safely out of the bay and headed south in deep water, all eyes clung to the spot where her whistle was bolted to the smoke stack. Soon, a white jet of steam shot out and was blown away on the southwest wind. Nothing more. All hearts sank. The Santa Maria was not coming back. Then suddenly a second whisp of steam appeared, and then a third. The mill crew threw their hats in the air, and then danced on them, yelling and shouting. Smith bellowed above the noise, "Let's get up steam and saw like hell. We got to have lumber ready when she docks again" (1:12). [1]

And so the Tillamook-San Francisco connection was made. By May of 1887, Joseph Smith's sawmill and planing mill employed forty men and produced 50,000 board feet in a ten-hour day. "The *Oregonian* reported that the mill was scheduled for improvement and a brand new steamer was about to make her first trip to California with a cargo of 330,000 feet" (Levesque 1:12). In 1888, agents for the Truckee Lumber Company of California approached Smith with a tempting offer, and on April 3, he sold his holdings (Levesque 1:23). The Truckee Company expanded production to between 30,000 and 50,000 board feet of lumber a day. The new owners entered a period of enlargement and expansion that lasted seventeen years.

By the end of the nineteenth century, timber had emerged as the dominant enterprise in the coastal Northwest. The industry was at first mainly represented by the cargo mills, such as Joseph Smith's, that had sprung up in harbors large and small along the Pacific Coast. They shipped lumber in sailing schooners, serving Pacific Rim markets like China, Japan, Australia, Chile, and southern California. Financed mostly by San Francisco money (White 1991, 259), these mills pulled the first wave of investment capital into the Pacific Northwest and encouraged the permanent settlement of areas that farmers and miners had bypassed (Cox 1974, x). After their decade-long heyday in the 1880s, the cargo mills were gradually supplanted by bigger mills as rail and steamships began to favor locations that could serve as both large ports and railheads, and as innovations in milling technology demanded expensive upgrades that drove smaller mill operators out of business. By the 1890s the West Coast lumber industry was being transformed from "the relatively simple sort of resource exploitation that it had long been" into the modern industrial force that it would become (Cox, 254). "Though the number of sawmills in the nation declined by 12 percent during the eighties, capital invested in the lumber industry increased by over 200 percent. The industry in the Far West got more than its share of the increase."

Land ownership was similarly dominated by outside interests, as we have seen. As the nineteenth century drew to a close, the Northwest's wealth of timber, especially the vast stands of Douglas-fir forests along the coast, was attracting the attention of a lumbering industry that had exhausted most of the choice timber in the East and upper Midwest (Levesque 1:48). Among the owners of Tillamook timber lands were some whose names ring a bell today: the Blodgetts of Grand Rapids and the Stimsons of Muskegon (Levesque 1:62). In 1891, the Tillamook *Headlight* reported that the sale of public-domain timber land in the county had produced almost half a million dollars (Levesque 1:64). In 1902, the Portland *Oregonian* estimated that lumbermen from Michigan and Wisconsin had invested $30 million in the development of the Northwest (Robbins 1988, 28). What the historian Richard White says of the West as a whole is also pertinent here: "Particularly as mining companies and lumber companies imitated railroad companies and became larger and larger enterprises controlled by eastern corporations, the western economy began to seem like a marionette controlled by eastern puppeteers" (White, 268).

By the late 1800s these lumbermen, having just about finished the job in Michigan and Minnesota, were turning their attention to the West, where there was plenty of timber and an abundance of water for transportation. The Midwestern lumbermen found a forest wholly unlike the pine woods of their home. The steepness of the canyons and the hugeness of the trees (a mature Douglas fir can stand 300 feet tall, and the red cedars were commonly ten or fifteen feet thick) presented problems these entrepreneurs had not encountered before (Schwantes 1989, 177). Early loggers in the West usually cut only the trees small enough to manage with axes and close enough in to splash down into a navigable waterway. They would slide the logs down into the water over a greased corduroy road of logs called a skid road (the etymology of the more colorful "skid row"), or float them downhill in water-filled wooden flumes. Sometimes they would build a temporary "splash dam" on a narrow tributary river, float the logs on the temporary pond, and then dynamite the dam, sending the whole pondful of logs tearing downhill (Schwantes, 177).

Three technical innovations of the 1880s, the narrow-gauge logging railroad, the steam donkey, and the two-man crosscut saw, allowed loggers to get farther back into the woods and cut more and bigger trees. High-lead logging, developed in the early part of the twentieth century, made possible further inroads into the virgin forest. In high-lead operations, logs were fastened to cables and dragged to a tall spar tree by a steam donkey engine. High-lead logging made it possible to collect trainfuls of logs at a central location and send them down to the mill all at once. Logging camps began to penetrate the previously inaccessible woods east of Tillamook Bay. Levesque's history mentions eight large logging companies—at least three of which also operated sawmills—as well as a dozen and a half smaller outfits operating in Tillamook County between 1911 and 1933. A spreading web of logging railroads pushed even farther up the steep coastal canyons, bringing formerly untouchable stands of timber within reach.

Nobody worried about overcutting; the timbered hillsides just seemed too vast. The log supply, according to an 1899 special edition of the Tillamook *Headlight*, was "practically inexhaustible for the next fifty years . . . Along this vast stretch of heavily timbered country the axman has not penetrated" (Levesque 1:41).

Logging was about the most dangerous occupation of the day, and working in a sawmill ranked right up next to it.[2] Early newspapers are filled with accounts of gruesome accidents in the woods and the mills. Many later writers have romanticized the logger's occupation. Storyteller Ellis Lucia, in *The Big Woods*, says loggers enjoyed "the challenge of destiny wrestling those big ones" (1975, 27). Lucia also gives a nod to grimmer reality: the logger lived his life at the mercy of an exploitative industry, his labors backbreaking, dirty, dangerous, and poorly paid. "The old-time lumber kings sacrificed countless lives getting the logs at high speed down to splash" (27).

The infant Tillamook lumbering industry hit a rocky period with the Panic of '93 (Levesque 1:22), but it slowly recovered during the next couple of decades. By about 1913 the local industry was thriving (Levesque 1:107). The coming of the railroad in 1911 had expanded markets tremendously. "In the period that followed, a modern local industry began to evolve at many points along this umbilical rail connection to Portland markets" (Levesque 1:109).

King Timber

All along the Northwest coast, timber came to dominate the culture of the early settlement days as it dominated the economy. Early logging resembled mining more than anything else. "Here was a natural resource only to be exploited, with little thought given to conservation or sustained yields," writes the historian Carlos Schwantes (1989, 175). It was a capital-intensive enterprise operating in an environment of ferocious competition and volatile markets. "Ruinous competition, overproduction, market chaos, and dependence on railroad rates to compete in distant markets plagued the lumber business" (Schwantes, 180).

The unstable economic environment fostered a culture of unrestrained exploitation, a cut-out-and-get-out mentality. In good times, King Timber encouraged a heady boosterism; most people in those days truly could not imagine that the hillsides might someday be bare. It reinforced the frontier notion of the unlimited blessings that are sure to flow when nature is mastered and turned to human advantage. In bad times, depressed prices forced down wages, which brought on militant labor activity (Schwantes, 180) and destabilized communities. The extreme vulnerability of the lumbering enterprise to fluctuations in the national and international economy made it a rough economic ride for early settlers of the Northwest coast (181). Ellis Lucia characterizes the times with this colorful metaphor: "Timber ruled with a fist of tough, fibrous, pitchy wood, so that all else—economic, social, and political patterns, the lives of nearly everyone—was molded, bent, and battered to its ends" (Lucia 1975, 15).

Mostly a Blessing

By the dawn of the twentieth century, Tillamook was enjoying some of the blessings of prosperity and civilization. In 1904 the town had graveled streets, electricity, telephone service (Tillamook Pioneer Association 1972, 182-3), and a population of 1,500. There were six churches, two schools, and three dozen commercial enterprises, including a music store and a jeweler. Along with lumbering, dairying was becoming an economic mainstay. The first cheese plant had been started in 1894; it processed the milk from 2,400 cows within a radius of four miles of the town of Tillamook (182).

By and large the development of the timber resource, whether by local enterprise or out-of-state investment, was welcomed by a frontier citizenry that enjoyed the rising standard of living it brought. The published comments of the mid-1880s were mostly favorable about the timber barons' large land ownerships (Levesque

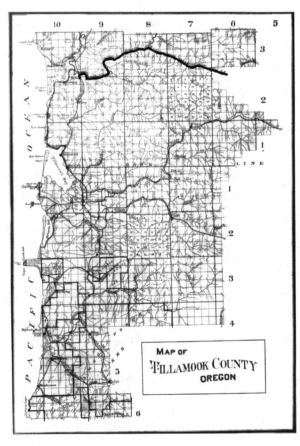

Map of Tillamook County drawn between 1897 and 1904, showing the route of the future Pacific Railway & Navigation line down the Salmonberry Canyon.

1:65). An 1892 article in the Tillamook *Headlight* chastised the lumbermen for land speculation, but the writer did not seem to mind their greed, or even their fraudulent practices, so much as their slowness in developing resources (Levesque 1:65-6). People wanted the prosperity that comes with the good times in a timber-based economy, and they seemed willing to put up with the social costs. "Most westerners," says Richard White, "saw the rapid development of the West as their greatest triumph" (White, 296).

"Tillamook is to be waked up this season," said the Yamhill *Reporter* in 1883: "The puff of the steam engine and the swir of the circular saw will be echoed through its stillness before many weeks as a lumberman is putting up a mill of immense capacity where one of the rivers enters the bay. . . . The erection of this first mill is a beginning of which the end cannot be seen. It is within reasonable probability that railroad communication will be established between Portland and Tillamook bay in a few years" (Tillamook Pioneer Association 1972, 185).

In fact, it took a little longer: the Pacific Railway and Navigation Co. started a rail line from the east side of the Coast Range in 1905. The rail line was finally finished in 1911 (Levesque 1:105). The train was nicknamed "Punk, Rotten, and Nasty" because, it is said, the combined effects of the steep grades, hairpin curves, breathtaking trestles, and smoke from the firebox made passengers queasy. With the coming of the railway, the town and the county were finally linked by land to the outside world, and the new century beckoned.

Notes

1. Levesque calls the Santa Maria a "steamer." It is likely she was a steam schooner—a sailing vessel retrofitted with a steam power plant in the stern. Thomas Cox (1974) has a fascinating chapter on the technological changes in the West Coast lumber industry, both ashore and at sea.

2. It is still dangerous, as the economist Tom Power points out: "The rate of disabling injuries in the lumber and wood products industry is 40 percent higher than in the construction industry and three times higher than in mining and manufacturing" (Power 1996, 146).

3

Tillamook Legend and Frontier Culture

THE TILLAMOOK BURN STORY IS A SET OF HISTORICAL EVENTS, like the ones we have just discussed. It is also a frontier legend, like Charles Oluf Olson's story of the hardworking pioneer Joseph Smith, who built a sawmill on a shoestring and sold it at a handsome profit five years later. The Tillamook Burn story, like the Joseph Smith story, resonates with many familiar frontier themes: risk-taking, hard work, individual enterprise, mastery of nature, faith in technology, and optimism about the future.

The dictionary definition of *frontier,* "that part of a settled or civilized country which lies next to an unexplored or undeveloped region," (Webster's 1974) is straightforward enough, but does not give much hint of the powerful influence of frontier mythologies on the way people think about a place. "Frontier" in the popular American imagination means a country larger than life, the promised land, the end of the rainbow, a place of big mountains and big men, a garden both utterly wild and irresistibly welcoming, a friendly Eden, a landscape molded by exceptionally strong and wise (or exceptionally weak and wicked) individuals.

The idea of the frontier has loomed large in American iconography ever since Columbus stepped off the boat. For religious dissenters and Crown-chartered capitalists, for starving Irish peasants and displaced Southern sharecroppers, the frontier was idealized as a place to escape the corrupt and oppressive forces of politics and economics that held sway in the old country or back East. Light out for the territories, the frontier promised, and you will be your own man, beholden to nobody.

"Frontier" has other, more-pragmatic indicators. A frontier economy is one based on resource extraction—lumbering, mining, farming, ranching. It is dependent on outside capital and outside markets (Robbins 1989) for its economic existence. Frontier social structures are fluid: people are mobile, settlements new, social boundaries permeable. Frontier cultural institutions—schools, libraries, newspapers, musical and artistic organizations—are underfunded and underdeveloped, relative to those in more settled places.

Finally, "frontier" denotes a worldview, a taken-for-granted set of attitudes and values. In the frontier worldview, nature is seen primarily as a storehouse of goods and, in a corollary image, as something to set oneself against, to master, and to manage. The principal measure of success on the frontier is how thoroughly wealth is extracted from nature—unsurprisingly, because resource extraction is the economic base of a frontier society. And because logging, mining, farming, and ranching call for physical prowess and a certain courage and daring, the frontier culture prizes physical strength and endurance of hardships. Individual endeavor, hard work, and risk-taking are seen as both necessary and sufficient for success.

The idea of the frontier has lent a mythical color to the ways in which Americans, especially Westerners, have interpreted the events of their own history. Its definition, character, and significance, and particularly its function as a lens through which the development of the West is viewed, have been the subject of furious debate among academics in recent years. This debate is an important one, for it challenges some key attitudes that we Americans, particularly those in the West, hold about ourselves as a nation and as a culture. The debate has unmasked some of the rationalization of motive and method behind westward expansion, and it has shifted the focus from the triumphs of the dominant group—European white people—to the social and environmental costs of their domination.

I want to spend some time discussing this debate, because it sets the scene for the main idea in this chapter: that the frontier worldview was the driving energy behind the Tillamook Burn reforestation effort, and that this energy also partly drives today's management plans. The philosophy and strategies that make up the plans for the Tillamook State Forest, in other words, draw heavily on frontier attitudes and values. Forest management on the Tillamook is a frontier story, in the larger sense of "story" proposed in the introduction.

I intend to qualify that assertion in several important ways. I am not suggesting, for instance, that modern forestry, on the Tillamook or elsewhere, is the functional equivalent of the "cut-out-and-get-out" logging that prevailed a hundred years ago. In fact it has stood as a bulwark, chiefly in theory but often in practice, against such depredations. Nor do I believe that the frontier worldview is the only philosophical foundation for modern forestry. Other worldviews have played an important role, including the one I call "arcadian."

Finally, I am not going to say, as some critical historians seem to, that our frontier heritage is irredeemably negative. I believe the traditional frontier worldview, despite serious blind spots, can serve our modern life well as a source of positive energy and confidence in what human hands and hearts can accomplish. What I am arguing is that modern forestry is a frontier story because it draws heavily on the cultural heritage that—for better or worse—has come down to us under the rubric of "frontier."

The Frontier Worldview Then

Much of what this century's scholars have thought and written about American history has rested on one very influential idea. In 1893 the historian Frederick Jackson Turner presented a paper at the Columbian World's Fair in Chicago, titled "The Significance of the Frontier in American History." In it he set forth a grand unifying historical theory: All of American social development can be explained by the presence of a large space that offered free land and resources and the opportunity for Americans to come in and seize them—in a word, Frontier. As Turner explained it:

> . . . the United States lies like a huge page in the history of society. Line by line as we read this continental page from West to East we find the record of social evolution. It begins with the Indian and the hunter; it goes on to tell of the disintegration of savagery by the entrance of the trader, the pathfinder of civilization; we read the annals of the pastoral stage in ranch life; the exploitation of the soil by the raising of unrotated crops of corn and wheat in sparsely settled farming communities; the intensive culture of the denser farm settlement; and finally the manufacturing organization with city and factory system (quoted in Meinig 1993, 258).

In short, a progression of predestined steps leading from primitive life to successively higher levels of civilization.

Turner's idea fit well with nineteenth-century thinking, because Americans already saw themselves as the model for human progress: "The ongoing drama of their westward expansion was, in effect, a reenactment of the human past" (257). Thus the unfolding of events along the frontier came to be interpreted as a mythological embodiment of the story of progress. Myth, says the historian Richard Slotkin, has the function of making the past

> metaphorically equivalent to the present; and the present appears simply as a repetition of persistently recurring structures identified with the past. Both past and present are reduced to single instances displaying a single "law" or principle of nature, which is seen as timeless in its relevance, and as transcending all historical contingencies (Slotkin, quoted in White 1991, 616).

Westerners have looked at their own history through the lens of myth. "Looking back from their old age on a period of momentous changes," says the historian Richard White,

> Anglo American settlers usually saw only the world transformed. They constructed from their memories a simple story of progress: "savagery" subdued, wilderness conquered, civilization planted, wealth created, and progress insured. Perhaps because only the most successful of these settlers had the luxury of writing memoirs or of being interviewed for the innumerable county histories, this remembered West emerges as a fluid, malleable place that people of ambition, determination, and intelligence shaped largely as they pleased (White, 181).

Turner's idea of the frontier had an important political dimension. Even before the Louisiana Purchase in 1803, Thomas Jefferson had nourished the dream of a nation of prosperous small farmers, politically free and economically independent because they owned their own land. Private ownership was seen as a bulwark against the tyranny of Europe, with its huge manorial estates and its miserable landless peasants. The West—the frontier—provided a seemingly limitless supply of land and resources for the defense of democracy. Turner saw the "closing" of the frontier—which he "ceremoniously" announced in 1893 (Hirt 1994, 301), as an alarming development, because it meant the probable end of "America's individualistic, libertarian political culture." Half a century later, Walter Prescott Webb, Turner's intellectual heir, reiterated these themes: the frontier's material blessings had made Americans prosperous and free; scarcity, he warned, would breed authoritarianism (Hirt, 301). Exploitation of natural resources, in other words, became a patriotic duty (an intriguing theme well developed in Hirt).

On a psychological level, the frontier came to be seen as both a refuge from modern culture and a source of revitalization for civilized life, which had become "overcivilized, sterile, and unreal."

It represented a source of virile energy, authenticity, moral order, and simple natural nobility (White, 621).[1] The idea of the frontier, then, carried a heavy burden of political and cultural expectations. It is not surprising that the real West came to take on a certain mythical coloration. The West's fabled emptiness (think of the lonely rimrock canyons in the typical western movie, or the huge, beautiful, human-free spaces in the photographs of Ansel Adams) fed this mythical vision by offering a *tabula rasa,* a blank slate upon which Americans could inscribe their destiny.

"In the conventional view," writes the historian William Robbins, "the West was opportunity, a lotus land and haven, a refuge for the discontented and outcast, a place of perpetual youth where life could begin over and over again."

In what became

> *the great American myth, above all, it was the promise of the West that loomed largest; for it was there that people would find the answer to their quest for a better life. Reality, in that sense, was less important than the symbols through which people perceived a larger design; indeed, in that scheme, symbol and myth passed for reality* (1989, 430).

The historian Richard Drinnon presents a more sinister view of the mythological West. In his *Facing West,* which is in effect a psychoanalysis of European-American imperialist motives, Drinnon argues that westward expansion was fueled by a furious and brutal energy that sprang from the repressed sexuality of white Europeans. Alienated from their own physical, sensual, and emotional selves, they projected their culturally unacceptable "shadow" qualities upon the darker-skinned people they encountered. Racism and violence, in this view, were not just unfortunate byproducts of frontier settlement; they were the central organizing principle of white-European-American oppression and domination, which continues to this day (Drinnon 1980, xv-xviii).

A less critical historian, Donald Meinig, points out that the Turner thesis, while useful in some ways, was the product of its time, "and with the hindsight of another century we now see things rather differently" (Meinig, 259). Turner lent a needed breadth to historical analysis by looking at economics and geography as well as politics, "but his simplistic, optimistic view of society as an organism evolving inexorably from simple to complex is now regarded as a serious misreading of the nature of society and history . . . "

Through the work of these and other scholars, we are beginning to reassess the received wisdom of traditional frontier history—the story that most Westerners my age absorbed without nuance or irony in grade school—from a different viewpoint. This alternative reading, well developed in Patricia Limerick's *The Legacy of Conquest* (1987), rejects the premise that Western history marched to some different drummer, that it was guided and shaped by something other than the economic and political institutions that guide and shape development in other parts of the world. Not high-flown ideology, say Limerick and her fellow scholars, but material realities created the West: struggles over control of raw materials, control of capital and technology to exploit them, control of transportation networks, control of political and military power, control of native Americans. This alternative perspective sees Western development as a phenomenon of world capitalism, focusing on the flow of resources and capital, the distance and domination of markets, and the inequities and hardships that ensued for most of those who were not white and European, as well as many who were (Robbins 1989, Stegner 1992, Schwantes 1989).

These analyses provide a much-needed corrective to the mythological elements of frontier history. They are a wake-up call to tell us that some dimensions of our old ideas are no longer valid, if they ever were. It is important to remember, though, that the critical view is also a story. It is a more complex, more subtle, and no doubt more accurate story than the frontier one, but still a story, and, as William Cronon has pointed out, a story cannot tell the whole truth.

It is important to keep this in mind, because there is a danger that the critical reading of our history can exaggerate the tragedy and shame of the Western heritage, even as the frontier myth exaggerates other, more positive qualities. The critical reading "may have a considerably wider application . . . and provide a useful introduction to a complex topic," says the evenhanded Donald Meinig, but "we must not reify it as 'the American frontier process'"(1259-64). Meinig's point, that the alternative reading sometimes fails to take into account important local and regional variations of the pattern, is applicable in a larger sense: if accepted universally and undiscerningly as "the truth," the critical reading of Western history risks being coopted as a myth itself—reduced to a set of "persistently recurring structures," as Slotkin has described, with the function of demonstrating, again and again, the obverse theme to the frontier myth: that white men are no damn good.

The critical historians I have cited are mostly careful not to do this—they remain grounded in historical reality and qualify their assertions carefully. Yet I sense that some of their appraisal has permeated the popular culture, without the important disclaimers.

We should not disdain the positive human qualities that are celebrated in the frontier myth even as we resolve to stay mindful of the environmental and human costs of that period of our history. Regardless of what one thinks of their personal motives, or of the economic forces that pulled them westward, the pioneers *were* courageous, inventive, energetic, strong, hardworking, confident in their abilities, realistic about the need to shape their environment to ensure their survival. We do not have to approve of the slaughter of Native Americans or applaud the slicking of trees off hillsides to appreciate these qualities and to appropriate them into our own lives.

The Frontier Worldview Today

Until very recently, the uncriticized mythological frontier worldview was the dominant framework through which Westerners perceived and acted on their reality. Indeed, for many people it is still the dominant framework. Because of its isolation, the West had a frontier economy and culture for much longer than most of the United States (Schwantes, 19). Some argue that the dominant role of resource extraction in the West's economy makes it in many ways a frontier still. In his 1989 history, *The Pacific Northwest,* Carlos Schwantes uses the concept of *hinterland* as a governing theme. By "hinterland," he means a region remote from centers of power and "tributary to more developed cities and regions" (xix). As we have seen, the development of the Tillamook region was retarded even more by the lateness of its linkage by rail to the Willamette Valley; the first railroad was not pushed through the Coast Range until 1911. It is in such hinterlands, the small, rural communities along the Pacific slope, that the frontier worldview has its strongest flavor.

Now for a disclaimer: when I talk about a "frontier worldview," I only describe it; I do not judge it. In the pages that follow, I will contrast the frontier worldview with a different one, emerging from a different set of root ideas about how the world works. My purpose is to show how a worldview emerges from the politics, economics, and culture of a time and place, how its roots both feed and are fed by it, and how it has the power to shape people's actions.

I also do not mean that, because they shared a worldview, everyone who lived in the West over the last 150 years had the same opinion about timber cutting or anything else that went on in their society. A worldview is larger than a political stance or a set of opinions. It is rather a mental lens or framework that people living in a given time and place use, mostly without thinking about it, to make sense of their world. It is the names they give things and the web of relationships spun by those names; it is the stories they tell themselves. A worldview is larger than a story, but a story can distill a worldview and present it in microcosm. In fact, that is one of the main functions of stories, in the sense that we are defining them.

Why do I bring up worldviews in a book about the Tillamook Forest? Because a worldview is the set of coded instructions for how we are to see the world; and how we see a thing has power to make a difference in how we think about it, and in what we do about it. Worldviews are important because they are *functional*—they inform, guide, and rationalize action (Johnson 1992, 36-38). A worldview presents certain choices as logical and reasonable, and devalues or discounts or eliminates other choices. If the teacher says my child has behavior problems, I will reach for a particular set of remedies; if the diagnosis is hyperactivity, I will likely reach for a different set of remedies. If my worldview tells me that a forest is a farm for trees, I will do one thing. If it tells me a forest is an ancient life form with which I can enter into an *I-Thou* relationship, I will probably do something else. So in describing the Tillamook Burn and reforestation story as a frontier story, I do not mean to say that the people who carried out this arduous and risky job were wrong or bad or even "old-fashioned." They simply saw the world the way they saw it, and did what their vision called them to do. (I should not say "simply" quite so simply, without saying also that what seems simple and inevitable in hindsight was probably, at the time, the product of complicated and contingent forces. I owe this insight to the critical historians).

Today we are beginning to see the world in a different way, even as the frontier view continues to shape our thoughts and actions in many ways. As a result, our collective vision about what to do seems less clear and compelling than it once did.

Frontier Roots

The Tillamook Burn story participates in the story of the frontier West, and that story is a piece of the worldview that undergirds European-American civilization. One important theme of that worldview, and the one that most concerns us here, is the domination and mastery of nature by human beings. Another is the celebration of the technology that helps us accomplish our manipulations of nature.

The idea that nature was there for man's taming became particularly pertinent with the arrival of English settlers in the New World, which seemed to many of them a fearsome and chaotic place. William Bradford, fresh off the Mayflower, called America a "hideous and desolate wilderness," according to the historian Roderick Nash. "Civilizing the new world," Nash writes in *Wilderness and the American Mind,* "meant enlightening darkness, ordering chaos, and changing evil into good" (Nash 1983, 411).

This ethic came to dominate American culture, as evidenced in the aggressive metaphors that were common until recently in discussions of the history and development of the West: *subduing* the earth, *harnessing* the rivers, *conquering* the wilderness, *pushing back* the chaos. "Such language animated the wilderness," Nash writes, "investing it with an almost conscious enmity toward men, who returned it in full measure" (414). Alexis de Toqueville, that most perceptive of America-watchers, observed in 1831 that Americans seemed to see "the wonders of inanimate nature" as nothing more than an obstacle to civilization. Americans, he speculated, lived too close to untamed nature to appreciate its beauty (Nash, 411).

For many generations, this frontier worldview told Americans their place in the order of things: they were to be the masters of nature, entitled to the fruits of conquest and entitled to use whatever tools were necessary. Yet even before the critical historians came along, the frontier worldview has been shaped by circumstances. It has been altered and softened in certain areas, as people came to see its ruinous consequences in particular situations. The movement to set aside federal forest reserves in the late nineteenth century, for example, arose in response to a complicated set of cultural developments, but one of the strongest was public dismay at how thoroughly and swiftly timber companies had ravaged the woodlands of the upper Midwest. People did not want the same thing to happen to the forests in the Pacific Northwest. The idea of forest conservation arose out of the Progressive movement of the last century, and it was envisioned as a philosophical and practical counterweight to the untrammeled forest exploitation that had taken place as part of the conquest of the frontier.[2]

Nevertheless, forest conservation still drew its ethic from the frontier ideology, focusing as it did on the utilitarian goal of maintaining "nature's ability to produce goods and services" rather than "the preservation of nature per se" (Hirt 1994, 32). The conservation movement reinforced the frontier theme of nature's continuing bounty as a necessary condition for liberty and democracy (Taylor 1992, 16). Gifford Pinchot, the first Forest Service chief and generally acknowledged father of Progressive conservation, opened his 1910 book *The Fight for Conservation* with the claim that "the conservation of natural resources is the basis, and the only permanent basis, of national success" (Taylor, 16). Conservation combined frontier ideology with the broader Progressive trends of professionalization, bureaucratization, scientific management and planning, efficiency, and stability (Hirt, 108). Stephen Fox offers this somewhat jaundiced take on conservation's driving vision:

> . . . the professional conservationists welcomed the urbanized present and future, describing bright prospects in the crisp, desiccated patois of engineering. Nature herself had no rights, . . . The world was, after all, made for man. "There are just two things on this material earth," said one professional, "—people and natural resources." User and used, in the spirit of the first chapter of Genesis (Fox 1981, 108).

Pinchot claimed to have coined the term "conservation" having chosen its root word carefully (Hirt, 32) to distinguish his program from a more-radical preservation agenda. The general acceptance of the term, says Fox, represented "the triumph of the utilitarian approach" (108). Conservation as applied to forests meant not preserving them from exploitation, but pursuing a more prudent, efficient, and farsighted exploitation that carried the additional goal of maintaining the forests' productive capacity for future generations.[3]

According to conservation ideology, humans still had the right to turn nature to their own purposes, but that right carried an important obligation to protect the land's productive capacity for the future. The conservation ideology is the frontier ethic softened by social constraints. The notion of nature's bounty as a condition of democracy is still there, enlightened by the duty to secure that bounty to future citizens. Optimism about human progress is still there, further leavened by faith in science, technology, and modern management.

The Tillamook story is a frontier story in this sense—a story about frontier values mediated through progressive ideals. In the Tillamook story, the price of mastery is the obligation to be a good master, a good steward of nature's bounty. The frontier was broken with plows and guns and barbed wire. In the Tillamook story, the taming was accomplished with chainsaws and skidders, but also with strategically placed firebreaks and nursery-grown seedlings and scientific silviculture—with mind as well as muscle. The Tillamook story stresses the heroism of the firefighting, the swift decisiveness of the reforestation experts, the people's faith in scientific forestry, their agreement about what this created forest was for, and the social blessings that would surely flow from the carefully managed tree farm that the Tillamook was expected to become. These emphasized elements play the melody and counterpoint of the frontier.

Arcadian Roots

We might like to think that environmentalism sprang full-grown from the brow of Earth Day in 1970. In fact, it is the contemporary expression of an alternate vision that has existed alongside, and in tension with, the frontier vision for almost three centuries. This alternate vision is a vision of nature as possessing an intrinsic worth apart from human utility, and even of nature as a living thing with whom humans may enter into a relationship. In America, this vision was expressed in the eighteenth and nineteenth centuries in the writings of John and William Bartram, John James Audubon, and especially Henry David Thoreau.

John Muir was the clarion voice for this arcadian sentiment, as the environmental historian Donald Worster terms it (1994, 3-25), in the nineteenth and early twentieth centuries. Raised in a strict (some would say abusive) Scots-immigrant Calvinist home, Muir became a prophet and evangelist for a mystical, ecstatic, experiential, non-human-centered version of nature conservation. For him, nature offered "an . . . essentially religious source of values and experiences" (Taylor, 91).

Muir saw no evidence in nature for the grim Christianity in which he had been raised. He was taught as a child that "man is productive of nothing but evil" (Fox 1981, 50), and was raised singing somber hymns that proclaimed the world's wicked vanity. Then as a young man (he was dodging the Civil War draft), Muir walked through Canada and saw the rare orchid *Calypso borealis*, "two white flowers against a background of yellow moss" (Fox, 43). The encounter changed his life. Muir noted in his journal, "I never before saw a plant so full of life; so perfectly spiritual, it seemed pure enough for the throne of its Creator. I felt as if I were in the presence of superior beings who loved me and beckoned me to come. I sat down beside them and wept for joy" (quoted in Fox, 43). Muir spent the rest of his life in service to that vision, working tirelessly for the preservation of wild places, doing his utmost keep them out of the hands of people who would use them for merely human material benefit.

Muir's preservationism was very different from the human-centered conservationism of Gifford Pinchot. "The world we are told was made for man," Muir wrote in his journal. "A presumption that is totally unsupported by facts. There is a very numerous class of men who are cast into painful fits of astonishment whenever they find anything, living or dead, in all God's universe, which they cannot eat or render in some way they call useful to themselves" (Fox, 52). The utilitarian bent of the more-dominant conservation ethic frustrated him: "To obtain a hearing on behalf of nature from any other stand-point than that of human use," he fumed after watching stockmen, lumbermen, and tourists invade his beloved Yosemite Valley, "is almost impossible" (Fox, 59).

Muir did not invent the arcadian ethic, but he revived and popularized a stream of thought that had existed since the Age of Reason (Worster 1977), and counterposed it to a movement that advanced the goals of nature conservation only in the context of a wider ideology of human use and benefit. The arcadian tradition has many disparate tributaries, and it covers a wide range of intellectual and emotional territory.[4] Along with Muir, thinkers like Aldo Leopold, Joseph Wood Krutch, and Rachel Carson brought the arcadian sentiment into the twentieth century. Essayists like John McPhee, Edward Abbey, Wendell Berry, Barry Lopez, and Bill McKibben are among its principal voices today.

The breadth of its concerns is represented well in Donald Worster's *Nature's Economy*, which treats the arcadian ethic as one of two opposing scientific traditions, and in Thomas Lyon's *This Incomperable Lande*, which traces its influence in nature writing since the seventeenth century. Lyon shows us the carefully researched natural histories of the Bartrams and Audubon, Muir's ecstatic response to nature's transcendent presence, and the cautionary voices of Carson, Abbey, and Berry (Lyon 1989, 3-74). These nature writings are the collective intellectual tradition of the environmental movement that came into the mainstream of American culture in the late 1960s. Diverse as they are, these sentiments have in common a consciousness of nature as something other than a metaphor for evil, a threat to survival, or a storehouse of material riches.

Environmentalism articulates a vision very different from the frontier vision (or what Worster calls, more harshly I think, the "imperial" vision) concerning the relationship between humans and their natural environment. Since its official birth on Earth Day 1970, "environmentalism" has become an overarching heading for a certain kind of aesthetic and emotional response to nature, a set of ethical values around the use and preservation of land, and a political movement devoted to validating that response and bringing those values into the cultural mainstream. The environmental ethic holds a brief for the wild over the tame, natural processes over human management, organic over mechanistic metaphors for the workings of nature, and the subjective experience of nature over a scientific or objective outlook.

A short digression is needed here. As is surely obvious by now, what I am building is a dichotomy of viewpoints which I am labeling "frontier" versus "arcadian." I go into the task knowing that dichomomies can be slippery things. At best they are simplifications; at worst they can distort reality by selective overemphasis and suppression. One wise thinker (it may have been G.K. Chesterton) said that whenever someone engaged him in conversation with, "Now, either a thing is A, or it is B," he immediately resolved not to believe a word the man said afterward.

Yet, as a botanist uses a dichotomous key when wading into a thicket of unfamiliar vegetation, a dichotomy of ideas can be a useful way to find your way around in a tangle of philosophies. Some dichotomies are better than others. I have already mentioned one that you hear often these days: "log-it-off" versus "lock-it-up." Such dichotomies are used with the intent of shutting down conversation. What I want to do instead is open the conversation up to divergent views and then examine them, compare them, and evaluate them. A dichotomy can be a useful way not only to identify a broad cleavage of thought, but to begin to find ways to bridge it (Hirt, 1).

So in that spirit I cautiously offer my dichotomy, knowing I am following the precedent of several others who have already weighed into this particular conversation. I have mentioned Donald Worster's "arcadian" versus "imperialist" tradition in science. Aldo Leopold puts forth his "A-B cleavage" (Leopold, 258-61). Paul Hirt offers the "ecological" versus the "agronomic" vision of the forest. Bob Taylor gives us the "pastoral" and "progressive" versions of conservationist thought.

What I am proposing in the arcadian-versus-frontier dichotomy is that these two strains of thought represent two distinct worldviews which nevertheless share significant moral underpinnings. By using it to frame the discussion, I am hoping to help people in each camp realize what they have in common with those in the other, so they can work toward a shared vision of what the Tillamook Forest ought to be.

The Environmentalist Critique

The impact of the environmental movement on the frontier world view is profound. Today it is rare to read any popular writing that talks about conquering nature or making the desert bloom, unless the writer's intent is ironic. It is much more common to read descriptions of natural settings that verge on the poetic and the mystical, such as this rhapsodic passage about a virgin forest, from the usually understated *The New Yorker*: "Above all, this forest is a remnant of the world as it was before man appeared, as it was when water was fit to drink and air was fit to breathe" (Caufield 1990). Much of the popular discourse about forestry—in newspaper stories, magazine articles, and casual conversation with friends—begins with the premise that modern forest management amounts to rape of the landscape. Writing in *Atlantic Monthly*, the nature writer Bill McKibben takes on the forest products industry in an article about the regeneration of logged-and-abandoned East Coast forests. With angry sarcasm he calls clear-cutting a "devastating 'management' technique" and deplores "(T)he . . . attack of industrial forestry" that has "afflicted the Maine woods . . . " and the "Bunyanesque rate of logging" that has taken place there. He urges his readers not to believe the claim of the timber companies (which is also the dominant rationale of modern forestry) that trees are a renewable resource. Rather, they should trust "the feeling in their gut that comes from looking at the ugly face of industrial forestry" (McKibben 1995).

Today, this ethic speaks to an increasingly large and influential segment of the society. The alternative is in some ways eclipsing the traditional, and the frontier ethic is becoming marginalized. Environmentalism has radically changed public sentiment about forestry practices, as any timber industry executive will tell you. Logging practices that were once routine and mostly applauded as good stewardship—large-scale clear-cutting and replanting, intensive salvage logging, burning of slash—are now excoriated for the damage they are assumed to inflict on forest soils, flora, and fauna.

The environmentalist critique goes further, however, than a condemnation of particular industrial practices. The movement has elevated a different way of thinking about humans and their natural environment, a different set of metaphors by which society's judgment is guided: the earth as a spaceship, with its obvious correlative message that natural resources are finite and on the brink of exhaustion; nature as a fragile and delicate dance of systems; humans (in the most extreme expression) as a cancer on the natural order. From within the framework of this set of metaphors, extraction of natural resources in general cannot be seen as heroic conquest, but only as environmentally unconscionable greed.

A worldview is functional—it opens certain avenues of action and closes off others. These shifts in meaning represent significant disturbances in our culture's worldview. They have had the effect of discrediting courses of action that once seemed right and good, and legitimizing others—such as leaving large blocks of forest untouched—that would have struck our pioneer ancestors as wasteful folly.

The advance of environmentalism in the culture has challenged the frontier worldview in another important way. It has been accompanied by—which is not to say it is entirely responsible for— an existential pessimism about the consequences of human activity on nature, and indeed, about every aspect of life. It is significant that the ascendency of the environmental movement coincides with the coming of the Age of Anxiety, or what some people call the postmodern age. The dropping of the atomic bombs at the end of the most destructive war in history, the awakening of concerns about world overpopulation and massive famine, the dawning awareness of limits on the productivity of natural systems, the shifting of scientific models away from assumptions of fundamental order and toward assumptions of fundamental dynamism, the overturning of traditional social and moral taboos, the increasing intrusion of (usually unpleasant) global happenings into our daily consciousness—all these have contributed to a pervasive sense of pessimism, a widespread feeling that life is whirling out of control. The arcadian model for nature helps allay this anxiety, by elevating nature from a storehouse of material goods (which those of us in the developed world have in plenty already) to a source of something we feel we lack—that is, *meaning.* In the arcadian ideal, nature can represent a source of meaning, an oracle from which humans can derive a set of moral values and ethical guidelines. It can even offer a kind of immortality, by making possible a relationship with a living thing that will endure long after we are dead.

The writer Bill McKibben (with his bestselling book *The End of Nature*) and other modern environmentalists have revived Muir's transcendental, essentially religious sensibility and his conviction that humans, by imposing their will upon nature, have hugely inflated their own importance (Taylor 1992, 93-94). The "deep ecologists" have taken this attitude several steps further in their claim to locate moral values within nature itself and to advocate a completely non-human-centered ethic toward it (Taylor, 95). Deep ecology "offers an alternative to the utilitarianism of progressive conservationism, as it looks to nature, rather than human desires, for philosphical first principles and moral guidance" (Taylor, 104).

The deep-ecologist stance, says Taylor, is fraught with contradictions and inconsistencies, and at its most extreme tends to be antiurban, antidemocratic, antirational, illiberal, technophobic, and downright misanthropic. Yet it appeals to many people nevertheless, because it criticizes the empty materialism of today's consumer society and offers instead a source of moral absolutes, assuaging, for some, a deep spiritual hunger.

The average environmentalist is not a deep ecologist, however, and it would be a mistake to conclude that environmentalism is nothing more than misplaced religion. People are drawn to the movement for a wide variety of reasons—to experience an ecstatic and mystical response to nature, to express a love of wilderness, to search for spiritual renewal, to set aside the best hiking places, to protect wildlife from extinction, to reinforce a sense of the interconnectedness of life, to indulge in a back-to-the-land fantasy, to express a disapproval of big business and the profit motive, and to escape, if only temporarily, the pressures of civilized life. "American attitudes toward nature," say Thomas Cox and others in *This Well-Wooded Land*,

> continued to be a mixture of many elements: Jeffersonian ideas, romanticism, transcendentalism, the antiurban Arcadian myth, a belief in progress and the inexhaustibility of the nation's resources, and more. As always, the particular blend varied from individual to individual. Those seeking to bring scientific management and utilization to forest resources often found themselves in conflict with those who had different priorities (Cox et al. 1985, 209).

That, in a nutshell, is precisely what's happening on the Tillamook now.

Environmentalism has furnished a platform for practical critiques of every aspect of industrial and commercial life. It has leveled many well-founded criticisms at the lumbering industry for its past and present practices. And it has offered an attractive alternative to the utilitarian tendency—still dominant today—to see the world in purely material terms.

Demands on the Forest

A more mundane factor in the rise of the arcadian ethic is that most people now live in cities. The frontier in fact is a hundred years gone. Standards of living are rising, even as people lose touch with the material base of their prosperity—the slaughterhouses, the sawmills, the smelters. The messy processes of resource extraction are less regularly on public display, and there is less of a link between the log felled on Tuesday and the paycheck on Friday, to reinforce the cutting of trees as a social good. For most people nowadays, the forest is a place to play, not a source of meat on the table and a roof over the head.

The arcadian ethic has put a different kind of demand on the forest, even as population growth and people's rising standards of living ensure a continuing brisk demand for the forest's more material blessings. Consumption of wood products has risen steadily since World War II. While per-capita consumption of lumber has leveled off in the last decade, in absolute terms it continues to rise. In 1960, Americans used about 30 billion board feet of softwood lumber, enough to build three million small-to-medium-sized three-bedroom houses. In 1990 the figure was 46 billion board feet (Haynes et al. 1995).

Houses are getting bigger. An average single-family house built in the early 1950s had about 1,150 square feet of floor space. A house built in 1990 had an average of 2,080 square feet, and average size is expected to grow to 2,275 square feet by the year 2040 (Haynes et al. 1995), increasing by 13 percent the amount of lumber used to build each house. For years the average three-bedroom house was assumed to contain about 10,000 board feet of wood. Today the figure is closer to 16,000 board feet ("Senate panel approves environmental exemptions," 1995). As for paper, consumption is on the rise even in this era of electronic communication. In 1952, each man, woman, and child in the United States used, on average, 369 pounds of paper annually. In 1991 the per-capita consumption had risen to 672 pounds (Haynes et al. 1995). That is equivalent to 336 reams of printer paper, or 10,752 first-class letters with envelopes, or 2,688 rolls of two-ply toilet paper.

In brief, demand on the forest has never been more intense, or more varied, than it is now. There are many more of us Americans than ever before, and we all want wood products to make our lives comfortable, and logs to keep mills running, and paychecks to support families, and tall trees, and clean water, and wildlife habitat, and pretty hiking trails, and . . . intangibles like the shiver of a tree's shadow on the shoulders, the soft scrape of moss on the back of the hand, the spring of duff underfoot, the shaft of sunlight streaming through the canopy. We want it all. And we are in deep and painful conflict about the role, purpose, and worth of forests in our lives.

Notes

1. Richard White (1991), in his chapter titled "The imagined West," does a good job of unpacking and analyzing these tacit cultural codings.

2. For a thorough and readable treatment of the complex dimensions of the conservationist/environmentalist movement in America, see Stephen Fox, *John Muir and his legacy* (1981).

3. Pinchot's conservation conflicted with another, sharply diverging view that its early adherents called "preservation" (and which I am calling the arcadian view). To them, preservation meant protecting natural settings from human use altogether, rather than exploiting their resources even in a

socially responsible manner. The difference between "conservation" and "preservation," says Stephen Fox, became blurred early in the century as "conservation" came to be applied to everything that needed environmental protection (108-9). Today, however, the distinction is regaining its clarity.

4. Bob Pepperman Taylor's *Our Limits Transgressed* (1992) offers a lucid analysis and comparison of the conservationist and environmentalist philosophies.

4

The Legend-spinners

Fire

THE FOREST COVERING THE TILLAMOOK COUNTRY BEFORE 1933 may have been the biggest swatch of contiguous virgin forest in Oregon and probably in the entire forty-eight states (Oregon Department of Forestry 1992). Official accounts of the fires seem to take this for fact. To make the statement without any qualification, however, is to mislead. Many people think the Douglas fir forests of the Pacific slope existed in a stable state over thousands of years and were disturbed only when European-Americans arrived.

This is not the case. These forests evolved in the presence of periodic and massive fires. The stands of pure Douglas fir and mixed Douglas fir and hemlock that the settlers found in the Coast Range forests had sprung up from the ashes of fires that may have occurred anywhere from a decade to five centuries before. A particular several-thousand-acre tract of forest might live and grow for 250 to 500 years before being flattened by fire again, and the cycle would begin with new seedlings sprouting out of the blackened earth.

The frequency of fires was influenced in turn by larger climatic patterns, and these also had the effect of reshuffling the forest's plant communities several times in the last 14,000 years (Spies et al., in press). Major shifts may have happened very rapidly, in the space of a few decades. Samples of pollen and ash found in a lakebed deposit in Lane County, Oregon, for example, suggest that a spruce forest was replaced by one dominated by Douglas fir in less than a century. The forest apparently reverted back to spruce after about 400 years. Evidence like this (even though it is too early to know whether it holds region-wide) makes the common notion of a stable state even less tenable.[1] Coast Range forests almost certainly existed in a slowly shifting mosaic of large and small patches of forest, ranging from shrubby areas to stands of dense, old trees.

In some places, along the fringes of forest next to the coast and the inland valleys, the forested landscape was aggressively managed by the original inhabitants. The Native Americans' management tool was fire, which has been used by humans in a deliberate and systematic way, here and on many other parts of the globe, for thousands of years (Pyne 1982). The Indians of the Northwest used fire to clear out the underbrush and create open habitat for game, to fell large pines and cedars for their own use, and to encourage the growth of blackberry and huckleberry patches (Walstad 1992, 31). As a result of Indian land management—as much shaped and constrained by their technology as ours is by our own—the landscape of western and southern Oregon was much more open, less wooded, than it is today, as the journals of pioneers will attest. An early Tillamook County settler noted that

> there was not a bush or a tree to be seen on all those hills, for the Indians kept it burned over every spring, but when the whites came, they stopped the fires for it destroyed the grass, and then the young spruces sprang up and grew as we now see them (Petersen 1994, 15).

Douglas fir does not grow well in shade—its own or that of any other tree species—and it germinates best on a duff-free, mineral-soil surface. Natural, large, periodic fires thus set the stage for the vast, even-aged Douglas fir forests that the early European explorers and settlers found when they got here.

The 1933 Tillamook fire, which burned 240,000 acres, was large by the standards of settled European-Americans, but it was not the largest fire that had occurred even in the brief history of white settlement of the Northwest. That record probably belongs to the Silverton fire of 1865 (Office of the Secretary of State 1994), which burned almost a million acres. Fires occurred fairly frequently along the Oregon coastal forests before and after European-American settlement. The Nestucca fire of 1848, the Siletz fire of 1849, and the Yaquina fire of 1853 together burned over a million and a half acres, about two and a half percent from Oregon's total land area of sixty-one million acres (Office of the Secretary of State 1994).

The patch of forest that would become the Tillamook Burn, however, had been spared from fire for at least 400 years. It was primarily composed of huge Douglas firs. The land was rugged and steep, which, along with poor timber markets during the Great Depression, kept the Tillamook forests from being logged as quickly as the lower-lying stands along the coastal rivers. The Tillamook was a fog-drenched, moss-draped, soft-floored ancient forest, cloaked in light-dappled shade.

The 1933 fire was not an aberration, but a continuation in a long-standing, though unpredictable, pattern of disturbance. That fact, had it occurred to the people of the Tillamook at the time, would have been small comfort. To them the Tillamook fires were monsters that destroyed their forest paradise and gobbled up their livelihood, billions of board feet of prime timber. This malevolent characterization of forest fire still dominates nearly all the writing and storytelling about forest fires in the Northwest, and indeed everywhere: there's almost no American alive who doesn't know the story of Bambi, the admonitions of Smokey Bear. Fire represents the antagonist in the Tillamook legend, the adversary over which human effort and skill finally won a great victory.

The Tillamook legend was spun by superb storytellers. Ellis Lucia, a Forest Grove newspaperman, cast the Burn and the reforestation effort as a heroic saga—in fact, he calls it "the saga of the Tillamook Burn" (xix) in his book, *Tillamook Burn Country* (1983). He tells of the hardy high-school and college students of Forest Grove who worked summers logging in the Burn. "Many virile young men," says Lucia, "hard of muscle from summers in The Burn, gave Pacific University and nearby high schools some of the toughest football teams on record" (xiv). Working on the Tillamook Burn became a rite of passage for a whole generation.

Another newspaperman who wrote about the Burn, Stewart Holbrook, is well known for his colorful and romantic writings about the early days of Northwest lumbering. On August 24, 1941, the eighth anniversary of the "blowup" of the 1933 fire, the *Sunday Oregonian* ran a story by Holbrook headed, "The Terrible Tillamook Fire." Alluding to the fire's alleged human cause, Holbrook wrote, "the gods must have wept" at the ignominious beginning of "a major forest tragedy in this or any other country" (Holbrook 1941).

William Stafford, later named Oregon's poet laureate, wrote a poem about the Tillamook Burn in 1958 (Stafford 1962). It begins "These mountains have heard God;/they burned for weeks. He spoke/in a tongue of flame . . . " Arthur W. Priaulx, a public-relations man for the West Coast Lumbermen's Association, may have had the greatest influence in shaping the Tillamook legend. Writing in the Portland *Oregonian* in 1946, Priaulx brought the three Tillamook fires vividly to life, calling the 1933 fire a "hot monster" and the snags "solemn markers in a graveyard" (Priaulx 1946). The purpose of the article was to mount a persuasive argument for a statewide effort, then only a controversial idea, to turn the Burn into "a vast 300,000-acre growing tree farm."

Priaulx makes his case in terms of sound business practice, perhaps as a preemptive strike against assertions of creeping socialism. The article shows that the timber industry was by and large behind the effort to reforest the Tillamook through a state bond issue. An earlier plan would have imposed a severance tax on timber to pay for the reforestation, but that idea was defeated after vigorous industry lobbying. The phrase, "tree farm," incidentally, had been coined only five years earlier by a Weyerhaeuser public-relations man, Roderic Olzendam, to christen the company's new conifer plantation near Montesano, Washington (Richen interview 1994).

It was Priaulx who dreamed up the idea of taking school children out to the Tillamook Burn, giving them shovels and hoedads, and setting them to work planting trees for a day. He arranged it with Donald W. Stotler, an administrator with the Portland public school district, who described the program's mission in this way: "Plant Trees and Grow Citizens." It started in 1950. The kids went out in yellow school buses and chartered Greyhounds (Lucia 1983, Gale interview 1995). Their pictures appeared regularly in the newspapers. The children kept coming for 20 years, more than 25,000 of them in all.

The "Plant Trees and Grow Citizens" program was a stroke of public-relations genius. It worked so well that the role of school children has been exaggerated in the lore of the Burn ever since. Today, when they drive down the Wilson River highway, these middle-aged car repairmen and college professors and computer programmers and secretaries look out at the expanse of young trees next to the highway and say to their own children, "I planted that forest." In fact children planted fewer than one percent of the seedlings that would grow to become the new Tillamook Forest (Fick and Martin interview 1993).

The Lyda Story

This is not to suggest that these people were inventing stories. Their accounts are factual. It is just that the facts of the Tillamook Burn fit so neatly into the prevailing cultural landscape that it would have been difficult not to trumpet the story in heroic strophes. It is instructive to look back and examine legend and fact together from the moody perspective of our own time, half a century down the road.

For instance, the legend of the 1933 fire invariably starts with the story of Elmer Lyda's logging outfit, operating up Gales Creek Canyon on that hot, dry August day. The fire hazard was extreme, and fire wardens had urged logging operations to halt for the day, but there was no law to compel it in those days. Lyda's crew, the story goes, was intending to haul in just one more log before shutting down. That log, scraping over a dry piece of slash, rubbed and flamed, and suddenly the woods were on fire. In his retelling of this story, Ellis Lucia points out that Elmer Lyda may have been unjustly blamed all these years. There was some evidence, he says, of another fire burning at the same time, deeper in the woods (xx). In any case, 1933 was a year of drought all across the country, and the forest was as dry as it could be. It wouldn't have taken much to spark a fire—a little lightning or a flicked cigarette could easily have done it. Fire, after all, is a periodic visitor to these forests. Elmer Lyda's loggers may have touched off the 1933 fire, but they did not "cause" it.

The Elmer Lyda story was used for years by the Keep Oregon Green organization as a cautionary tale about human carelessness in the woods. Human culpability is an important theme of the Tillamook legend, because it reinforces the idea of human domination of nature. As humans have power over their environment, so they bear responsibility for controlling natural events. Today we are inclined more to emphasize nature itself as being in control, as knowing what is right for the forest. This ethic is one element of the arcadian worldview about the place of humans in the natural order. It also may be a reaction, perhaps an extreme one, against the frontier myth of conquest and domination. In any case, today's discourse about forests, especially at the scientific level, tends to treat fire not as a foreign enemy but as an essential element of the Douglas fir forest ecosystem. "We're learning fires are not the all-consuming, all-destructive things we thought they were in the past," says the forest ecologist Dave Perry of Oregon State University (Pryne 1994). This would have seemed a strange notion to the men who fought the Tillamook fires.

In another example of legend juxtaposed on history, Lucia tells us that the 1948 constitutional amendment for the reforestation bond issue was passed "unhesitatingly." In fact, it was a squeaker. The amendment was approved statewide by only 1,875 votes out

Collage of newspaper headlines after the 1945 fire.

of 420,000 cast, and it did not pass in Tillamook County (Fick and Martin 1992), which might have expected to benefit the most. The "yes" votes from the counties of Multnomah, Lane, and Benton carried the legislation (Levesque 1985, 2:865). Multnomah and Lane counties are, respectively, the homes of Portland and Eugene, the state's two most populous cities.

A bond issue was not the only idea suggested. The minority report of the governor's 1946 special committee had proposed levying a severance tax on the timber industry amounting to twenty-five cents a thousand board feet. The spokesman for the minority was Morton Tompkins, master of the Oregon State Grange, who strongly believed the industry "should be now, and should have been for a long time, assuming their responsibilities of such a program" (Levesque, 2:849). Tompkins figured the tax would bring in between one and a half and two million dollars a year. "Argument was made that this was unfair to the timber industry," he said in the report. "In this I cannot concur." Governor Snell proposed a twenty-cent-per-thousand tax to be used for rehabilitating the Burn and also for fire control and research.

Naturally the lumbermen objected to the tax. "Quietly and smoothly behind the scenes," reported the Gresham *Outlook,* "timber interests are carrying on a high powered campaign in opposition to Governor Earl Snell's proposal to levy a severance tax . . . " The newspapers, however, were generally positive about the idea. The *Oregon Voter* responded to the governor's proposal with this editorial opinion:

> *Oregon, now the foremost forest state of the Union, can become a grand benefactor of posterity, or it can neglect a great mission which peculiarly confronts it. . . . Far-sighted leaders see the mission and the opportunity clearly. Of course it is possible, as some observers believe, that the people of 1975 will not have much need for lumber and wood products. That theory is too much of a strain upon our intelligence. The people of this generation must proceed in the belief that timber and wood products still will be vitally needed a generation hence* (Levesque, 2:852).

The governor wooed the recalcitrant timbermen in a talk at the 1947 Pacific Logging Conference. "I know that as logging operators, you are vitally interested in the young forests and the forests we expect to grow," he said. "The operator and the timber cannot be separated" (Levesque, 2:854). Nevertheless, pressure from industry succeeded in getting the proposed tax reduced to ten cents a thousand board feet. That version passed the House easily, but hearings on the Senate version brought out strong opposition from the timbermen. The president of Willamette Valley Tree Farms testified that the tax "will put a substantial mortgage on funds that otherwise would be expended for private reforestation programs" (856). Others objected to placing the burden for reforestation on a single industry. The bill's prospects looked dim.

Then, three days before the vote was scheduled in the Legislature, state treasurer Fred Paulus came up with the solution: a constitutional amendment authorizing the bond issue. The severance tax idea was dropped (although it did not go away), and on April 5, the last day of the legislative session, the bill passed both houses almost unanimously. It was approved by the voters— narrowly, as we have seen—in the November general election.

The legend proclaims that the people of Oregon acted with one voice, eagerly taxing themselves for the sake of restoring the Tillamook Burn. Then as now, things were more complicated. Nothing on the scale of this reforestation scheme had ever been attempted before. Public ownership of timber lands was viewed with suspicion by many. Roosevelt's New Deal was emphasizing increased federal ownership of land, to the dismay of most people in the timber industry (Levesque, 1:370). They and other business people tended to look askance upon any government interference with free enterprise. Many Oregonians probably thought the idea was an unwarranted intrusion of the state into local affairs, and a foolish waste of money besides (Lucia 1983, xxiii). Some local people may not have trusted the state to keep its end of the bargain and hand over the money when the new trees grew big enough to log.

The Salvage Story

The salvage efforts are another example of events given a mythical burnishing. The salvage logging was written up in approving tones in the newspapers of the time (Holbrook 1941, Priaulx 1946). Stewart Holbrook calls it "a cheering part of an otherwise dismal picture." Lucia casts it as a heroic struggle to reclaim for the war effort timber that would otherwise have been wasted (xxii, 114). Heroism, in this case, turned out to be profitable. In December of 1933, four months after the first fire, the Tillamook's largest timber landowners, including Weyerhaeuser Co. and John W. Blodgett, a Midwestern timber magnate, formed the Tillamook Salvage Pool, soon renamed the Consolidated Timber Company (Levesque 1985). Consolidated's partners came up with about $3.5 million to build logging railroads and truck roads and to buy equipment. The general manager was Lloyd Crosby, a cousin of the famous singer. Bing Crosby had worked in the woods on a survey crew in 1921 and 1922. "He was a good worker," Lloyd Crosby later recalled, "although he twice hacked himself with an axe and had to be hospitalized. He used to sing in the woods—developed his voice that way. We didn't think he was much good, but he fooled us all" (Levesque, 1:327).

Over the next 13 years, Consolidated and as many as 200 smaller operators (Pyne 1982) salvaged about four billion board feet of sound Douglas fir logs, about a third of the estimated toll taken by the fires (Oregon Department of Forestry 1993). The value of the wood was, of course, much less than it would have been had it not burned. But World War II and the postwar building boom had sent timber prices skyward. The price of stumpage more than doubled between 1946 and 1951 alone, going from $5 a thousand board feet (Priaulx 1946) to $12 a thousand (Beh 1951). In all, salvage logging from the Tillamook yielded almost $100 million (calculated in 1993 dollars) from 1934 to 1955 (Oregon Department of Forestry 1993).

The speed and efficiency of Consolidated's logging operation were "legendary," according to Lucia (86). The Consolidated logging camp at Glenwood, northwest of Forest Grove, was a "brawling highball center of salvage operations" (90) through which millions of board feet of timber were transshipped. Much of the salvaged Tillamook timber went to the Portland shipyards to be used as keels and spars for Navy ships and as construction scaffolding. In these uses the Tillamook timber had an advantage, because the unbucked, tree-length logs could be carried to tidewater over the rail lines that Consolidated Timber had pushed into the Burn country. Some of the best logs were peeled into fine-grained, knot-free veneer and used to make plywood for barracks (Arnold 1942). Much of the timber was processed by mills in the towns ringing the Burn: Tillamook, Seaside, Astoria, Forest Grove, Hillsboro, Carlton, McMinnville (Lucia 1983, 104). In 1943, Consolidated Timber Company received the Army-Navy "E" award for its high production efforts to defeat Hitler and the Japanese (115). The award was presented at the Glenwood camp "under wartime security" (114), and the event was heralded by a sixty-piece brass band.

The smaller salvage operators did well for themselves, too. Because prices kept going up, loggers would go back in to the same areas again and again to pick up wood they had left behind on the last entry. This piecemeal salvage activity hampered the state's early reforestation efforts (Oregon Department of Forestry 1993, 14). Salvaged timber continued to dribble out of the Burn until 1971. In all, about 7.5 billion board feet of timber were removed, more than half the amount that would have been available had the four Tillamook fires never happened (Oregon Department of Forestry 1993, 22). What is glossed over, in the Tillamook legend's emphasis on the "killing" of billions of board feet of timber, is that half the board footage was recovered in salvage, and these logs made very fine timber indeed. The salvaged wood was just as much a resource as the green timber would have been, and even though there was less of it, it fetched high wartime prices.

Today salvage logging after a wildfire is controversial. Some scientists and most environmental activists say the forest ought to be left alone to repair itself after a fire, which is after all a natural event for a forest ("Scientists advise against proposed dead timber cut," 1995). The dead wood, they say, is nature's way of nourishing the recovering ecosystem. Referring to the Wenatchee National Forest fire of 1994, Dave Perry, the forest ecologist, said, "If we salvage, it will probably lengthen the period of time before the area provides habitat for old-growth-dependent species again" (Pryne 1994). For their part, timber company owners argue that the dead trees have to be taken out not only because they're valuable but because they would otherwise harbor diseases and insects that would threaten the forest's health—by which they mean the health of the remaining live trees ("Salvage logging bill passes in House," 1995). Like most other forest issues, this one is far from settled, but one ecological study of the Tillamook Burn concluded that the heavy salvage logging in the Tillamook country did more damage to soils and streams than the fires ever did (Oregon Department of Forestry 1992).

The Management Story

The Oregon Department of Forestry is now making plans to manage the Tillamook and other state forests in northwestern Oregon under a set of strategies called, collectively, structure-based management (SBM). We will look at these strategies in detail in the next chapter, but essentially, SBM calls for using the traditional tools of silviculture—clear-cutting, partial cutting, thinning, planting, and vegetation control—to foster a "dynamic balance" of forest types across the landscape. These forest types will range from planted clear-cuts to thinned middle-aged stands to structurally complex older stands that will, in theory, have most of the structural attributes of old growth.

SBM is a new approach, and highly experimental—decisions are driven by desired forest structures rather than desired quantities of timber. Realizing the public's approval is important, the department is committing itself to openness at every stage of the planning, by inviting interested individuals and a wide variety of recreation and environmentalist groups to participate. If the Northwest Oregon forest plan, now a draft, is adopted as expected in 1999, the Tillamook foresters will begin a task that will take the next several decades: converting a mostly even-aged young plantation to a forest that is structurally and biologically diverse. Their goal, and their promise, is to create a forest that can provide abundant timber, healthy wildlife habitat, pure water, pretty scenery, rich recreational opportunities—everything.

That promise, and the notion of using human effort and skill to achieve it, are products of the same myth that stresses the heroism of the frontier. I have already drawn a line from traditional frontier mythology through the Progressive conservation movement to the Tillamook Burn rehabilitation. By calling the Tillamook's management plan a "story," I'm extending that line forward to link the plan to its frontier heritage. I believe the forest's managers would not object to this link. I think they would agree that the task before them will require all the positive frontier virtues—courage, persistence, hard work, technical know-how, technology, and the confidence that this forest can and will produce wealth for future generations. And if their plan works, they will be right.

Will it work? Some people think the idea of managing forests amounts to war against nature—I am thinking now of Bill McKibben and the deep ecologists. I do not agree with them. The technic of forestry has evolved alongside society's evolving environmental consciousness (Society of American Foresters 1993). Foresters, no less than botanists and biologists, have learned a great deal over the past few decades about the complexity of natural processes in a forest. At the time the Tillamook Burn was reforested, such things as the role of fungi and other microorganisms in healthy forest soils, the importance to salmon and trout of dead wood in streams, and the damaging soil compaction produced by heavy log-skidding equipment were not part of a forester's knowledge. Today's

Louisiana-Pacific advertisement acknowledging State Forester Ed Schroeder's role in creating the new Tillamook Forest. Schroeder was the Northwest Oregon District Forester from 1945 to 1955.

management plans for public forests, including the structure-based management scheme being planned for the Tillamook, pay attention to forest soils, streams, and wildlife habitat, and make conscious tradeoffs in timber yield to protect these resources (Oregon Department of Forestry 1998a, Seven key elements 1994).

I should point out, however, that these advances in forestry research and practice have not been always so purposeful in their intention or so enlightened in their execution as hindsight makes them seem. The management story is often told (especially by those who make their living as forest scientists or managers or timber executives) in a way that makes the accumulation of forestry knowledge sound like a logical, orderly, and inevitable progression. In real life, forestry science, like all science, is more often a halting forward-and-back process of limited discoveries, unexpected failures, inexplicable successes, and fortuitous accidents. The body of knowledge about forests is richer than ever before, but its accumulation was not governed by the rational planning of scientists and managers.

Professional myopia—believing uncritically in one's own story—can cause problems. Paul Hirt, one of the historians we met in Chapter 3 (and one of the most critical of them), mounts a scathing indictment against the Forest Service for presiding over "an orgy of unsustainable logging" during the 1970s and 1980s. All during this time, he says, the agency was blinded by a "conspiracy of optimism," a belief that with ever more intensive management foresters could produce enough outputs of everything to please everybody (Hirt 1994, 294).

Why did this happen? Foresters were not cynical collaborators in irresponsible logging, Hirt says; it is just that they had "a psychological investment in the efficacy of intensive management" so powerful it filtered every assumption and perception. Enough science existed in support of their faith in technological mastery over nature that "foresters could assert an empirical foundation— and therefore unquestioned legitimacy—to their beliefs," Hirt says. But for the most part, "forest researchers were only asking the kinds of questions that would advance the conspiracy of optimism." Any research that pointed to flaws in their practices was "consigned to marginality" or deferred for further study (294).

None of this is to fault the information or judgment of the forestry department's managers as they make their long-range plans for state forests in northwestern Oregon. The evidence suggests that they are doing everything right—keeping on top of the research, embracing an innovative approach, and sharing their every move with the public.

The Tillamook legend promises *timber forever.* The new management plans now being formed for the Tillamook promise timber *and* everything else, forever. That goal is audacious enough to give anyone a moment's pause.

Fifty years ago, the visionary wildlife biologist Aldo Leopold noted that rational manipulations of landscapes tend to be confounded by unintended consequences. Nature, he had come to see, is mystifyingly more complex than the traditional linear, cause-and-effect-based management philosophy of the time could hope to understand (Lyon 1989, 76). The Tillamook's managers will do well to keep this principle in mind. The history of modern forestry is very short, and the time it takes to grow a mature forest is very, very long. And yet the management plan for the Tillamook Forest, shaped by history and legend, is aiming for a forestry that can sustain both the forest and the people who use it, forever. That is something never before accomplished in human history.

Notes

1. It also makes us ponder whether pre-settlement conditions are an appropriate reference point for management. "It would be impossible to recreate the coastal forest that existed at some point in the past, even if we could describe previous forest conditions perfectly (which we cannot) or knew the role of Native American activity precisely (which we do not)" (Spies et al.).

5

Field Trip: Mark Labhart
"I just call it a win-win."

ALL THROUGH THESE LAST FEW TURBULENT DECADES, THE Tillamook State Forest has been placidly growing, oblivious to the crosscurrents of politics and economics, unaware of changing worldviews and paradigms, putting on wood the way a trust fund gathers interest. The Tillamook Forest, a poster child for the scientific forestry of the 1950s, is now coming of age in a world in which both of those words—"scientific" and "forestry"—carry a somewhat different emotional resonance.

Its original reason for being—to furnish trees for timber—is succeeding beyond question. The seedlings planted and the seed scattered from airplanes in the 1950s and 1960s, along with those pockets of trees that came back naturally, are now fast-growing, thickly-planted stands of Douglas fir. Mark Labhart is proud of those trees, proud of what they represent, and proud of what they promise. "This is essentially a man-made forest," he says. "It was created by human beings. It was totally ruined, and this"—he sweeps an arm toward the green-stippled hills beyond the windshield—"is how it came back. And the story doesn't end there. It goes on. It's a story of good forest management."

It is a beautiful August day, and I am riding in Labhart's Department of Forestry pickup. We are headed east out of Tillamook, along the Wilson River highway, into a tumbled curtain of green. Mark Labhart is the district forester for the Department's Tillamook District, which puts him in charge of managing 250,513 of the Tillamook State Forest's 364,000 acres of trees. Most of the trees are still very young, but the forest has already seen some logging activity in the form of thinning. Young Douglas fir in coastal forests—whether planted or naturally regenerated—tend to be packed into very dense stands. Thinning the forest now is both good business and good forest management, Labhart says, and if it's done right, it's easy on the eye.

He pulls off the highway next to a stand of young Douglas fir. The trees are about twelve inches in diameter, and fifteen or sixteen feet apart. The stand was thinned a few years ago, and now, to the casual eye, the forest looks untouched, parklike. The remaining trees, with their competition reduced, will grow much faster. "This is an example of a light thinning we did right along the highway, just so we could show the public what it looks like," says Labhart.

The first sale of timber from the Tillamook Burn was offered in 1983. By the end of 1997, a total of 7,166 acres had been thinned, and another 13,679 were under contract. Thinned logs are turned into small-dimension lumber and pulp chips. Sales are awarded to the highest bidder; only bids that exceed the state's management costs are considered. "We don't run below-cost sales," says Labhart. Between 1987 and 1996, about 343,000 board feet of timber was harvested from the part of the state forest that lies in Tillamook County (Oregon Department of Forestry 1998a, VII-6). The timber fetched about $95 million. Harvest levels are expected to hold steady for the next decade or two and then begin to rise. If everything goes as planned, the promise of *timber forever* would seem to be coming true.

About 10 miles east of the city of Tillamook, well up on the west flank of the Coast Range, Labhart turns abruptly. We leave the pavement and jolt up a narrow, rocky road. The August sun filters through the tree canopy, and the air becomes cooler. A few miles in, just where the road hangs a hairpin turn to the left, Labhart stops and points out the cab window. Up to the left is a steep slope with a scattering of young Douglas fir trees interspersed with clumps of salal and sword fern. "Look at that hillside right there," says Labhart, getting out of the truck. "Everything we've been driving along since we left the road has been helicopter-logged. If you come up through here, you can see the results of the recent logging"—he gestures toward stumps of about twelve inches in diameter—"but if you're looking at it from a distance, all you're going to see is a forest."

Specifications of all timber sales are set by Labhart and his staff of foresters. They wanted the loggers to use helicopters for this job— the most expensive method—because this slope is so steep. "You don't want to put big equipment up there; you'd tear up the whole hillside. And it would be very difficult to build roads. Roads are the number-one cause of erosion and sedimentation problems. So if you can limit the amount of roads you're building, the better off you are."

Labhart compares helicopter logging to one tool in a well-stocked toolbox. "I use analogies a lot," he says, "because people relate to them. When you're building something, and all you've got is a hammer and a saw, it's a little difficult. But if you can reach in your toolbox because you want to drill a hole in a board, and you've got a drill in there, you're that much better off. And then if you reach in there and you say, 'I need a little drill bit, I don't need a big drill bit,' then you're *that* much better off. The idea is to keep as many tools in your toolbox as you can, so that the product you build will be the best product it can be."

The product in this case is a "working forest," a term encountered frequently in the management plans and in the conversation of the Tillamook's foresters. The central assumption of the "working forest" idea was until recently an unapologetic "timber first." But public hearings have brought out a heavily negative reaction to that notion, and right now the precise position of timber in the balance of other forest values is a subject of intense debate.

By law, the Tillamook Burn and other forest lands that were transferred from the counties to the state back in the 1940s—the co-called Chapter 530 lands, named after the statute that governs their acquisition—must be managed to achieve "the greatest permanent value" to the state of Oregon. In 1997 the Board of Forestry began a process of drafting a formal administrative rule to nail down just exactly what "greatest permanent value" means. In January of 1998, after rejecting two earlier draft versions, the Board adopted a rule that defines "greatest permanent value" as "healthy, productive, and sustainable forest ecosystems that over time and across the landscape provide a full range of social, economic, and environmental benefits to the people of Oregon."

The rule goes on to list six benefits—the first being "Sustainable and predictable production of forest products that generate revenues for the benefit of the state, counties, and local taxing districts." The list also mentions "properly functioning aquatic habitats," wildlife habitats, "productive" soil and clean air and water, flood and erosion protection, and recreation. To achieve the greatest permanent value, the rule says, the state forester is directed to "maintain these lands as forest lands and actively manage them in a sound environmental manner . . . " (Oregon Administrative Rules, 629:59).

The final version backs away somewhat from the stronger timber emphasis of a previous draft rule, which called for "the growing and harvesting of forest tree species as *the leading use* for the benefit of the counties and the people of the state of Oregon" [emphasis mine]. Even though that version promised to manage for timber "consistent with protecting, maintaining, and enhancing other forest values," it was withdrawn in November of 1997 after a chorus of opposition from conservation groups. Environmentalists, unsurprisingly, oppose putting timber ahead of wildlife and the other values of a public forest.

In this new rule, the Forestry Board has made it clear that the "working forest" philosophy remains central to its management philosophy. But that doesn't mean timber *only*, says Mark Labhart. A "working forest" means that other uses and values—wildlife, water quality, recreation, scenery—are, with good management, fully compatible with timber production. "I just call it a win-win," he says. "My vision is that we can have a win-win out here. We can have a forest that produces products, that provides jobs to the communities, and that continues that trust-like relationship we have with the counties. We can have abundant wildlife, fisheries, recreational opportunities, and pretty scenery, all at the same time. You just need to do that a little differently than was done in years past."

Labhart is a tall, straight man in his mid-forties with prematurely gray hair and piercing brown eyes. His patrician profile and silver mustache make him look a little like Gifford Pinchot, the first Chief of the Forest Service and an early champion of scientific forestry. If you were told to look at a lineup of men and pick out the forester, you would probably pick Mark Labhart.

He is at ease in the woods, ducking under branches, identifying wild shrubs, and he is equally at ease in conversation, explaining forestry philosophies and techniques in simple analogies—a toolbox, a patch of corn in the garden, a city park whose managers must be responsive to the wishes of many citizens. "The difference between this forest and a city park, though," he says, "is in, 'What was that public land set up for?' This forest was deeded to the state by the counties to be managed for timber. So if people come to me and say, 'This is just like a big park,' well, no, that's not what the counties deeded the land to the state for, to be set aside. It was deeded to be managed. And the dilemma for me—the excitement for me—is how to manage that land for that purpose, but also to manage it in such a way that the environmentalists say, 'You're doing a good job out there.'"

Timber Pays

We emerge from the forest by another gravel road, travel down the highway a few more miles, turn off again, this time to the north, and cross the Wilson River into Jones Creek Park. The park, says Labhart, offers a good example of how Tillamook foresters balance objectives and achieve win-wins.

The forestry department has operated the Jones Creek campground and several others since the 1950s. The campgrounds catered mostly to elk hunters, anglers, and families seeking low-cost, primitive-style camping. A budget crunch in the early 1980s forced the department to cut out what campground maintenance there had been, and the mostly family-centered clientele of the parks gave way to a wilder crowd, drinkers and fighters and vandals and gang-bangers. There were gunfights, rapes, and other unsavory behavior. In 1991 the legislature called for a comprehensive recreation plan for the Tillamook State Forest. Since then, the Forest's campgrounds have been undergoing a rehabilitation.

Jones Creek used to be a littered pit of four-wheel-drive and dirt-bike tracks weaving around and through the gully-banked creek. Now the streamside vegetation has been replanted, and a barricade of logs and rocks keeps vehicles out of the creek. The park features sturdy concrete "vault" toilets (looking indeed like cemetery vaults turned on end) and picnic tables and garbage cans anchored by chains to rings in concrete blocks. Today there are only a few cars in the park, no tents. It's quiet. The Wilson River sparkles and murmurs over its bed of stone-scattered basalt. "Look," says Labhart. "There's a fawn."

A resident campground host equipped with a radio now provides a welcoming face and some measure of protection. Two sheriff's deputies patrol the campgrounds and the Forest's roads. The lawless behavior is gradually subsiding, the troublemakers going somewhere else. "Now I would feel comfortable bringing my family here," says Labhart. "Before, I wouldn't have." A ten-dollar-a-night fee helps pay for the improvements, but the bulk of the cost of maintaining the campgrounds comes from timber dollars. "We'd have to close this park if we didn't have the money from the forest revenues to do the work." Besides recreational programs, he says, timber revenues also fund fisheries improvement and watershed restoration projects, and the Forest's educational and interpretive programs.

We cross the highway again and climb the hill to a gentle slope of young trees. This is the site of a recent commercial thinning. The felled trees were hauled out with a tractor, the most common and cheapest method. Tractor logging typically draws a lot of criticism from the public for its unaesthetic character, but this site looks pleasant enough, with widely spaced trees and green underbrush. "Now the immediate thought when somebody says, 'This was Cat-logged,' is, 'Whoa, my Lord, that's terrible!'" says Labhart. "Well, I brought the Sierra Club, the Forest Conservation Council, and the Coast Range Association up here on a tour. We looked at some clear-cuts, and of course they didn't like clear-cuts. But when we came to this thinning, I said, 'Well, here's what we're doing; what do you think?' And they were okay with it. The visual part was pleasing to them."

As for wildlife habitat—a major concern of the environmental groups—there's some research going on that Labhart is watching with interest. Early results of these studies (some of which are being conducted on the Tillamook) indicate that certain ways of thinning young Douglas fir stands and encouraging the growth of new trees and other plants underneath the remaining trees will create old-growth-like conditions in relatively young forests—say, about 80 to 120 years old.

Related studies are showing that wildlife associated with old forests may not care whether the forest is really old—only that it have the architecture of an old forest, the big trees, multiple canopy layers, fallen logs, and snags that are the characteristic attributes of old growth. If this research proves its promise, it means that skillful silviculture can "create" a forest that looks like old growth, and has some of the important functions of old growth, in less than half the time it takes nature to do the job—a structurally complex forest that would, in theory, suit spotted owls and marbled murrelets just fine.

Labhart walks up into the woods, his pant legs swishing through blackberry vines. "Looks kind of like a park, doesn't it?" In fact it looks like an unusually open Douglas fir stand, roomy enough to walk under the shoulders of the trees, which are tall, straight, and vigorous-looking. "Our philosophy is called thinning from below. That means we take out the weakest trees and leave the best for the future."

This thinning operation, Labhart says, is the start of a sequence of management manipulations that will take decades to complete and will call for decisions at several points along the way. In another ten to twenty years, depending on how fast the stand is growing, the tree crowns will lengthen and broaden, spreading out so that they're touching, and the canopy will close. Then the loggers will come back in and thin out more trees and open the stand up again. New trees will be planted or grow naturally underneath the thinned overstory. These, along with the shrubs, ferns, and other native vegetation, will create a rich mix of species in the understory.

As the new trees grow, the stand will gain structural complexity, developing two or more canopy layers and an understory with a variety of hardwoods and shrubs. The stand will be more visually appealing, and it will become home to a different set of wildlife species. As it approaches 100 or so, the stand will begin to approximate the structure of old growth. The trees will be bigger, the canopy intricately layered, and there will be more snags and dead wood.

"I would figure on this stand, we'd come in with one more commercial thinning, probably replant underneath, let that stand grow up to a certain height, then come back in and take off the overstory and let the younger stand grow up. Or you could just leave the stand as it is and wait, and eventually clear-cut it," and then start over again with an even-aged stand of seedlings. A lot of forest visitors ask about clear-cutting. Does Labhart expect to be clear-cutting more as these forests mature? Clear-cutting, he replies, is another tool in the toolbox. "Right now, our philosophy of forest management is a combination of commercial thinning and clear-cutting. Right now it's about ninety percent commercial thinning; there's very little clear-cutting. These stands are too young for clear-cutting. They need thinning. So that's what we're going to be doing for at least the next 10 or 20 years, and probably beyond that." Eventually, "our plan is that about five to fifteen percent of the landscape would be in clear-cuts, which means that most of the forest would be in other stand structures" at any given moment.

Structure-based Management

What Labhart has just described—the successive thinnings, the nurturing of understory conifers and shrubs, the range of forest types across the landscape—are the key components of "structure-based management," or SBM, as it's commonly abbreviated. Mike Schnee, a member of the Oregon Department of Forestry team developing the state forest plan for northwestern Oregon, defines SBM in this way: "It's active management to achieve a range of forest types and landscape arrangements to provide for integrated management of many forest resources."

SBM is the main silvicultural idea used by the Tillamook's foresters as they plan what they want the Forest to look like over the next decades. "What we're doing," Schnee explains, "is taking the practices we have historically used to manage for timber, and adapting those to develop the landscape design and stand structures that correlate to a range of wildlife habitats. The idea is to integrate habitat development with timber management. We figure we can do this maybe seventy to eighty percent of the time." The rest of the time, management activities will take place without a commercial timber objective, Schnee says. "A case in point is our riparian [streamside] management areas. The objective in these areas is to maintain and enhance the riparian habitat" for the fish and other creatures that live in or near the stream. "So any management activities we do in those areas must meet that test."

And indeed, "management activities" do not always include cutting trees. In this summer's Operation Stump Drop, foresters trucked large chunks of wood from other places in the forest and dropped them into the Trask River with a helicopter to improve the stream's functioning as fish habitat. Because the fires and the salvage logging so thoroughly denuded the landscape, many streams and riparian areas in the Tillamook lack enough living or dead conifers to contribute to future large woody debris in the stream. Woody debris is an important element of habitat health for salmon species, and the remnants of logs or stumps from conifer trees make the best kind of woody debris.

Philosophical Roots

Structure-based management is one of the practical applications of recent intellectual disturbances in the forestry academy collectively known as New Forestry. Growing out of the work of University of Washington ecologist Jerry Franklin and others, New Forestry emphasizes the idea of a forest as a highly complex system of biological functions—an ecosystem—rather than primarily a factory for timber.

New Forestry considers the forest's functions over long time spans and wide spatial scales, and it stresses the importance of maintaining a variety of structural patterns. In other words, according to New Forestry principles, a healthy forest ecosystem will have not only young, pure-species stands, and not only stands of big, old trees, but stands of mixed sizes and species all along the age spectrum.

Encouraging a diversity of sizes, ages, and plant species across the forest landscape is thought to maintain a healthy diversity of life, and such a diverse landscape will function better as habitat to a broad range of wildlife. New Forestry also emphasizes the social aspects of forestry, the need for the public to take part in forestry decisions that affect their lives (Brooks and Grant 1992, 3-7).

New Forestry theorists do not rule out any of the conventional activities of management, including the cutting of trees. Nor do they rule out any of the conventional tools of silviculture. But they urge foresters to use those activities and tools within a philosophical framework that considers the forest as an ecological, economic, and social entity. Society's thinking about forests, they say, should consider the complexity of a forest's workings at every level, the effects of patterns of disturbance—both human-caused and natural—across the landscape and over time, the habitat needs of forest wildlife, and the right of citizens to participate in decisions about forests.

Structure-based management is one way to put some of the concepts of New Forestry into real, on-the-ground forests. According to Chadwick Oliver, the University of Washington silviculturist whose work provides its theoretical basis, structure-based management means using silvicultural operations—cutting and planting of trees—to maintain "a target distribution of structures across the landscape in a dynamic balance" over an indefinite time span (Oliver 1992).

The main underlying principle of structure-based management is that a forest is a living, growing thing. Mark Labhart puts it this way: "Forests are not vast stands of old growth that stay that way forever." Rather, a forest exists in a dynamic, unstable state all the time. A hands-off stance, therefore, will not produce or maintain a steady state—the forest will continue to change according to its own natural processes. Left to itself, the forest may or may not continue to meet the desires and needs of humans in the course of working out its own destiny—whether these desires and needs be defined as a flow of wood products or a tree-covered landscape teeming with biodiversity. If humans want these things, say SBM advocates like Mike Schnee, it's up to humans to do what it takes to create them, working with a knowledge of and respect for the forest's own biological processes and constraints.

This point is very much in keeping with the progressive-conservation tradition, which speaks of the right and obligation of humans to manage forests for human benefit. What is left unvoiced in this formulation is the arcadian point that some people would *prefer* that forests be left to work out their destiny without the help of people—even if the forest in question got started with a lot of human help, and even if the biological diversity of that forest might well be improved by a bit more human intervention.

To Oregon Department of Forestry managers, who sit firmly in the progressive-conservation tradition, SBM is a way to have most of the good things people want from the state's forests, at the same time and from generally the same place. SBM, says Mark Labhart, uses tested forest management techniques that, when applied in a carefully-planned manner over time, create a mosaic of forest stand structures across the landscape, from older forests to new plantations.

"These techniques," he says, "are designed to produce a wide range of values and products—revenue for the counties from timber, and also songbirds, threatened and endangered species habitat, clear, cold water, recreation sites, scenic areas—a whole range of things." What's more, he says, it is a way to smooth out the boom-and-bust cycles that have historically plagued timber economies, a way to secure both a legacy of biodiversity and the economic vitality of timber-dependent regions (Oliver 1992).

To Mark Labhart, structure-based management resolves the *either/or* dilemma created by society's polarized thinking about forests. "We believe pretty strongly that the 'old' vision of either/or—that you can use the forest *either* for timber *or* wildlife habitat, but not for both—will result in a state of natural resource gridlock like the one we've witnessed on federal lands in recent years," he says. "We've tried to avoid this gridlock by providing a practical, balanced, and scientifically defensible forest-management approach."

Such an approach "does not minimize the importance of timber management," says the most recent draft of the management plan for northwestern Oregon's forests. Rather, "it takes the proactive view that appropriate forest management activities, properly applied, can be used to produce a diversified forest landscape and a sustainable timber harvest" (Oregon Department of Forestry 1998a).

Traveling Mosaic

The discussion needs to become more technical at this point. I ask the reader to bear with me as I describe how structure-based management would create a more complicated and diverse Tillamook Forest.

The draft management plan calls for designating each of the forest's stands as one of five types: regeneration, closed single canopy, understory, layered, and older forest structure. These stand types represent the diversity of forest structure historically found in Coast Range forests.

The stand types are listed in ascending order of structural development. "Regeneration" means an area left open by logging or natural disturbance. A clear-cut would be the most obvious example—although the Tillamook's foresters point out that today's clear-cuts aren't like the ones of twenty years ago. Says Mike Schnee: "A regeneration site would contain green trees, snags, down wood—structural and biological legacies from the previous stand." About five to fifteen percent of the forest will be in regeneration areas.

"Closed single canopy" means a single-aged stand of young trees growing closely enough that some of the trees are beginning to die from shading and competition. About ten to twenty percent of the forest is targeted for this stand type.

"Understory" means a stand in which some of the trees have died or been thinned out, making light and nutrients available to new trees and other plants beneath the canopy. About fifteen to thirty-five percent of the Tillamook will fall into this category.

A "layered" stand develops from an understory stand as the trees, shrubs, and herbs in the understory become more numerous and vigorous, and finally two or more canopy layers emerge. About twenty to thirty percent will fall into this stand type.

Finally, with many large trees, a multilayered canopy, and many snags and fallen logs, a stand achieves "older forest structure" condition. About twenty to thirty percent of the Tillamook will be of this stand type, including most of the land next to the rivers.

Foresters will work to develop these stand types, in roughly these proportions, on each major river basin. The stand types would remain generally balanced across the landscape, but they would exist in different places at different times in the life of the forest—producing what Mike Schnee calls a "traveling mosaic" of forest structures "flowing" into and out of different locations.

For example, a ninety-year-old forest with two or more ages of Douglas fir trees might be clear-cut, with trees and snags left for wildlife, and planted with seedlings. Thus its type would change from "layered" to "regeneration." Within the same decade, a closed-single-canopy stand might be thinned to hasten it on its way to an understory condition, while a ten-year-old regeneration stand might be left to assume a closed-single-canopy condition. A 120-year-old stand might be thinned to create the openness characteristic of older forests, or it might be left the way it is for another several decades.

SBM calls for using every tool in the silviculturist's toolbox. However, harvesting decisions would be driven not by a desired timber volume, but by a desired set of forest structures across the landscape. Therefore the harvest rate under SBM would be slower than under plantation-style forest management, and the timber volume removed would be lower, at least in the beginning decades, while the promised "dynamic balance" is being achieved.

The prototype plan for the Trask basin provides an example of how the SBM idea might play out over the next several years. The basin consists of about 56,000 acres drained by the Trask River, which flows into Tillamook Bay. Most of it burned in at least one of the Tillamook fires; the 1951 fire was wholly in the Trask basin.

Because of the basin's fire history, most of its trees are young Douglas firs planted in close formation. About ninety-one percent of the forest in the basin is in closed-single-canopy stands. Less than one percent is in the regeneration stage. About five percent is in the understory stage, and none is in older forest structure.

More than 15,000 acres on the Trask basin have been precommercially thinned, beginning in 1985. ("Precommercial" means the trees removed are too small to be marketable.) In the past five years there have been four commercial thinnings and one clear-cutting of hardwoods. Currently 3,500 acres of thinning sales and 200 acres of regeneration cuts are under contract. Next year another 4,500 acres of thinning and 300 acres of regeneration cuts may be put up for sale. That adds up to 8,500 acres, or between one-sixth and one-seventh of the Trask basin's forest land, slated for either thinning or clear-cutting in the next two years. The pacing of these activities, particularly the thinning, will start fast but slow down over the next few decades as more of the younger plantation stands are moved into the understory or layered-stand structures.

The Trask also has about 3,000 acres of older, mixed-species stands that lend themselves to thinning. The goal in these stands is to

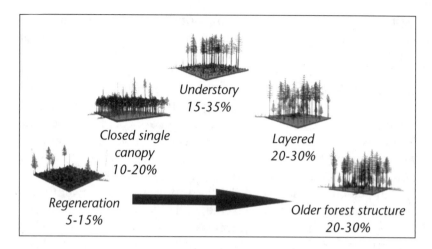

The five stand types specified in the structure-based management plan for northwestern Oregon state forests.

1) A regeneration stand is an area left open by logging or natural disturbance.

2) In a closed-single-canopy stand, young, even-aged trees are growing closely together, and some are beginning to lose the competitive race for sunlight and nutrients.

3) In an understory stand, some of the trees have died or been thinned out, and the rest grow faster by taking advantage of the increased light and nutrients.

4) In a layered stand, an understory of trees, shrubs, and other plants eventually grows to become a second canopy layer.

5) Older forest structure is achieved when the stand has large trees, several canopy layers, and many snags and fallen logs.

hasten understory development and bring on a layered, multispecies condition, after which the stands will eventually grow into older forest structure.

Most of the management on the basin thus falls under the heading of "biodiversity pathway," meaning an emphasis on partial cuts and underplantings to bring on the more-complex forest structures as quickly as possible. The ultimate goal is to bring the Trask basin to its "desired future condition:" an ongoing balance of ten percent of the land in the regeneration stage (where it stays for about thirteen years, or until the young trees reach the next stage), fifteen percent in the closed-single-canopy stage, and twenty-five percent each in understory, layered, and older forest structure. The desired future condition on the Trask should be achieved in fifty to seventy years, if the management proceeds along roughly the lines described above.

There are complications. A fungal disease called Swiss needle cast has infected large areas of coastal Douglas fir forest, including about forty percent of stands on the Trask basin. The disease is spreading fastest in stands of Douglas fir that were planted in the coastal "fog belt," historically dominated by western hemlock and Sitka spruce. It does not seem to kill the trees (nobody knows for sure yet), but it retards their growth severely. The plan calls for the regeneration logging to be concentrated in the most-diseased stands, because they're growing so poorly anyway that they offer little potential for future timber production. Less severely diseased stands could be thinned and underplanted with shade-tolerant trees that resist the fungus, like western hemlock, or they could be left alone for a while.

Habitat Conservation Plan

A more urgent consideration is that coastal coho, a threatened salmon species, use the North Fork, South Fork, and East Fork of the Trask as habitat. The Trask and its tributaries are also home to chum, spring and fall chinook, summer and winter steelhead, and sea-run and cutthroat trout. Because the dwindling coho are on the federal threatened list, the Tillamook's foresters must manage the streams so as to give its populations a good chance at recovery. The Tillamook's riparian management strategies are spelled out in a draft Habitat Conservation Plan which the department is negotiating with the federal agencies charged with enforcing the endangered-species law.

This Habitat Conservation Plan, or HCP, will become part of the plan for the northwestern Oregon state forests. It will also include recovery strategies for thirteen other wildlife species, two of which (the northern spotted owl and the marbled murrelet) are on the federal threatened list; the rest are unlisted but regarded as sensitive. The combined, final document is expected to come before the Forestry Board for approval in October of 1999.

The provisions for stream management in the draft HCP are complicated and controversial, so they bear a bit of examination here (Oregon Department of Forestry 1998b). First of all, fish-bearing streams (called Type F, in foresters' jargon) and the riparian areas adjacent to them are divided into four zones: the river itself (called the aquatic zone, and including the whole of the channel that contains water during high flows), the streambank, the inner RMA (riparian management area) zone, and the outer RMA zone.

The streambank on fish-bearing streams is designated as that portion extending from the water's edge out to 25 feet on both sides of the stream. The inner RMA zone extends from 25 feet to 100 feet on both sides, and the outer RMA zone extends from 100 to 170 feet on both sides. Non-fish-bearing streams (Type N) have similar designated zones, but they are narrower. Type N streams also are subject to a host of other classifications and variations in management approach.

continued on page 86

Trask Basin: Current and desired future condition, by stand type.

	Current condition	Desired future condition	Current condition	Desired future condition
	percent		acres	
Regeneration	>1%	10%	315	5,639
Closed Single	85%*	15%	47,962*	8,458
Canopy	9%**		5,054**	
Understory	5%	25%	2,608	14,097
Layered	<1%	25%	313	14,097
Older Forest	0%	25%	0	14,097
Structure				

* conifer
** hardwood

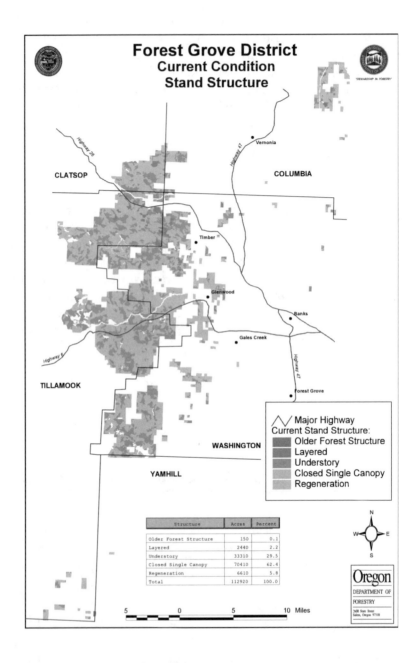

Forest Grove District current condition (this page) and desired future condition (facing page).

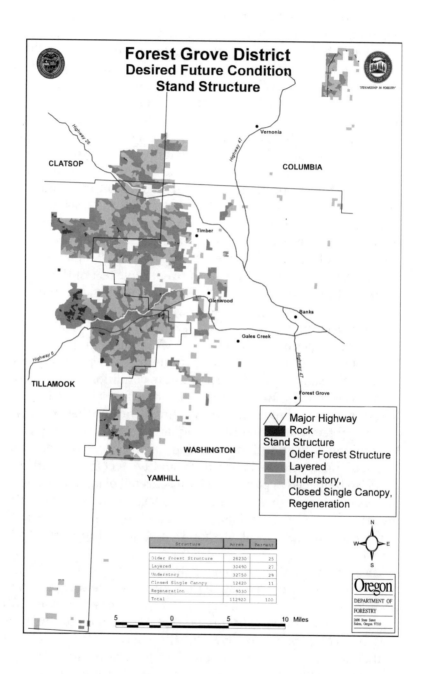

Forest Grove District
Desired Future Condition
Stand Structure

Vernonia

CLATSOP

COLUMBIA

Timber

Glenwood

Banks

Gales Creek

TILLAMOOK

Forest Grove

WASHINGTON

YAMHILL

Major Highway
Rock
Stand Structure
Older Forest Structure
Layered
Understory,
Closed Single Canopy,
Regeneration

Structure	Acres	Percent
Older Forest Structure	28230	25
Layered	30490	27
Understory	32750	29
Closed Single Canopy	12420	11
Regeneration	9030	
Total	112920	100

5   0   5   10 Miles

Oregon
DEPARTMENT OF
FORESTRY
2600 State Street
Salem, Oregon 97310

The forestry department's philosophy on riparian zones, as with the forest as a whole, is to manage actively. On fish-bearing streams, the plan calls for protecting the stream and its banks and then managing the inner and outer riparian areas as managers deem appropriate for developing mature forest conditions. The management activities they choose must work toward achieving the desired future condition in the basin. Management also must promote "properly functioning aquatic systems." That means enhancing streambank stability, promoting shading of the water, achieving current or future large woody debris in the stream, or securing sufficient nutrients to feed the fish and the amphibians, insects, and other creatures that live in or near the stream.

Under special circumstances, even certain streambank zones—right next to the water—may see management activity. For example, if the streambank is dominated by hardwoods, the plan permits thinning out the alder even within twenty-five feet of the stream, as long as the goal is to convert the stand to conifers, and as long as the operation is done gently, to avoid disturbing wildlife habitat (Oregon Department of Forestry 1998b, VI:17).

Thinning is permitted in the inner RMA zone, 25 to 100 feet away from the stream, with several restrictions: the goal must be to advance the stand toward "desired future condition;" only partial cutting is permitted, and none at all if mature forest is already there; loggers may make only two entries to finish the job; they must take care to protect water quality and aquatic habitat; and they must leave all the slash and all the trees that suffered incidental damage. The outer riparian areas, between 100 and 170 feet from the stream, may also be logged as part of the basin's overall plan. In these areas loggers must leave at least ten trees or snags to the acre, minimize disturbance to the ground, and retain all the slash on the site to return nutrients to the soil (Oregon Department of Forestry 1998b, VI:17).

The notion of actively managing riparian areas has drawn the fire of environmentalists, who say all riparian areas should be preserved from logging altogether. They point out that President Clinton's plan for federal forests calls for 300-foot no-touch buffers in areas that are ecologically sensitive. But the Tillamook's foresters are confident that their management plans for streams have "a high probability of maintaining and restoring properly functioning aquatic habitat for salmonids and other native fish and aquatic life," in the words of the department's forest plan coordinator, Ross Holloway.

Mike Schnee adds, "We believe that over the long haul, this [active-management] approach offers the greatest promise to eliminate the need for a Habitat Conservation Plan." By creating a structurally and biologically complex forest, he says, foresters will "develop a landscape in which healthy habitat is available for all native species."

Scientific Review

ODF has promised to make its structure-based management plans as scientifically sound as possible. Early in 1998 the department voluntarily submitted the draft HCP to a twenty-six-member scientific panel. The review team included experts on northern spotted owls, marbled murrelets, and other terrestrial and aquatic wildlife, as well as scientists trained in botany, silviculture, ecology, geomorphology, hydrology, and landscape ecology.

Their job was to probe the HCP mercilessly—to find the holes so that the forestry department could fix them. And probe they did, says John Hayes, Oregon State University wildlife biologist who coordinated the team and wrote the report. Hayes notes in the report's introduction: "It is important to emphasize that many positive aspects of the ODF documents were identified by the reviewers. With a handful of exceptions, the reviewers expressed general favor with the overall direction presented in the HCP, and several indicated that the approaches outlined represented major progress" in forest management. "The emphasis on areas of concern is [an] attempt to provide guidance for considerations of areas that may be improved upon, and should not be construed as indicative that the existing documents are without merit." Yet the sum of the scientists' remarks makes it clear that the forestry department has more work to do.

The scientists raised a number of concerns about whether the conservation plans outlined in the HCP would in fact provide enough healthy habitat for wildlife species that are threatened or sensitive. The range of their opinions is too diverse and the level of their assessments too detailed to summarize very thoroughly here, but several broad themes emerged in their more than 300-page report (Hayes 1998). The panel was concerned that the HCP did not provide enough quantifiable measures to evaluate whether the structure-based management plans would really do what they are supposed to do. They thought the strategies for the spotted owl and marbled murrelet, in particular, were not strong enough to contribute to the recovery of those threatened species.

While the scientists agreed the structure-based management scheme would probably create the various forest structures as planned, they pointed out that it is impossible to know whether the birds and other wildlife would actually find these structures to be usable habitat. Some expressed doubt about the "traveling mosaic" notion—the idea that wildlife would be able to follow their habitat around on the landscape as the forest stands moved into and out of the various structure types. Some thought the patch sizes of different forest structure were too small, and the disturbances from harvesting too frequent. The panel also pointed out several places in the HCP where they felt the scientific justification for management strategies was thin—in particular the plans for managing aquatic and riparian areas.

Several of the scientists proposed reserving blocks of land as a conservative approach to restoring wildlife habitat, and one, Reed Noss of the Conservation Biology Institute, suggested that the department revisit the idea of managing western Oregon state forests primarily as habitat reserves, with no timber harvest at all.

The HCP is also receiving a review from a Forestry Board-appointed group called the Public Interest Committee, whose members represent county elected officials, environmentalists, recreation groups, and the timber industry. The next step for ODF managers is to revise the HCP in light of the scientists' concerns and the comments from the Public Interest Committee. Then they will submit it to the U.S. Fish and Wildlife Service and the National Marine Fisheries Service for approval; that process will include an opportunity for additional public comment. Then they will revise it again, and finally the HCP will be incorporated into the department's long-range management plan for northwestern Oregon forests.

The department hopes to submit the Northwest Oregon State Forests Management Plan, with the HCP included, to the Board of Forestry for approval in late 1999. By early 2000, if all goes without a major hitch, the plan should be written into Oregon law.

A Change in Philosophy

If the Tillamook foresters succeed in their goal to practice structure-based management, and if SBM fulfills its promise, the Tillamook Forest will look very different in 100 years. Gone will be the vast sweep of young plantations across acres of hillsides. Instead, here will be a patch of young plantation with its canopy just beginning to close. Over there will be a stand of Douglas fir fifty to seventy years old, with a deepening understory of vine maple, sword fern, and huckleberry. Along the creek bottom will be a mixed stand of alder and maple interspersed with big, old Douglas fir. Here and there will be patches of alder, planted in places where *Phellinus* root rot has killed the Douglas fir. (*Phellinus,* a very persistent soil fungus that causes a root disease fatal to Douglas fir, is a big problem in Oregon's coastal forests.) Across the valley will be a stand dominated by 140-year-old Douglas fir but full of other species of trees and shrubs, and starting to assume the characteristic look of old growth—spongy fallen logs, intermediate canopy layers, towering snags, and a thick layer of duff on the forest floor.

There was a time when the Tillamook's management philosophy leaned more toward industrial, tree-farm-style forestry. The Tillamook's first plan—called a "timber management plan"—was drafted in 1984 and shelved a few years later, after the northern spotted owl, a denizen of older Northwest forests, was declared threatened under the Endangered Species Act. In 1991 came federal Judge William Dwyer's injunction against timber sales on federal forests in areas that might be habitat for the owl. The Oregon Department of Forestry regarded the ruling as handwriting on the wall, and state foresters made a decision to plan for the Tillamook and other state forests in anticipation that endangered species would have to be considered in management plans. That meant the 1984 plan was defunct.

State foresters also took a lesson in public relations from the painful experience of the Forest Service. Many National Forest plans, developed by in-house experts and presented full-blown to a skeptical public, ended up paralyzed in a welter of appeals and lawsuits. So the managers of the Northwest Oregon Area, the administrative division responsible for the Tillamook, decided to take a more open approach. They have developed the new management plan in stages proceeding from the general to the specific, starting with "guiding principles" and moving down through "resource goals," "vision," "resource strategies," and "implementation." At every stage the department has called public meetings and listened to people's concerns.

For example, a public meeting was held in Tillamook, the last in a sequence of six held in various Oregon towns during the first months of 1998. It drew about 120 people, including loggers, industry representatives, townspeople, county commissioners, environmentalists, and at least one state legislator. About a dozen people from the Department of Forestry were there, including Mark Labhart and Mike Schnee.

At one end of the room—a cramped conference room at the Tillamook Shilo Inn—was an overhead projector and screen; at the other, a long table spread with white linen and set with coffee urns, cups, and platters of fruit and cookies. Angling off from the refreshments was another table piled high with documents—the Western Oregon State Forests Habitat Conservation Plan, the Northwest Oregon State Forests Management Plan, and several others. If you stack the forest plan and HCP drafts together they make a weighty four-inch-thick pile. A blizzard of paper seems to be the price of good public relations.

Before the meeting, Mark Labhart circled the room, shaking hands and chatting; he seemed to know many of the people there. Then he opened the meeting by thanking everyone for coming. "You're showing that you care about the future of the Tillamook Forest." He added, "We're a big player in this county; we own about half the county." Then he introduced Mike Schnee. Schnee is a compact, quick-moving man of medium height, with a vivid tanned face, large dark eyes, and a ready smile. Like the rest of the forestry department people, he had put in a full day's work already. He'd then driven to Tillamook from his Philomath office for this evening's meeting.

Schnee gave a quick outline of the structure-based management concept and how managers plan to apply it on the Tillamook. Then he brought the audience up to date on the draft management plan. "There are no real changes in most of the concepts since our last round of meetings," he said, "but we've done a lot of refining and clarifying. Two areas where there've been significant improvements are the aquatic and riparian management strategies and the monitoring and adaptive management section." He added, "We've also included 'remnant old growth' in the components we'll be managing for, along with snags and woody debris. Even though, as you all know, there isn't much remnant old growth out there."

He listed a few more changes, then yielded to Ross Holloway, the Northwest Forest Plan coordinator. Holloway outlined the main strategies in the draft HCP for managing the streams and also the lakes, ponds, bogs, springs, seeps, wetlands, and estuaries that together make up the forest's riparian areas.

Then Schnee took the floor again for questions. The state representative, Tim Josi, raised his hand and complimented the department for "responsible forest management." How much riparian land, he wanted to know, would be set aside or restricted altogether from timber harvest? It's very preliminary yet, replied Schnee, but early estimates put the amount of land covered by streams, banks, and inner riparian zones at about eight or nine percent of the landscape. "We're starting on a complete watershed assessment; we'll be working on it over the next three or four years."

A woman wanted to know if the money to pay for all this expensive planning was being "siphoned away" from the county's share of the timber receipts. No, replied Ross Holloway: the counties still get approximately two-thirds of all the money, just as the original deal said. The planning costs come out of the state's one-third.

Then another woman raised her hand and asked a question that took Schnee aback for a moment. Is sustainable timber harvest really possible? she asked. "Or is it, you know, just a concept?" Her soft voice, tentative and self-conscious, made it clear she wasn't being ironic; she really wanted to know. "I mean, can it really work? Because I've never seen it."

Schnee, who had perhaps been expecting something a little more technical, a little easier, paused to gather his thoughts. Then he answered emphatically, *Yes.* "Yes, it is possible," he said. "It's more than possible. Following this structure-based management plan, and with careful monitoring and adaptive management, I am confident—we are confident—that we can manage this forest sustainably over the long haul, for the benefit of all the wildlife who live in it, and for the economic benefit of the people in the counties and of all Oregonians."

After a few more questions and a break, the group reassembled at two "listening posts," easels equipped with newsprint tablets, surrounded by concentric half-circles of chairs. One department staffer solicited comments from the audience, and another wrote each person's comment with a marking pen: "I support the management strategies." "No clear-cutting." "More clear-cutting to provide food for big game." "Leave one basin unmanaged as a control for long-term fish productivity." "I appreciate the opportunity for public input."

One man said, "I'm not sure how to put this into the form of a comment, but I hope you make sure you can achieve all these goals you have in the plans. I mean," he said, groping for the right words, "being sure your goals are compatible. Because sometimes it's really just a contest of resources. Do you know what I mean? And then, timber companies have to be able to plan for the future." He wasn't sure what he was really trying to say, he went on with a self-deprecating smile, but the plan needs to recognize that conflicting opinions sometimes can't be resolved. Sometimes goals aren't compatible. "And that's just the way it is." In short, sometimes you can't have a win-win.

Audacious

Structure-based management is an exercise in sheer stark ambition. To embark now upon an untried way to manage this forest over the long haul is just about as audacious as it was to embark upon an untried scheme to reclothe the burned landscape with trees in the 1950s. Like that ambition, this one rests on many unproven assumptions. No one has done a controlled study of structure-based management on the ground—there hasn't been enough time yet. SBM uses tested forest management techniques, but no one has tried an approach like this, one that combines these techniques in such a complicated way over such a large acreage for such a long time. And yet—being bold paid off once. Why not again?

Once again the Tillamook is a laboratory. And its managers are sticking their necks out, planning and creating a forest they will never see in its maturity. "I don't know what forestry is going to be like 15 or 20 years from now, or 50 or 100 years from now," says Mark Labhart. "It's going to be different, I know that. What we're doing with our management now, you see, is we're preserving options for the future."

Visitor's Center

The sun is in our windshield as Labhart and I head for the town of Tillamook and the ocean. Our last stop is a shaded grove of large alder, maple, and Douglas fir on the south bank of the river. Labhart pulls the pickup into a narrow turnout. Then he says, abruptly, "Wait! What was that?" and backs the truck up the highway's shoulder at about twenty-five miles an hour. I swivel my head backward as we bump along, but see nothing. "Bald eagle," says Labhart. "Oops—it's gone. Did you see it? No? Too bad."

We are at the site of the future Tillamook State Forest Visitor's Center. The trees are a remnant of those left standing after the 1933 fire, a shred of history right here next to the river. The $12.5 million new center—to be paid for out of private contributions, not state funds—will tell the department's version of the Tillamook story: the catastrophe of the fires, the tragedy of the ruined timber, the heroism of the reforestation, and the good management that promises to provide Oregon with timber—and diverse, healthy forests—forever.

Labhart believes that, for most people, hearing this story and then seeing a "working forest" in operation will be enough to convince them. "I believe very strongly that you can have managed forests and good environmental values, and I think most of the public agrees with me," he says. "The public wants a win-win; they want forests to be sustainable. But we are going to have to rebuild people's emotional bank account. And so we say, 'Just come out here and let us show you. Let us demonstrate it. Let us prove it to you.' And most of the time people walk away saying, 'This is okay. I can live with this.'"

6

Field Trip: Bill Emmingham
Creating Biodiversity

O NE OF THE METAPHORS YOU OFTEN HEAR PEOPLE USE ABOUT the Tillamook Forest is "laboratory." The Tillamook is a laboratory for untried reforestation methods, for innovative county-state partnerships, for progressive forest management. Sometimes the phrase is more than a metaphor. Today the Tillamook is literally a laboratory—the place is crawling with scientists. For all its woodsy remoteness and sun-dappled serenity, the Tillamook is an intensely studied landscape. Today I am riding in one of five thirteen-passenger vans over the washboarded roads of the Tillamook and two adjoining forests, winding through thickets of young Douglas fir. The vans are carrying scientists from Oregon State University's school of forestry and the Forest Service research station in Corvallis, along with a slew of forest managers from public agencies—the Forest Service and the BLM, the Oregon and Washington forestry agencies, the Seattle water bureau—and private timber companies.

Also along are thirteen displaced timber workers from the city of Tillamook, former fallers, buckers, choker setters, and sawmill workers, men who once made a good living in Tillamook's timber industry. Now they are paid students in a federal program called Ecosystem Workforce, funded by President Clinton's 1993 Northwest Forest Plan. The program is intended to teach them new skills to market themselves in this unfamiliar marketplace that forestry is becoming.

It's Halloween, a bright, cold day, and we are visiting study sites where the scientists are doing experiments on the young, mostly single-species Douglas fir stands on the Tillamook Forest and other forests in the area. The aim is to lend this tree-farm-like planting some measure of the kind of diversity that comes to a natural forest after many years.

It isn't only public opinion that is down on monocultures. Much of the research coming out of the forestry universities these days says that large, single-species plantations are ecologically undesirable. Dave Perry, an Oregon State University forest ecologist, maintains that biological diversity—a rich mix of species and sufficient numbers of each population to maintain it—should be a principal goal of forestry, not just a by-product of a primary focus on timber production. Diversity is important in keeping a robust habitat for forest wildlife, especially for the bacteria, fungi, bugs, and other small life forms on which the big ones depend—"the little things that run the world," says Perry, quoting the Harvard biologist E. O. Wilson. More practically, a diverse forest is more resistant to pests. "Uniformity," Perry says, "sets the lunch table for pathogens."

What does biodiversity look like in a forest? It looks messy, for one thing, not like the neat herringbone ranks of young trees on the Tillamook's canyonsides. Diversity starts with different species of trees and other plants, standing dead snags, lots of chunks and branches on the forest floor, a mixture of ages and sizes of trees, and scars from periodic natural disturbances, like trees scorched in a fire or blown down by a windstorm and left unsalvaged to rot. The scars from the big Tillamook fires are pretty well hidden now by the cloak of new green. Can this vast Douglas fir plantation be turned into the kind of messy, diverse landscape that scientists, and the public, are calling for? These scientists say, yes, there's a good likelihood it can be done. The way to do it is with silviculture—"forest architecture," as it is sometimes called. In this case the main strategy for creating diversity is thinning, which in the hands of a silviculturist can be a precision tool.

Thinning, in a forest as in a garden, means taking out some of the young plants so that the others will get more light and more nutrients and therefore grow better. These scientists are trying out all kinds of thinning strategies in this young forest—thinning at various ages, leaving the remaining trees spaced at various intervals, planting and cultivating various species of trees and other plants beneath the taller trees.

If the scientists are right, a patch of thinned young forest will eventually—pretty soon, actually—come to resemble a stand of old forest. The resemblance to old growth, structurally speaking, should be close enough that wildlife such as the northern spotted owl will thrive in these manipulated stands. In other words, thinning will create a forest that will, if all goes well, have that characteristically rich old-growth diversity of structure and species: an uneven mix of tree ages, sizes, and kinds, an array of standing dead snags, a layered canopy, and lots of decaying wood on the forest floor.

The process is expected to take 50 to 100 years, which is quite rapid, considering that it takes nature 300 or 400 years to do the job. And these moist, temperate forest lands are a perfect place to try it. Trees grow faster in the Coast Range than almost anywhere else. In the Cascades it might take a Douglas fir 200 years to reach 170 feet tall, the height at which old-growth habitat characteristics start to develop. A Coast Range Douglas fir can grow this tall in 70 to 100 years (Spies et al., in press).

In the meantime, those thinnings will make good timber. Not as much timber as a conventional plantation would yield, but still enough to be profitable, enough to make this rather fussy management scenario worth all the trouble. That is the theory, at least.

These thinning-based strategies are the key to the Tillamook State Forest's proposed structure-based management philosophy. They are the key to the promise of the Tillamook—both abundant timber and healthy forest ecosystems—and the key to what Tillamook district forester Mark Labhart likes to call "a win-win."

Our first stop is a hillside on the Siuslaw National Forest, which borders the Tillamook on the south and southwest. We're at the site of a thinning study called Wildcat. We climb down and stretch and head for the boxes of sweet rolls and the urns of coffee set out on the floorboards of one of the vans. It's already nine o'clock on a sunny day, but the coffee still steams in the cold air.

The Siuslaw was until recently one of the most productive of all federal forests from a timber point of view. Then came the listing of the northern spotted owl, and in 1991, federal Judge William Dwyer halted all logging in areas that might be owl habitat. The ruling had the effect of temporarily shutting down most logging on federal forests (Beuter 1994).

As a result of this and the whole furious debate on the role of federal forests in the economy and the biological heritage of the Northwest, President Bill Clinton convened a team of biologists, economists, and social scientists that came to be called the Forest Ecosystem Management Assessment Team, or FEMAT. The team's findings were woven into the president's Northwest Forest Plan, which designated certain parts of the Northwest's national forests as "Late-successional Reserve." Most of the Siuslaw ended up under this designation.

"Late-successional" means "older forests." But right now, because of past logging and wildfire, "there's just not much old growth left out here," explains Forest Service silviculturist Stu Johnston as we curl our fingers around our coffee cups. Before these thinning trials began, "we had very uniform plantations to start with, maybe 300 trees per acre, twelve-inch-diameter, mostly Douglas fir." To increase the diversity, the stands were thinned and underplanted with hemlock and Douglas fir. The value of the thinned logs, incidentally, covered the cost of the thinning operation.

The thinning trials on the Wildcat site called for taking these dense stands down to 100, 60, and 30 trees to the acre, plus leaving some stands untouched as controls. The scientists are taking measurements at every stage of the operation. They are trying to document precisely how the forest changes with each different degree of thinning—how fast the remaining trees grow, how much sunlight filters through the canopy, how well the different species of seedlings do when planted or released underneath, how the mosses, ferns, forbs, and shrubs on the forest floor respond to the logging. In similar thinning trials on the Tillamook, they want to see what effect the logging has on the wildlife that live in these forests, the flying squirrels, the Townsend's solitaires, the rough-skinned newts.

More Than One Way to Manage

We hike down a steep, brushy hillside dotted with widely scattered Douglas fir. This is a study site that was thinned very heavily. Here and there, Douglas fir seedlings poke up through the shrubs and grasses. They are encased in tubes of orange plastic netting to keep the deer from eating them. A few of the seedlings have become entangled in the netting and look as if they're doing poorly.

Bill Emmingham steps up onto a stump, holding a portable P.A. system. This study, he tells us, is a trial of seedlings of six conifer species (grand fir, Douglas fir, Sitka spruce, western hemlock, western red cedar, and Pacific yew), planted in the thinned areas and in the unthinned controls. He's also testing two hardwood species, red alder and bigleaf maple. After a year, he says, most of the seedlings are doing well in the thinned stands—better in the heavier-thinned ones because there's more light. Based on what is already known about these species, Emmingham expects the Douglas fir seedlings eventually to lose their competitive race against the grand fir, spruce, hemlock, and cedar as the crowns of the overstory trees begin to close. But further thinning in the future, he believes, can keep Douglas fir growing in the mix. Douglas fir is a sun-loving tree, which is why it does so well in plantations after clear-cutting, "but it can also grow well at moderate light levels in thinned stands," says Emmingham.

Bill Emmingham is an Oregon State University silviculturist and a leader on this tour. He is an athletic-looking man in his fifties, with deep smile lines around his blue eyes, a thick, neatly trimmed silver beard, and an engaging grin. He runs several miles a week on his lunch hours, and his bearing and physique show it. He has a deliberate, careful way of talking, an air of weighing his words, and—perhaps because of this—a gift for explaining complicated forestry concepts in language that a non-expert can understand.

"What we're doing in these experiments," he later explains to me, "is developing alternative methods of forestry and identifying the tradeoffs they imply. That's really where the silviculture profession should be going. As researchers, in the past, we were wrong to focus exclusively on one thing—the even-aged, plantation approach to growing Douglas fir. Now that our culture is giving us the clear message to manage for diversity, we have an opportunity to explore different approaches."

Emmingham has found models for his work in the managed forests of Europe, especially Switzerland, Germany, and France. "The Europeans," he says, "have had centuries to refine their silvicultural methods to suit their own economic and social needs and their own tree species." He's looked at European methods in the context of the young, second-growth forests of the Northwest, and in light of the economic and social ways of our much younger culture. There are lessons we could learn, he says. "I've come to believe that we could manage our forests in more ways than most people can imagine."

Now, standing on his stump, Emmingham fields questions from the audience: "Are you using weevil-resistant stock for the spruce?" ("No—it wasn't available at the time.") "Why did you plant yew?" ("It was a catchy thing at the time; there was research money available—because of a concern that natural stands of yew would be decimated because of the cancer-curing potential of the bark—so we took advantage of it.") "I want to know how you're keeping your seedlings from being eaten alive by deer, like ours are." ("The tubes are helping some, but otherwise I don't know. This year the deer and elk haven't come in as much on this site.") By the way, he says, please don't straighten the bent seedlings or disturb them in any way; this study is supposed to resemble real-life conditions as much as possible.

The Ecosystem Workforce group of displaced timber workers stands quietly, listening. They don't talk to the scientists much. They don't ask questions. They stand and listen, arms folded, polite.

The next site lies at the end of a steep switchback trail winding uphill through denser woods. The Ecosystem Workforce men are right in front of me. They are almost all young; only one man looks to be over fifty. They wear their blue jeans with ripped-off cuffs, striped denim loggers' shirts, suspenders, and billed caps, like a proud uniform. Many are ponytailed, bearded, earringed. A few have a three-inch disk straining the denim in a white circle on a hip pocket: a Copenhagen can. The rest are smokers, and they light up as they file down the trail, talking about hunting. "You go along the ridgetops and they'll just drop down the other side and you'll never see 'em," said one. "I guess you could shoot into the brush where they are and get one. But I like to see what I'm shooting."

I ask one young man who he is and why he's here. His name is Steve Anderson[1], and he grew up in Astoria and Tillamook. His wife is a cook at an assisted-living center in Tillamook. They have a four-year-old daughter, and a baby on the way. "I had a job at a hardwood mill," Anderson says, "but I got laid off twice, and then when I got back on I was working graveyard four days a week, and the day shift got all the overtime. So I quit and went to work for this program. The pay is better."

Anderson is cautiously optimistic about his prospects after he finishes the program, which is teaching him skills like how to identify a tree that might host a cavity-nesting bird, how to lay out an exacting thinning sale in a wildlife habitat area, and how to manage a small business. The men are also building footbridges, clearing trails, and doing other important but often low-priority work on the Tillamook and Siuslaw forests.

"They're going to teach us skills so we can into business for ourselves as forestry contractors if we want to," says Anderson. "Private industry, if they're going to bid on sales on the state and federal forests, they're going to need people with these skills, who know how to mark wildlife trees and do commercial thinning like they're showing us here. There will be a demand. So I'm pretty hopeful this will work out for me."

Bad Times for Timber Workers

It wasn't until the late 1980s that the spotted-owl debate brought Northwest forests into national headlines. But lumber and wood products workers in the region had been hurting since before then, ever since the early '80s, when the state's economy took a nosedive. In 1982, employment in wood products in the three northwestern Oregon counties, including Tillamook, had dropped to 2,100, down from 3,510 in 1977 (Oregon Employment Department 1993, 22). Lumber and wood products were hit especially hard by the nationwide downturn of 1980-82; layoffs, shutdowns, and closures were common. By 1989 there were a few more forest-related jobs in the northwestern area (2,490 of them), but over the next three years another 750 bled away (Oregon Employment Department 1996, 26). A few were added back in during the brighter economy of the mid-1990s, but most of the job growth in Tillamook County during that time was in retail and services—there were plenty of jobs for waiters and waitresses, sales staff, maids, housekeepers, cashiers, kitchen help. In contrast, of the eighteen occupations on the "dislocated" list in the 1996 Oregon Employment Department report, half were timber-related jobs. There used to be six wood-products mills in Tillamook County; now there are two.

Sometimes people's anger over lost jobs and economic hardship found a convenient scapegoat in the northern spotted owl. But in fact the hard times all through the 1980s were forcing mills to get efficient or get out. The resulting improvements in manufacturing productivity accounted for more than half the lumber and wood-products jobs lost in the region after 1980, according to state employment statistics (Oregon Employment Department 1996, 26).

This is not to say the owl's listing made no difference. After the owl was listed as threatened in 1990, a government panel headed by Forest Service biologist (and later the agency's chief) Jack Ward Thomas recommended setting aside 7.7 million acres of federal forest as protected habitat. In 1991 came the court injunction halting all timber sales in areas that might be owl habitat. Federal Judge William Dwyer lifted the injunction in 1994 after finding that the President's forest plan satisfied the requirement for owl habitat. But the President's plan most assuredly does not return the Forest Service to business as usual. It protects up to eighty percent of remaining old-growth forests, setting harvest levels at 1.2 billion board feet—down seventy percent from the levels of the prosperous 1970s (Oregon Employment Department 1993, 27).

There is only a little federal forest in Tillamook County. A splash of the Siuslaw National Forest falls along its southwestern edge, and there is a little BLM land also in the southern part of the county. The changing timber economy has a different face in northwestern Oregon, where most of the forest land is either private or state-owned and most of the trees on it are very young. In fact, the timber economy in Tillamook and Clatsop counties is expected to fare better in the future than in most other parts of Oregon because so many young trees are approaching harvesting age. But whether and when they will be harvested depends much on federal and state policy—in particular, whether the state forestry department's long-range management plan is adopted as proposed. In the meantime, there is no escaping the dwindling availability, at least for the next few years, of jobs in the mills and the woods, in Tillamook County and all over the Pacific Northwest. All of which leaves Steve Anderson and his classmates in need of a different set of skills for the future.

Meticulous Measurements

In front of us, researcher Kathy Maas is talking about what happens to the overstory trees, the ones that are left after the thinning. The trees in the heaviest-thinned plots (that is, those in which the fewest trees are left) are expected to develop longer, thicker crowns than the trees in the other plots. The crown is the part of the tree from the tip to the lowest branch. Long crowns are an old-growth characteristic, a desirable habitat element for red tree voles, small mammals that live their whole lives in the tops of Douglas fir trees.

Another researcher, Sam Chan, talks about the shrubs, herbs, wood litter, and bare soil beneath the trees, the meticulous measurements he and his colleagues have taken, their careful calculations of the relative amounts of each of these things on the forest floor. Chan talks about the importance of tiny variations in conditions from site to site—the steepness of the ground, the direction of its slope, the amount of light coming in through the canopy, how much bare soil is exposed, now much woody debris is on the site, the temperature of the ground. Light is especially critical for the growing seedlings. Chan took the light readings in his plots with two instruments to get more precision. "It's important to make sure your thinning will create the regeneration you want." Getting the light readings right the first time, he says, is a lot easier and cheaper than going back and starting over. These studies are closing in on the precise point at which Douglas fir seedlings, well known to be intolerant of shade, can survive and grow below a thinned overstory. "Early results indicate that with the light available under a heavy thinning, Douglas fir do just fine," says Bill Emmingham. "And it's important to note that even the shade-tolerant species like hemlock and cedar didn't do well in the heavy shade of the unthinned stands." Creating a forest stand where both sun-loving and shade-loving conifer seedlings can thrive, he says, is the first step toward creating a managed forest with more biological diversity—more kinds of trees and shrubs and forbs, more kinds of wildlife.

Clear-cutting as a Solution

Under the plantation-style clear-cut and plant methodology, of course, there is no worrying about light. Douglas fir's intolerance of shade is not a silvicultural decree, as is sometimes argued. But it is a biological fact that leads many silviculturists to defend clear-cutting, properly done, as the most reliable method of regenerating coastal Douglas fir forests.

In the predominant public sentiment, which now generally finds it repugnant, clear-cutting is nothing more than a quick and cheap way to scalp logs off hillsides. The silvicultural meaning of the term is more emotionally neutral and more all-encompassing. To a silviculturist, clear-cutting is a *reproduction method*—a definition that focuses attention on the new stand that will grow after the logging is done. The meaning of the term seems obvious, writes David Smith in *The Practice of Silviculture* (1986), but lately it has slipped into "a semantic morass" because of loose usage and negative connotations.

In the 1940s and 1950s, clear-cutting was seen as the most reliable, straightforward way to get a new stand of trees growing, leaving "as little as possible to chance or nature" (Smith 1986, 371). Before the Tillamook Burn, when there was little reforestation technology to speak of, it was assumed that Douglas fir would grow back naturally in most instances. New trees would naturally regenerate from seeds stored in the soil, or blown in, or dropped from seed trees left on the site or nearby. That is the way coastal forests have regenerated themselves all during the eleven thousand years that Douglas fir has spread itself across the Coast Range (Spies et al., in press). Reseeding is nature's way of growing a new conifer forest after a fire, flood, or windstorm.

But even in nature, Douglas fir doesn't always regenerate reliably. Besides, logging is different from fires and floods. Because many of the cut-over sites in the 1930s and 1940s were full of dry slash and brush and unlogged trees—logging was less efficient back then—Douglas fir regrowth from seed was spotty in many places. There wasn't enough bare soil to sprout seeds, or enough light to grow them, or there was too much competition for them to thrive.

Also during this time, a system of selectively cutting old-growth stands came into common use, under the rubric of "maturity selection" (Munger 1941, cited in Guldin 1996). The idea was to extract "financially overmature" Douglas fir logs from virgin stands on the west side, releasing the remaining trees to grow faster into their own financial maturity. The problem was, they did not. A 1956 analysis by Forest Service silviculturist Leo Isaac found that the bigger and older the residual trees were, the less likely they were to increase their growth after partial logging. Moreover, cutting a few big trees from thick stands inevitably damaged the remaining trees, and shade-tolerant shrubs and hardwoods flooded into the gaps.

What may be most important is that there was virtually no reforestation research going on at the time, and so these efforts lacked the scientific and technical backup that might have helped them succeed. The failure of the maturity-selection system soured silviculturists on the whole idea of selective cutting, an attitude that persists today among many within the forestry community. "By the 1950s," says Smith, "the whole episode was recognized as a fiasco to be quietly forgotten."

At the time, the main obstacle to reforestation seemed to be messy, careless, or greedy logging. Clear-cutting was envisioned as a way to mimic the effects of a natural catastrophe—sweeping the land clean and giving the young Douglas fir a head start, either with naturally blown-in seeds or with planted seedlings. Reinforcing the conservationist bent of this idea, deer and elk typically flooded into newly planted clear-cuts because there were plenty of young shrubs and tender plants for them to eat. In those days, when wildlife was mostly thought of as "game," this seemed a pretty good indication that clear-cutting was environmentally benign.

Clear-cutting, and indeed many of the tools of intensive silviculture, were developed and refined in the crucible of the Tillamook Burn reforestation. Foresters learned a lot in a hurry (and often the hard way) about how to match seedlings to the right elevation, slope, and aspect, how to protect them against field mice and deer, how to fertilize them, how to control the other plants that competed with them for water, nutrients, and light.

To be sure, there was all along some doubt about the ecological wisdom of clear-cuts. Through the 1970s and 1980s, as clear-cuts began to spread across more and more acreage (much of it federal forest land), scientists began to take a dimmer view, linking clear-cutting to erosion, flooding, landslides, and blow-down of trees.

The Forest Service strategy at the time was to try to soften the impact of clear-cutting, visually as well as ecologically, by making the units smaller and by scattering them within a matrix of intact forest, like raisins in an oatmeal cookie. But this produced a fragmented, deeply roaded, edge-riddled forest landscape that was nothing like the original forest in its size or its ecological integrity. The alarm over this fragmentation of the old-growth forest was one of the concerns that produced research leading to New Forestry in the 1980s.

Scientists were also concerned about the extreme efficiency of clear-cutting, the very quality that had recommended it as a scientific methodology of reforestation. Experiments in the 1970s began to show that cleaning all the slash from the land and pulling debris out of the streams—the best, most enlightened logging practice of the day—actually stripped vital nutrients from the soil and water. Finally, many of today's ecologists point out that clear-cuts don't really mimic forest fires very well. There's a crucial difference: wildfires, unless they are very intense or repeated, tend to leave some of the plant nutrients on the site. Clear-cutting, unless significant quantities of slash are left behind, tends to take them away.

In response to these findings, many silviculturists now are leaning harder on selective cutting for harvesting and regrowing timber. These scientists are also realists, aware that forestry is a very public enterprise that must enjoy at least some degree of public permission. Still, most academic and practicing foresters—including Bill Emmingham—maintain that clear-cutting is a legitimate silvicultural tool if applied at the right time and place.

Some people object to clear-cutting merely on the grounds that it is driven more by profit concerns than by reproduction concerns. Well, yes. The forestry enterprise as a whole is driven by profit concerns. If there were no profit in it, there would be no cutting of trees at all (or very little, perhaps, for subsistence purposes), no need to reforest, and no need for a forestry profession as we now understand the concept.

"Forestry" *means* that copious basket of science, technology, tools, and techniques directed toward managing forests for the extraction of products—although not all who call themselves foresters are necessarily devoted to that end. In this country forestry is carried out mostly within the tradition of private enterprise, which means profit as the driving motive. Clear-cutting is one of the tools in the basket, and if conducted in good faith it can function as a check on the pure exercise of the profit motive by offering an achievable vision of a future forest. Can clear-cutting be a cover for greedy, exploitative, unsustainable logging? Of course, if it is done in the wrong place for the wrong reasons. In dishonest hands any tool can be a weapon.

Clear-cutting was conceived and born in an era where the pressing problems of forestry and society were the same: preventing forest fires, reforesting a burned or cut-over landscape, and furnishing abundant, cheap timber to a world rebuilding itself after World War II. In that era clear-cutting seemed both desirable and necessary. It was not a problem, but a solution.

Bone-deep Knowledge

Howard Beck[1] grew up in that world. "Look at that. Up there. That's a beautiful sight." Howard Beck is the fiftyish-looking man in the Ecosystem Workforce group. He is pointing at a clear-cut, a slash of brown up on the hillside. "Think of it in a few years. It'll be beautiful." We are back in the van, headed up the highway to the next site. "Think what the Tillamook used to look like," he says. "It used to look like the Sahara Desert. Now it's all green." He and the others in the van—they are all Ecosystem Workforce people—nod in assent. They talk about the landscape with the knowledge of those who know they are a living part of it. "Look at all that alder up there," says one man. "They ought to log that off." Another says, "Alder's more dangerous to log than fir. Splits and kicks back at you." "Yeah, they should log it," says Beck. "But there'd probably be some other *bird* they'd have to protect."

The men joke loudly among themselves about little things, inside jokes. One of them unwraps a candy bar, which provokes hoots and jeering from the others. They rib him good-naturedly: "Stealin' the Halloween candy from the little kids, hey?" Then, quickly serious, they talk about which mills in the area are open, which have been bought out or closed down, who's been laid off, who is logging and where, who is buying logs. It occurs to me that these men have a bone-deep knowledge of this place that all the scientists, meticulous as their measurements are, will never have.

Howard Beck is wearing cut-off ("stagged") pants, a red plaid shirt over a gray pullover sweater, gray wool socks, and a billed orange cap with "Husqvarna,"the brand name of a line of chainsaws, stitched across the front. He planted trees on the Tillamook as a schoolboy, after the 1951 fire, and started working in the woods as a faller in 1960. "It's all I've ever done," he says. He was about to lose his job when he applied for the Ecosystem Workforce group and was selected. Is the course of studies helping him? He politely ducks the question. He's clearly dubious about some of the newer forestry techniques being exhibited on this tour. "It's pretty interesting," he says, "but what are the deer and the elk going to eat?"

He tells how his cutting crew used to take down all the snags and yard them off the unit as a matter of course. It was just flat good logging, he says; if they didn't do it, guys would get hurt. "Now they leave them for the spotted owl and the *marbelet.* Because birds are more important than people, I guess."

"If We Build It, They Will Come"

Bill Emmingham has the microphone again. We're standing in an older, thinned stand on a ridge not far from a hillside that was aerial-seeded after the Burn. The seeding was uneven; you can still see a faint zebra-stripe pattern across the hill, two different shades of green. It's chilly in under the trees. Emmingham is talking about using silviculture to mimic most of the disturbances that were part of the evolutionary history of these forests. Managers can do a lot of different things at different scales, he says, from cutting a single tree here and there, to thinning lightly, to thinning heavily, to patch-cutting, to "messy" clear-cuts that leave snags and dead wood behind. And it's all for the wildlife, which, if everything goes as planned, will move in and thrive. "The idea of structural diversity," says Emmingham, "is, 'If you build it, they will come.'"

It may seem ironic to talk about managing a forest so that it looks and feels unmanaged. To Bill Emmingham, it is simply what forest scientists are supposed to do—to be responsive to what the society is asking forests to provide, and at the same time to protect the forest's ecological integrity. Emmingham does not call such a forest "natural," for "natural" is a culturally influenced notion and a devilishly hard one to pin down. Being a scientist, he likes to keep his terminology precise. "A lot of people have the idea that if you leave nature alone it will achieve some sort of equilibrium that humans will find appealing," he says. "But that represents a lapse in reasoning. All ecosystems are in a state of constant change. On top of that, the human impact on our environment has already been profound. With our highways, our wheat fields, our dams, our cities, we've shifted the presettlement disturbance regimes all around. It's unrealistic to assume that doing nothing will restore some 'natural' state of things." Instead of appealing to an unattainable ideal of naturalness, he says, "we need to take responsibility for identifying what's *desirable,* and then use our best science and our most careful management to change our surroundings accordingly."

The birds seem to like the thinning, say researchers Jennifer Weeks and Mike Adam. At least, these scientists counted more birds—both greater numbers and more species—in the thinned stands than they found before the logging, and that surprised them. We're now looking at birds, amphibians, flying squirrels, and *Phellinus* root rot, and the day is waning. We're on a steep road, in deep shade, and it is really cold. People have their hands in their armpits and they're stamping their feet. Three young people on dirt bikes tear past us down the hill.

"We found more birds this year, after the thinning," says Jennifer Weeks. They counted twenty-four species of birds before the logging, she says, and thirty-eight species afterward. Some of the species that increased in number are normally found in younger forest anyway, the researchers point out. But one, the Hammond's flycatcher, is sometimes thought to be associated with old growth. These findings, they stress, are preliminary and subject to change; birds, after all, move around. It will take several more years of monitoring to document reliably how birds are responding to the thinning experiments.

Another dirt-biker roars up the hill, not looking at us as we press to the sides of the road.

For his presentation, Doug Gomez, the small-mammal researcher, dons a pair of fuzzy squirrel ears, a collar, and a striped tail, trying to add a touch of humor at the end of a long day. "The northern flying squirrel is very important," he says, "because it's the main prey species for the spotted owl." Flying squirrels nest in cavities in snags or stumps and feed on lichens and fungi, buds and berries. "Will the structural characteristics provided by thinning suffice for them? That's what we're trying to find out." He speaks earnestly, nodding his head; he's forgotten the bobbing squirrel ears. He says he captured many more flying squirrels in the year after thinning than in the year before. His finding held true in all stands, including the unthinned control plots. Maybe a natural year-to-year fluctuation? Nobody knows yet.

Amphibian numbers, on the other hand, were down, says Nobuya Suzuki. He and colleague John Hayes found generally fewer animals in the thinned stands than in the unthinned controls. The rough-skinned newt and a couple of salamander species were exceptions, but so few of the salamanders were caught in either place that it was impossible to generalize from the findings. Suzuki and Hayes are also doing a retrospective study of other forest stands that were thinned between 10 and 20 years ago.

Suzuki suggests we bear in mind that thinning might disturb important habitat components on the forest floor, like leaf litter, moss, small plants, and shrubs. "Commercial thinning creates vertical structure," says Suzuki, "but these guys don't fly, so they don't care. You have to look at the horizontal scale."

Of course, everybody stresses, these findings are preliminary. They're all preliminary. Can precision thinning produce both timber for humans and a forest that wildlife will want to live in? The verdict won't be in for years. But then, the history of forestry is a history of managing with incomplete information, says Jerry Franklin, the chief avatar of New Forestry. At a seminar held at Oregon State University a few months before this tour, Franklin told a standing-room-only audience that the notion that forest management rests on proven principles is "a professional mythology." Said Franklin: "We never have all the information we want. And we can't wait till all the evidence is in. The best we can do is to move ahead and learn while we're doing." The alternative, he said, "is to continue doing what doesn't work."

Notes

1. Names have been changed to protect the privacy of participants.

7

The Search for Sustainability

THE WORD "SUSTAINABLE" IS A BUZZWORD NOWADAYS. ITS current fashionable status might make it seem that the search for sustainability in all kinds of natural resource endeavors—farming, fisheries, forestry—is something that just now occurred to people at this moment in history. In fact, the search for a humane, stable, and lasting way to extract and enjoy the fruits of the earth has been going on for a long, long time.

Before we start on this historical quest, let us consider what we mean by "sustainable." Many people fling the word around without knowing quite what they mean. That makes me suspect that sustainability is one of those ideas that gets fuzzier the harder you look at it—rather like faint stars that disappear under direct gaze, the ones you can see out of the tail of your eye if you look just slightly away. Perhaps "sustainable" will be easier to define in peripheral vision, by focusing instead on those dimensions of it that sit a little off to the side.

The first such dimension is "sustainability of what?" In their 1991 essay, "What should forests sustain? Eight answers," Richard Gale and Sheila Cordray offer a range of ideas, from "dominant product sustainability" through "human benefit sustainability," "self-sufficient sustainability," "ecosystem type sustainability," and down to "ecosystem-centered sustainability." These answers start at what I am calling the frontier extreme of a spectrum and end at the arcadian extreme. Gale and Cordray's Option #5, "self-sufficient sustainability," is (obviously) about in the middle. It defines sustainability as maintaining the long-term integrity of an ecosystem while providing for some extraction of products for human benefit. That definition gets close to the sort of sustainability that seems most reasonable to me. It is also the sort of sustainability the Tillamook's foresters seem to be trying to achieve.

Secondly, we should ask, sustainability within what thresholds of time and space? Change in nature happens over moments, days, years, decades, centuries, millennia, eons. The judgment of whether something is sustainable depends on your perspective. Events that appear unstable in the short term—like a fire that burns over many thousands of acres in a forest—take on the appearance of stability when viewed from a longer perspective as part of a pattern, when it's understood that fires come and go in a recurring though not a regular fashion. At least in the Pacific Northwest, at least in these last several thousand years, periodic fires have not destroyed the forest. The forest has been sustained—that is, has continued in a forested condition, and so far as we know, it has continued to have a wide range of ages and structures of forest vegetation present at some place on the landscape all the time.

On the other hand, some things that may seem sustainable to us are, over the long term, highly unsustainable. We use the phrase "solid ground" without thinking much about it, but the earth's crust might look more like a pot of jam coming to a boil if we could watch it from the moon for ten million years. Nevertheless, viewed from within our limited lifespan the earth seems reassuringly solid. For us, living on it is a sustainable activity.

For humans to define "sustainability" for forests, we must locate ourselves within a time perspective that makes sense for humans and forests—from, say, eighty years, a human lifespan, to about 500 years, a roughly average lifespan for a conifer tree in a coastal Oregon forest. We must also choose a space perspective, and that is a little harder, for there is room for human concern about forests small and large, everywhere on earth. If I had to choose arbitrarily, I would say, pick a contiguous forested landscape that is big enough to have a physical and biological integrity, not only trees but rivers, animals, shrubs, moss, hillsides, canyons. And let it be a forest that people are fond of, attached to, that they live next to, use, and love. The Tillamook qualifies on both counts.

The third dimension is, sustainability based on what root assumptions? One of the most influential stories on how plant communities develop is Frederic Clements' model of ecological succession. A forest progresses through several "seral" stages until it reaches a "climax" state and remains there in indefinite equilibrium. Clements' theory is complicated, subtle, coherent, and very useful, and I am not doing it justice here (see Worster 1994 for an introduction to Clements and his work), but my point is that the theory of ecological succession depends on a root assumption of order and harmony in natural processes. This idea represents very well the spirit of Clements' formative times, the late nineteenth and early twentieth centuries.

Our times are different. For the past few decades, biologists have been exploring nature's workings in light of the opposite root idea, that of fundamental disequilibrium. They are focusing more on the role of disturbance in natural communities than on orderly succession processes (Worster 1994). It is important that we be aware of the root assumptions underlying our ideas—that is the theme of this book, after all—but I don't think we have to solve this conundrum in order to find a working definition of "sustainable." There seems empirically to be a measure of order and predictability to the functioning of a forest, when the forest is viewed at a scale of time and space which we humans find imaginable. "Sustainability" in this context means doing things that promote both the continued existence of the forest in its forested condition and the continued presence of all its vegetation ages and structures on the landscape in some rough functional equilibrium. At the same time, "sustainability" means actively doing things to promote the ongoing welfare—however it be defined—of the people who have some connection with and stake in the forest.

Some might argue that the human race is approaching sustainability of its forests in some places; for instance, in the forests of Germany and Scandinavia, which, like ours, suffered a period of unsustainable exploitation but now have been managed carefully, if intensively, over several generations. And I might agree, if my interlocutor were able to convince me that preserving or recreating some remnant of the prehistoric forest is not important. Likewise, some argue that forest management in the United States is sustainable because there is more wood growing today than there was at the turn of the century. This is true, but that definition of "sustainability" fails the test of scale, and perhaps also the test of representative forest structures. Much of the lands across North American that were once covered by virgin forests has been replanted or regenerated and is now occupied by young and middle-aged trees. That is certainly a good thing, but it does not add up to sustainability for people who live near large, intensively logged acreages of what used to be, very recently, old growth. However, I do think the human race is groping its way toward sustainability, as I hope to show in this chapter.

This is an admittedly brief and vague definition. Like everything else I am telling you about the Tillamook, it is intended not as a universal truth, but as a limited and situational framework to aid understanding. It may not tell us when or if we have arrived at "sustainability," but it ought to be able to tell us whether or not we are going in the right direction.

The Staff of Life

Let us now look at the long and mostly futile search for sustainability over the many centuries that humans have lived on the earth. Trees have been the staff of civilized life for over five thousand years, from ancient times up until the glory days of the British Empire. "Wood, in fact, is the unsung hero of the technological revolution that has brought us from a stone and bone culture to our present age," writes John Perlin in *A Forest Journey* (1991). Houses, public buildings, roads, ships, docks, iron smelters, brick and ceramic factories, agricultural tools, hot baths—all the accoutrements of civilized life, and many of its luxuries—depended on wood.

The story of the ancient world, as told by Perlin, is a story of civilizations advancing, forests receding, and, most often, the subsequent decline of these civilizations as their thirst for wood outstripped the supply. Sometimes the dwindling forests prompted desperate and ultimately futile measures to conserve. Infrequently, a society successfully substituted another material for wood, as the British did in the early seventeenth century, when it began to exploit its resources of coal and continued thereby to fuel the Industrial Revolution.

The strivings of ancient kingdoms to assure an abundant wood supply contributed to the kinds of geopolitical jostlings that accompany the search for oil today. The Bible tells of the building of King Solomon's house, "of the Forest of Lebanon, . . . built upon three rows of cedar pillars, with cedar beams upon the pillars. And it was covered with cedar above the chambers that were upon the forty-five pillars, fifteen in each row." Solomon's Hall of Judgment "was finished with cedar from floor to rafters" (Bible, 1 Kings 7:2-7). The cedar came from the kingdom of Tyre, on the Mediterranean coast, where it was a mainstay of the economy. Solomon paid for the wood with wheat and fine beaten olive oil (1 Kings 5:10-11)—probably not the first exchange of raw materials for finished goods, and certainly not the last. To do the logging and milling of the wood, he conscripted thirty thousand forced laborers (1 Kings 6:13 and n.). Their subsequent resentment at this ill-treatment may have contributed to Israel's secession from the southern kingdom in the tenth century B.C. (1 Kings 12:1-20).

The Romans built their city on once-wooded hills (Perlin 1991, 103). As the city grew and more surrounding land was cleared for farming, the forests retreated "farther and farther up the mountains" (Lucretius, quoted in Perlin, 105-6). Cicero, a statesman of the late

Roman Republic, was an early conservationist, arguing that keeping Rome's native woodlands in public ownership was a matter of national security (Perlin, 107). But he was overruled by proponents of Rome's mounting colonialist policy. The Roman Republic spread into an empire, colonizing northern Italy, Spain, Gaul, Germany, Britain, and North Africa, in part to capture their abundant forest resources.

England in early Tudor times had plenty of wood, enough to export to Holland, Flanders, and northern France. When Henry VIII ascended the throne in 1509, "no lack of timber was felt or feared," in the admiring words of the Venetian ambassador to the Tudor court (Perlin, 163). But under Henry, Elizabeth, and the first Stuarts, England embarked upon a period of rapid development and colonization. The growth of its iron works, shipping, copper and lead smelting, glassworks, and building construction began to deplete England's famous woods (Perlin, 163-77).

John Norden, surveyor of the royal forests, wrote in the early seventeenth century that the oak forests "hath universally received a mortal blow within the time of my memory" (Perlin, 177-9). Observing "the great consuming of woods" and "the neglect of planting woods," Norden advocated mandatory reforestation. The law must compel owners "to plant for every sum of acres a number of trees or to sow or set a quantity of ground with acorns." But then as now, there was no immediate profit in reforestation. In most instances the land was more valuable as pasture, increasing the incentive to waste the timber on it.

The scarcity of wood had become a national issue in the early part of James I's reign, in the first decades of the seventeenth century. A conservationist of the time, Arthur Standish, argued a link between deforestation and famine, and he came up with a plan to preserve the remaining woods and plant new ones. His tract, *The Commons' Complaint,* caught the eye of the King. James adopted a conservationist policy, arguing for preservation laws and prohibiting the use of timber for firewood, building, and glassworks. But he used the royal forests as a source of revenue to support his lavish standard of living, and his conservation sentiments went mostly unheeded.

All through this time English industrialists were looking farther afield for wood to fuel their factories. They found it in the north of England and in Ireland, which was then full of "great woods or low shrubs and thickets" (quoted in Perlin, 197). Ireland was flooded with English lumbermen seeking wood for fishing boats, barrels, and charcoal for the ironworks they established there. Irish wood was so cheap that iron produced in Ireland had a large competitive advantage over English iron. A survey of forests in England and Ireland showed a great deforestation of Irish woods between 1603, the year James took the throne, and 1641. So many trees were taken that, in one observer's words, "you may travel whole days without seeing any woods or trees . . " (Perlin, 213).

The New World

In 1662 came an impassioned appeal for a national reforestation policy. John Evelyn's *Silva, Or, a Discourse of Forest-Trees and the Propagation of Timber in His Majesties Dominions* became a landmark document in both forest policy and silvicultural technique. Evelyn wrote a chapter on each species of English tree, and included detailed techniques for planting and harvesting. *Silva* was a bestseller, speaking as it did to a public vitally interested in saving England's woods. Evelyn's efforts accomplished some reforestation, but the scarcity and high price of wood continued to drive England, like Rome, overseas to look for other sources—principally to the New World.

America was a gold mine of timber. England needed New England trees for masts for the Royal Navy after the supply in Scandinavia became too scarce and the trees too small. America, with abundant wood for charcoal, also provided a place to locate English ironworks so as to ease the pressure on England's own scarce forests—a plan that had the approval of John Evelyn. In effect, Britain exported the environmental costs of her timber consumption along with a culture of unsustainable resource exploitation.

The transplanted iron foundries represented only one of many pressures of development on the woods of America. The clearing of land for farms and cities, the use of wood for brewing and distilling, baking and rendering, brickmaking and tanning and salt extraction, for housing and factory construction, building of wagon roads and bridges, carriages and carts, schooners and fishing boats, keelboats and barges—all these activities were necessary to the building of a new civilization in a new land, and they gobbled up wood at a furious rate. The developing economy of the New World cut a wide swath across America's forest primeval which had so awed the first European visitors.

The appearance of steam engines and railroads in the young United States greatly increased the national appetite for wood.

Railroads needed wooden ties and wood to fire the boilers. The railroads also punched open the West, inviting settlers to come into the Ohio Valley, Indiana, Illinois and the Midwest, the Lake States, the Great Plains, and beyond. Settlers cleared the woods away so they could farm.

An alarm was sounded in 1867 about the wasting of the nation's forests. In his report to the Wisconsin legislature titled *Disasterous Effects of the Destruction of Forest Trees Now Going on So Rapidly in the State of Wisconsin,* Increase Lapham pointed to "the experience of other countries, ancient and modern, whose forests have been improvidently destroyed . . . " (Perlin, 354). The 1880 U.S. census contained a later and more dire report on the condition of America's forests. It cited widespread deforestation everywhere east of the Mississippi and north of the Ohio. The report's author, Charles Sargent, argued for preservation of forests on ecological grounds, a prophetic plea. The forest is important in maintaining the flow of rivers and preventing erosion of the soil, he wrote. "The whole community will suffer widespread calamity which no precautions taken after the mischief has been done can avert or future expenditure prevent." Sargent went on to warn: "The American people must learn that a forest, whatever its extent and resources, can be exhausted in a surprisingly short space of time through total disregard in its treatment" (Perlin, 360).

National Forests

By the end of the nineteenth century, America's profligate ways with its woods had provoked nationwide concern. By 1890, the Western land rush was on full steam, and the wholesale transfer of public lands into private ownership had attracted national attention (Office of the Attorney General 1997, 5). Forests in particular were thrust into the spotlight in 1908, when President Theodore Roosevelt called a conference of the nation's governors to discuss the urgent problem of forest depletion. "This nation began with the belief that its landed possessions were illimitable," he told the governors. "We began with an unapproached heritage of forests; more than half the timber is gone" (Roosevelt 1908).

In 1891 Congress had authorized President Benjamin Harrison to set aside forested public lands as "forest reserves." The first one was the Bull Run reserve, set aside in 1892 (it is now the Bull Run watershed in the Mount Hood National Forest, the source of

Portland's drinking water). In 1897 Congress passed the Organic Act, spelling out measures for protection and management of the newly created federal forest reserves. By 1901 about fifty million acres had been reserved from disposal. When Roosevelt became president in that year, he set aside another 150 million acres of forest land.

In 1905 the lands were transferred to the Department of Agriculture, and in 1907 they became the National Forests. These forests were to be managed by a professional cadre of foresters according to the highest Progressive principles, to secure "the permanent good of the whole people and [not] . . . the temporary benefit of individuals or companies" (Office of the Attorney General 1997, 16). This professional cadre became the U.S. Forest Service.

The man who steered the Forest Service's course and shaped its culture perhaps more than any other was the handsome, Yale-educated, European-trained, high-principled forest steward who became Theodore Roosevelt's Chief Forester, Gifford Pinchot. Pinchot's Progressive ideals of perpetual stewardship for "the permanent good of the whole people" came to be embodied in a concept called "sustained yield," by which the new National Forests were to be managed. The objective of sustained yield, put simply, was to balance the harvest against the anticipated growth of a forest over time—a theoretical guarantee of forests forever.

The sustained-yield idea, further articulated by David T. Mason in the 1920s, envisioned a "conversion period" for harvesting the West's huge inventories of older forests, "decadent" because they had stopped growing new wood, and converting them into young, fast-growing stands that would provide a continuous supply of timber for future generations (Beuter 1994, 17). In the words of Mason, often called the "father" of sustained yield, the task was to "keep . . . forest soils regularly engaged in the work of growing trees so that dependent communities may have maximum permanent prosperity" (Mason 1927, cited in Cheek 1996, 3). Mason's view shifted the emphasis from sustaining forests to sustaining forest products—thereby guaranteeing perpetual prosperity (in theory) to those towns where the mills were located. He also envisioned coordination between public and private forest management to promote community stability (Clary 1986, 85-86).

Sustained yield became the defining philosophy of Forest Service management. Because National Forests were publicly owned, and managed by publicly employed, professional foresters—putting the whole process, in theory at least, above politics—sustained yield held out the promise, finally, of a sustainable, humane forestry. It promised to curb the power of big capital, soften the boom-and-bust cycles that were so familiar to forest economies up until then, and turn the forest into a stable and perpetual source of wealth for dependent communities.

A Troublesome Concept

Sustained yield has throughout its long life been a troublesome concept to carry out or even to define. It has suffered from a disconnect between its political and its technical implications; it has been regarded variously as a philosophy, a set of economic principles, a management toolkit, and a social-welfare policy to attain a variety of objectives. "Any misunderstanding regarding sustained yield," writes the economist Con Schallau, "stems from a belief that (a) there is a consensus regarding its meaning and (b) it is the principal means to maximize net benefits from public forests" (Schallau 1989).

At first, sustained yield was regarded as an antidote to the "cut-out-and-get-out" practices of the timber barons and the main means for the Forest Service, on behalf of the national welfare, to avert a "timber famine." The phrase is a coinage of Gifford Pinchot's, and his alarm about an impending shortage of timber fueled his crusade against the greedy and wasteful ways of private timber companies (Greeley 1951, 69). Then, in the 1920s and 1930s, says the economist Schallau, sustained yield became a way to avert a timber *surplus* by withholding public timber from the private market and by discouraging smaller operators from competing with the bigger landholding companies in the West (Schallau 1989).

Sustained yield's mandate to promote community stability was made explicit in the Sustained Yield Forest Management Act of 1944. This was the law that created sustained-yield units, formal agreements between the Forest Service and certain lumber companies that guaranteed a steady supply of federal timber to local mills with the goal of securing local economic stability. However, community stability did not necessarily always ensue. Sustained yield's assumption that mill towns need only a reliable timber supply to keep them prosperous may overlook the role of other factors, such as a sound transportation and communication network and a tradition of strong local leadership, says Kristin Aldred Cheek, who studied federal sustained-yield units in Oregon and northern California (Cheek 1996). "What was already in place in the local [sustained-yield-unit] community was a key factor" in its general well-being, she writes.[1]

The economist Tom Power forcefully challenges the conventional wisdom that timber supply is directly correlated with a community's well-being:

> [It] is not what usually determines the level of employment and income in the wood products industry. . . [and so] attempts to influence local economic well-being by manipulating the acreage allocated to timber management are like trying to push something with a wet noodle. The tools in the hands of federal land managers are too weak compared with the market forces that buffet the wood products industry (Power 1996, 159). [2]

In fact, some researchers maintain that sustained-yield policies have the perverse effect of making towns *less* stable, by undermining their resiliency to change (Force et al. 1993, cited in Cheek 1986).

Writing about the Forest Service in the Eisenhower years, the historian Paul Hirt says everybody who had a stake in the national forests "supported the policy of sustained yield—even though nobody was quite sure what it meant or how it should be applied" (Hirt 1994, 170). The timber industry espoused one definition (focused, unsurprisingly, on yield of timber) while conservation groups offered another, "a nonhierarchical definition . . . that implied equal consideration of all uses." To this group, sustained yield meant sustaining of the forest's biological function rather than its economic production (Hirt, 171).

Congress tried to clarify things in the Multiple Use-Sustained Yield Act of 1960: "'Sustained yield of several products and services' means the achievement and maintenance in perpetuity of a high-level annual or regular periodic output of the various renewable resources of the national forests without impairment of the productivity of the land." This definition begs the understanding of other crucial concepts, and as a result it is subject to a variety of interpretations, depending on how one understands the meaning of "high-level," "renewable," "resource," "impairment," and "productivity." With the Multiple Use-Sustained Yield Act, sustained yield underwent yet another identity shift: the Forest Service assumed the burden of public expectation to produce sustained yield of *all* forest resources, not only timber. That expectation, codified into law, exponentially increased the complexity of federal forest planning.

Hirt charges that the sustained yield concept, applied operationally to timber management, has encouraged the Forest Service to overcut the National Forests by overestimating the productivity of future young plantations. Sustained yield was calculated in a way that balanced the rate of harvest with the *potential* growth of the new, young trees that would replace those cut. The problem, says Hirt, was that Forest Service managers consistently assumed a best-case scenario:

> If the forester was told to assume [that the new trees] would be managed intensively in the future—that fire suppression by the agency would eliminate 90 percent of the natural fire loss; that greater use of pesticides would reduce insect and disease losses by another 90 percent; that cutover areas would be immediately replanted with genetically engineered, faster growing, commercially desirable tree species; that because of new utilization technology trees could be harvested at 60 years of age rather than 100; that careful logging would increase utilization; and that the negative effects of timber cutting on other multiple uses would be mitigated—then, under these new assumptions, the allowable cut could be much higher. (Hirt, 56-57).

Thus, whether a forest was being managed according to sustained yield or not depended on the assumptions that entered the calculation. Too often those assumptions were unrealistic (Hirt, p. 57).[3] Sustained yield has often collided with market forces or conservation principles, or both. Some techniques that have been justified in the name of sustained yield, like the systematic liquidation of old growth on federal forests, have dismayed and angered many citizens—in whose name the Forest Service claimed to be acting—and stirred painful second thoughts in many professional foresters.

Yet for all its conceptual fuzziness and practical contradictions, sustained yield has been a very important idea, the central idea that shaped the mission and practice of the Forest Service and its policies on timber harvesting up through the 1980s. Sustained yield has reflected a hope, never very well realized, that timber harvesting can be done in a way that will support and sustain communities. It voices a persistent and quixotic faith that a stable and humane forestry can be found.

Oregon Takes Up the Conservation Challenge

The 1909 Oregon legislature responded to President Roosevelt's conservation challenge by creating the Oregon Conservation Commission. Its job was "ascertaining and making known the natural resources of the State of Oregon . . . to the end that [they] may be conserved and put to the highest use" (Office of the Attorney General, p. 6). The commission lost no time getting to work. Its first report, in 1910, criticized the state for failing to protect forests from fire, failing to discourage waste in logging and milling, and failing to promote reforestation (Office of the Attorney General 1997, 6).

The report resounded with the high principles of the Progressive movement. It set forth the view that Oregon's forests, even the privately owned ones, were a public resource carrying public responsibilities. The 1912 report continued in this vein:

> *Oregon's forests are the assets of all its citizens. The lumberman or timber owner is, economically, only their agent in using them. The lumberman can change or move his business, but the people as a whole have a stake in forest preservation that is unalienable and paramount. . . . The question involved is not one of personal property but one of a community resource* (1912 report, quoted in Oregon Office of the Attorney General, 6).

The Conservation Commission recommended that Oregon appoint a trained state forester, create a fire-prevention program, make a systematic study of forest conditions, and educate the public on important forest issues. It also recommended cutting taxes on deforested lands to encourage owners to reforest them instead of abandoning them. And it made the first recommendations that the state begin to acquire cut-over or burned-over forest lands to rehabilitate.

In 1911 the legislature followed through by creating a comprehensive Forest Code and a new office of State Forester. The first man to hold that office was the visionary Francis Elliott, appointed in 1912 by an equally farsighted governor, Oswald West.

Elliott immediately took up the tasks recommended by the Conservation Commission, and pursued some ideas of his own. One of his first and most lasting acts was to establish the first Oregon state forest, creating it out of a block of land in Coos and Douglas counties that had been burned in the Coos Bay fire of 1868. The Millicoma tract, as it was called, was in federal hands at the time. Elliott offered to trade about 70,000 scattered acres of Oregon's remaining Common School lands (the two sections of each township that had been reserved for school funding when Oregon became a state) for the Millicoma tract. The land swap, which required two acts of Congress, gave Oregon the Francis A. Elliott State Forest, which today reaches to 92,000 acres.

Acquiring the Land

From the beginning, Elliott saw his task as bigger than fire protection or reforestation or education. His job was to create a state forestry system that would satisfy the requirements of private industry and protect the public welfare at the same time (Office of the Attorney General, 10). "Oregon should profit by the experiences of older states who exploited their forest resources with no thought for the future," he wrote in his second annual report to the governor in 1912. "The permanence of a great industry depends upon steps being taken speedily to bring this about" (Office of the Attorney General, 9).

Elliott soon identified the main obstacle to a stable forestry: unstable land ownership patterns that resulted from cut-out-and-get-out logging. Timber landowners in those days had no notion of managing forest land for the long term—there was no financial incentive for it. Once the timber was cut and sold, the land was worthless. The 1919 state forester's report mentions "millions of acres of land good for nothing else except the growing of forest crops, which is being rapidly mined by the owners and then left unproductive, an economic loss to the owners and to the state." Elliott confirmed the 1912 Conservation Commission's recommendation: Oregon should begin acquiring and reforesting logged-off and unproductive land immediately.

The legislature passed the first land acquisitions law in 1925. It said Oregon could accept gifts of forest land as long as the titles were clear. The problem was that most of the lands were encumbered by delinquent taxes. In the end the state did not acquire any lands under the 1925 law. But the law is important because it set forth, for the first time, the purpose for which state forest lands should be managed: "for forestry purposes or for the conservation of water or watershed protection, or for public parks or campgrounds." It was the first time Oregon law had spelled out a principle of multiple use for state forests (Office of the Attorney General, 12).

The problem of cut-over lands kept getting worse through the 1920s. On the eve of the Depression, an estimated two and a half million acres of forest land were lying unproductive, and another 125,000 acres were being logged and abandoned every year. What was more, tax foreclosures were dumping more and more of this land into county ownership. In 1926 more than one-third of the land in Tillamook County was tax-delinquent. The 1929 legislature provided some tax relief to landowners and kept about a million acres in private ownership that might otherwise have ended up in foreclosure, but it did not address the problem of already delinquent lands.

Harder times in the early 1930s made things worse. Massive foreclosures created a budget nightmare for the cash-strapped counties. They owned millions of acres of worthless, ugly, cut-over land, a massive brushfire waiting to happen, a liability for which they were responsible. Their plight was exacerbated by a state property tax that the state of Oregon levied on counties at the time. The counties found themselves owing tax money they could not collect from delinquent landowners. At the same time, Oregon's timber industry was on the skids—lumber production dropped by more than two-thirds between 1929 and 1932 (Office of the Attorney General, 14-16).

Encouraging Long-term Stewardship

All through this time, state forestry officials and legislators were wrestling with the question that had occupied Francis Elliott: What should Oregon do to create a timber economy that was both profitable and humane? What kind of forestry would satisfy private industry and protect the public welfare? Two things were seen as crucial requirements: stabilized land ownership and a legal and economic environment that would promote long-term land stewardship.

The idea that the state should own and manage forest land was viewed as a fitting solution to Oregon's forestry problems. Indeed, state ownership came to be seen as a social obligation to the people of Oregon. "The state is not meeting its social responsibilities of assuring permanent industries and communities," said the 1936 state forester's report, "so long as it permits continuation of an economic system that is directly antagonistic to good forestry practice." By 1936, there was a burgeoning consensus that the state had a crucial role to play as both landowner and forest regulator.

With the Acquisition Act of 1939, Oregon finally found a working mechanism to stabilize the forest land base by bringing thousands of acres of land into state ownership. The law resolved the problem of delinquent tax payments. It also set up a formula whereby the county in which the land was located would get most of the net proceeds from the future sale of timber. The state let the counties keep temporary salvage rights to any timber left standing on the land. This formerly worthless wood had suddenly become valuable in the mid-1940s, because of booming wartime markets. With the counties' approval and cooperation, the state took ownership of about 550,000 acres of cut-over and burned-over land over the next ten years. More than half that land was from the Tillamook Burn (Office of the Attorney General, 20-25).

Then the debate turned to the question of who would pay for the massive rehabilitation that was needed. As outlined in greater detail in Chapter 4, a scheme for a severance tax on timber was floated, then abandoned after heavy opposition from timber companies. Instead, the legislature proposed to issue $25 million in bonds—a clear statement that the responsibility for reforestation rested on all Oregon's citizens, and not just on the timber industry. In the end $12 million worth of bonds were issued. The bond question required a constitutional amendment, which had to be put to a statewide vote. The measure passed by a very narrow margin—1,875 votes out of almost half a million cast. It failed in Tillamook and Clatsop counties, where much of the cut-over timber land lay. Then as now, it was not easy to get consensus on how to achieve a stable and sustainable forestry.

Struggling Toward a Model

The quest for sustainability in Oregon's forests was born in the era of Progressive idealism, a time when people had become disillusioned about the capabilities and motives of private enterprise in conserving natural resources and securing a stable and humane economy based on them. In his speech to the governors in 1908, President Roosevelt made it clear that he expected the public to have a hand in the management and protection of natural resources.

But just what sort of role the public should play, at what levels, and to what purposes, has been the focus of the struggle for sustainability of our Western forests in this century. Ever since

Roosevelt, local, state, and federal governments have wrestled with forestry's tough problems—delinquent landowners, market swings, overcutting, ruinous forestry practices. In the process, they have worked out various roles for themselves in the forestry enterprise, and various relationships with one another and with private industry. Some of the ensuing arrangements seem to have advanced the objective of sustainability at least partway. Imagine, for example, what Oregon might look like today if all its forest lands had passed into private ownership a century ago.

In this chapter we have heard the story of how sustained yield came to be the guiding principle of Forest Service management, and the story of how Oregon devised a plan to coax worthless and abandoned land back into productivity. These stories are not offered here as unqualified successes. Yet there may be lessons in them that can help us avoid some of the mistakes our ancestors made in the past thirty centuries of unsustainable forestry.

Notes

1. Cheek found, nevertheless, that there was much favorable opinion about sustained-yield policies among residents of communities where sustained-yield units were in operation. She studied Lakeview-Paisley, OR, and Big Valley, CA, the sites of two federal sustained-yield units.

2. It should be remembered that research in economics and indeed in any discipline involves aggregating data and abstracting general principles. A logger laid off in 1992 from a company dependent on National Forest timber may find it hard to regard the situation with Power's philosophical detachment. Power is not saying that shifts in federal timber-harvesting policy make no difference in the lives of the people who live near federal forests. In the short term, at least, they can make a drastic difference. He is arguing that government attempts to increase the flow of federal timber through a community do not necessarily promote its long-term stability, and may even keep it from developing the broad economic base that could make it truly stable in the long run.

3. It should be noted that Hirt's complaint is not that sustained yield is a bad idea, but that it was carried out in bad faith.

8

Field Trip: Sybil Ackerman
Saving the Tillamook Forest

HI, I'M BOB, AND I'M HERE BECAUSE I LOVE FOREST ECOSYSTEMS."

"I'm Bonnie. I saw this forest when it was the Tillamook Burn, and I firmly believe that we have an obligation to protect it now."

"My name is Kenneth, and I came to see this forest so when they cut it down I'll know what it looked like originally."

We are going around the circle, about 40 of us who have come to the Gales Creek campground to take part in what's billed as "a summer hike to save the Tillamook State Forest." It's a glorious July morning, and the day promises to be hot.

"I'm Jenny, and I'm here because I love Oregon's forests. They're part of God's creation, and I want to protect them."

"I'm Kristin, and I'm new to Oregon; I moved out from Pennsylvania to study environmental law, and I'm trying to get out into all the wild areas."

"I'm Kevin, and I believe strongly in respecting God's creation."

A picnic table is spread with literature from the National Wildlife Federation, the Sierra Club, the Coast Range Association, Oregon Trout, the Oregon Natural Resources Council, and other environmentalist organizations. One flyer bears the headline: "Help save our state forests!" It tells of the Oregon Board of Forestry's plan "to consider declaring timber harvest the NUMBER ONE use of state lands." This, says the flyer, "would badly damage the Tillamook State Forest, Oregon's most productive breeding region for coastal salmon and one of the largest contiguous temperate rainforests remaining in the lower forty-eight states."

"My name's Betsy, and I think forests near urban areas are in a sense lucky because there are people who will care for them. I think people have to make the effort to get out into more remote areas and protect them too."

"I find forests to be very spiritual places. Although I don't attend church, this is my temple."

"I'm Rhonda, and these are my children, Cody and Jasmine. I'm here to educate them and show them how beautiful this forest is and how much it needs to be saved."

A slim, dark-haired young woman with wire-rimmed glasses listens intently as each person speaks. Then she says, "Thank you, thank you all. This is a really wonderful group of people. I want to tell you that the phone calls I get every day from you guys really keep me going, because you just care. You care about the forest, and it's so important, because you are the ones who can protect it."

The young woman is Sybil Ackerman, the endangered-species coordinator for the National Wildlife Federation's Portland office. It is she who organized this hike. We stand in a circle in the shady parking lot, listening to the murmur of Gales Creek behind us, as she tell us why saving this forest is so important. Her speech is measured, quiet, determined.

Three Issues at Stake

There are three complicated issues at stake here, Ackerman tells the assembled hikers. She outlines the history of the Tillamook Burn: how the counties entrusted the burned-over lands to the state to manage and are now counting on a flow of revenue from the timber when it's harvested. "They are really, really expecting a lot of money," she says, which means recreation, wildlife, and the other values of the Tillamook Forest are in danger of being overlooked.

The second issue is the long-range management plan now being developed by the Oregon Department of Forestry. Under this plan, she says, the forestry department would harvest ninety percent of the Tillamook and Clatsop State Forests over time. "Now they're not going to clear-cut it all—they have this plan called structure-based management, which means they're going to have specific percentages of structure throughout the forest. They're going to have something called old-growth forest *structure*, which is supposed to *look* like an old-growth forest, but it's definitely *not* an old-growth forest."

The counties and the forestry department both, she says, have a lot to gain from cutting the timber, and nothing to gain from preserving the forest. "It's important to remember that this structure-based management plan is a new idea. And we don't know how it's going to work. A lot of conservationists think it will increase the risk of species going extinct." Some of the hikers nod in agreement. Cody and Jasmine are beginning to pull restlessly at their mother's hands, and a dog yips somewhere outside the circle.

Finally, she says, there's the Habitat Conservation Plan now being worked out by the state forestry department and federal agencies. "They can't cut the forest the way they want to without getting an exemption from the Endangered Species Act. And this exemption, or permit, will allow the Oregon Department of Forestry to go ahead with the long-range management plan, provided they explain how they're going to protect spotted owls and marbled murrelets and salmon that live on this forest."

The forestry department, Ackerman says, has not convinced her and many other environmentalists that its structure-based management scheme will adequately protect these species. "And if they get this Habitat Conservation Plan, it means they may not have to change their management plan, even if the species that live in this forest continue to dwindle toward extinction."

She mentions a forthcoming Board of Forestry meeting and asks everybody to come and show their support. She also invites the hikers to another environmental gathering that she has organized next week at Rockaway Beach, out on the coast north of the town of Tillamook. Representatives of the Oregon Department of Forestry will be there, she says, along with representatives of the U.S. Fish and Wildlife Service and the National Marine Fisheries Service, the two federal agencies charged with enforcing the Endangered Species Act.

"We'll learn a little bit about the Habitat Conservation Plan," Ackerman says, "and we'll be able to ask some very pointed questions about the issue. It's important that all of you who can, make an effort to get there. Because they have not yet heard from people who care about species."

Like many gathered in the circle at Gales Creek today, Sybil Ackerman says "fah-rest," with a softly aspirated "ah-h," rather than "forrrrest," in the growling, hard-R'd Northwestern pronunciation. The initial vowel reveals the subtle but unmistakable accent of a place a long ways east of here. Sybil tells me later, over Thai noodles and vegetables (she is a vegetarian) that she was raised in New Haven and New York City, oldest child and only daughter of two law professors now on the faculty at Yale. Educated at private schools, she earned her undergraduate degree in environmental studies at the Claremont colleges in southern California. She is twenty-seven years old. "So I'm really the stereotype of the young Eastern liberal enviro." She smiles with warm brown eyes behind wire-rimmed glasses, applying the sometimes-pejorative term to herself in a wry, undercutting sort of way. "But I do make an effort to listen to people, really listen to what they're saying. I believe in working through things. If you can't convince people to do something willingly, then there's no point."

Growing up, Ackerman was an independent-minded, animal-loving child who at first didn't connect her personal passion with the idea that animals might need a larger, more powerful, and more political affection. "I didn't made the jump to environmentalism in high school, and so when I got to college I didn't know what I wanted to do with my life." She spent the summer after her freshman year at the Cape Cod National Seashore, inventorying populations and habitat conditions of piping plovers, an endangered bird, and least terns, which are on the threatened list. The personal and the political came together for her that summer. "Every day for three months I went out and watched these birds," she says. "And I absolutely fell in love with them."

The sand-colored piping plovers, she says, are hard for a novice to spot. "On my first day I went out with the scientists, and they could see them but I couldn't, and I said, 'Oh, no, how in the world am I going to watch these guys if I can't even see them?' But then I got so I could really see—I could see the diversity of the landscape much better. And the least terns—they were really cute! They're really loud birds; they go 'squawk squawk squawk' all the time, and whenever I'd go up to their nest to check their eggs, they'd poop on my head. It was so funny."

When the plovers and terns were nesting and hatching their young, it was Ackerman's job to block off the beach to keep dune-buggy drivers out. The National Park Service was doing what it had to do to protect the birds, but there was a big uproar. "The vehicle people protested, they petitioned, they had big signs, they threatened to kill the birds. The park police had to come in to protect them. They called it Operation Piping Plover." The controversy both appalled and fascinated her. "I was so impressed by how the law could save these birds in spite of this huge public outcry." She also saw that the law doesn't always go far enough—the protest succeeded in loosening the restrictions on dune buggies. "They opened up a lot more beach to vehicles, and the vehicles ended up killing a couple of pairs of birds. I know, because I watched them every day. I know which ones died." And yet, she says, "all those birds would've died if it hadn't been for the law."

She went back to school, declared a major in environmental studies, and began to delve into the Endangered Species Act. She did her senior thesis on a Habitat Conservation Plan developed for the Stephens' kangaroo rat. During the summers she worked for the Nature Conservancy and for a public-interest research group. One summer she volunteered for the United Nations Environmental Program in Nairobi, where she helped assess the 1992 environmental summit conference in Rio de Janeiro and wrote a paper on the International Tropical Timber Agreement.

She took a year off after graduation to work for a mass-transit organization in Sacramento, and then returned to Portland to study environmental law at Lewis and Clark College. She went to work for the National Wildlife Federation a year and a half before she received her degree in the spring of 1997—keeping a grueling schedule of working during the day and taking classes and studying at night.

She finds Portland a delightful change from the East Coast and Los Angeles. "It's not a big city as cities go—it's a nice city, and there are so many wonderful places to go when you want to get away. So many unspoiled places nearby."

Raising Consciousness

Sybil Ackerman seems very good at what she does, which is energizing and organizing popular support for the protection of wildlife, the Federation's main concern. It's her job to plan outings like the hike at Gales Creek and the endangered-species forum at Rockaway Beach—lining up speakers, coordinating schedules, arranging carpools, briefing volunteers, making coffee. It is also her job to raise the consciousness of politicians and bureaucrats about the Federation's agenda. So she testifies at public hearings, lobbies state legislators, calls on staffers at the forestry department, presses her cause with tactful persistence. At one recent Board of Forestry meeting, Ackerman spoke of her concern that the Habitat Conservation Plan for western Oregon state forests was being developed too much behind closed doors. "I hear you say that you will eventually have public hearings on the HCP," she said, "and I want you to know I would love to help with these. I still have concerns about the lack of public input into the process right now."

Her testimony was so persuasive that the Board decided to take her advice. They moved discussions about the Habitat Conservation Plan, which until then had been an internal department matter, onto the agenda of the long-range forest planning process, now being carried out with the help of an eight-member advisory panel. Ackerman was gratified with the Board's gesture but unsatisfied with its action. "There are many interests that aren't represented on that advisory panel right now and should be," she says. "Municipalities, anglers, recreationists, labor, schools."

More recently the Board appointed a 12-member Public Interest Committee to offer "technical and policy advice" on the HCP, and named Ackerman to it. That panel has members representing two timber organizations, two counties, three environmental groups, a four-wheel-drive recreational association, a commercial-fishing trade group, and an Indian tribal confederation, as well as one member from the Department of Forestry and one from the public at large.

Ackerman does her work with candor, courtesy, and good humor, avoiding harsh words and confrontational stances, welcoming like-minded people to the cause, politely debating with those who disagree. "Some of my colleagues in the conservation community think I'm too accommodating of other points of view," she says. "It's not that I don't get upset with what's happening to the environment. I care so *much* about the forest that sometimes it's hard to detach and get perspective. But I really try to always hear what the other side is saying. Because if we can't find a common-ground solution, we won't find a solution at all. It'll be a quick fix, and it'll end up backfiring on us."

Asking a Blessing

It's almost time for the hike. But before we break our circle, Ackerman introduces Jenny Holmes, who represents an organization called Interfaith Network for Earth Concerns. Holmes will offer a blessing for this gathering.

"For many people today," she begins, "our experience of the natural world is where we find God. The Tillamook Forest isn't Yosemite, but parts of it are still remnants of the freshness of creation, and they remind us that creation can be restored." She asks for a moment of silence. For a long minute we stand quiet, heads bowed, hearing nothing but the sound of Gales Creek sliding over its bed and the hum of cars out on Highway 6. The Holmes' quiet voice fills the air. "O Creator, O you who make all life holy, this universe is alive with your goodness. Help us to more fully share in this life. Open up our mind and all of our senses, that you might give voice to all you have given us. I wait you here and now. Amen."

We raise our heads and wait for instructions. Those who want a challenging workout, says Ackerman, can climb Elk Mountain with Charles here. Charles is a burly, handsome man in his late thirties who looks fit enough to climb Everest. Those who want a slightly easier pace are directed to the trail that winds up Gales Creek Canyon as far as the highway. Tim, a tall, wiry young man, will be the leader. I take my place in line behind Tim and am joined by a friendly couple in their late 40s. They introduce themselves: Vince and Carol, just moved up from the San Francisco Bay area "for the opportunities," Vince explains. Professional or personal? I ask. "Both," says Vince cryptically, fixing me with intense dark eyes. He hands me a business card, which reveals that he works for a real-estate office in one of Portland's suburbs.

Vince and Carol have been here two months, and they absolutely love it. "The quality of life," Carol fills in, talking with her hands. "It's just fantastic. I grew up with concrete all around me. I didn't see a real forest till I came West. And then the Bay area"— she dismisses it with a wave of polished fingernails. "It's gotten so crowded and crazy." She talks with the nasal timbre of a native Brooklyner, which in fact she is. She is tiny and vivid, with bright lipstick, a tropical bird in a flock of sparrow-toned Northwesterners.

Vince and Carol seem mildly awed to learn that I was born and raised in Oregon. Most everyone they've met so far seems, like themselves, to be from somewhere else. Carol immediately assures me that they are not the kind of people who come in and trash a beautiful place. "I know some people here resent all the people from California moving up here," she says, almost apologetically. "But we're good people—really we are." Her friendliness and her deference to my old-timer status are awkwardly touching. I would be ashamed, I tell Carol and Vince, if anyone has been rude enough to make them feel unwelcome here.

The Gales Creek trail winds for three miles through big second-growth Douglas firs along the south bank of the creek up to the highway. It was in this canyon that the first fire started in 1933. Flames crawled down the south-facing slope of what was then a logged-over slashfield, jumped the creek, crawled back up the other side, and crossed the highway.

Today a carpet of duff lies between the trail and the creek, scattered with sword fern and salal. Huge cedar stumps, ghosts from the centuries-old forest that once occupied this place, loom next to the trail, their heartwood broken down and spilling powdery red dust. Feathery fronds of red huckleberry spring from their craggy, crumbling tops. We speak in low tones; the shade and the coolness under the trees make it unseemly to shout. It's hard to believe that sixty-five years ago this canyon was a smoking ruin.

I catch up with Jenny Holmes. I want to talk to her about how environmental issues become issues of faith for her. She is a slender woman with an open, blue-eyed face, a winsome smile, and a slow, thoughtful way of speaking.

"One of the key things the faith community brings to the discussion about the environment," she says, "is the sense that creation is valued for itself, because it is good, because it was created by God. We have to care about the creatures for themselves, for the whole, not just for their value to humankind."

For a long time, she says, there's been a strong tradition in the Christian heritage that the earth and its resources were simply dead matter, put here for humans to exploit. "But looking at the Scriptures again, there's clearly a call to *protect* creation—not just because it's useful to us, but because it's fundamentally good and not something that needs our improvement."

The Christian "subdue the earth" tradition was fingered a long time ago as a culprit in environmental degradation. In a 1967 essay, the historian Lynn White, Jr. traced the origin of exploitative thinking about the earth to medieval Europe—"a culture saturated with Christian thinking" (Fox 1981, 359). He then worked back from there to Judeo-Christian anthropocentric philosophy, locating the root cause in early notions about a God who endowed only one of his creatures, Man, with a soul. White asserted that Christianity's conquest of paganism had stripped nature of its spiritual element. It had replaced cyclical and repetitive concepts of time with the idea of a linear progression, opening the door to the concepts of progress and endeavor. "By destroying pagan animism," White wrote, "Christianity made it possible to exploit nature in a mood of indifference to the feelings of natural objects" (Fox, 359).

Yet for a less exploitative alternative, White looked elsewhere in the Christian tradition: to St. Francis of Assisi, with his radical simplicity and his teaching of "our Sister, Mother Earth, who doth sustain us and keep us, and bring forth divers fruits, and flowers of many colors . . . " (Plassmann and Vann 1954). St. Francis, he said, is an exemplar of the proper human relationship to the natural world.

White's thesis made a splash in scholarly and environmental circles. Critics observed that Christians weren't the only environmental bad actors. They "pointed out non-Christian cultures with sorry records of land abuse, and other Christian cultures with better records than the industrial West" (Fox, 359-360). Others noted that the Biblical injunction to "multiply and subdue the earth" is not necessarily a license for exploitation, and that the Bible has many other passages that affirm God's love and concern for the whole of creation. The materialistic bent of Christian thinking, said these critics, came not from the Age of Faith, but from the Age of Reason: from Descartes, with his matter-spirit dualism, and Francis Bacon, with his scientific method, his celebration of technology, and his exhortation to turn the fruits of nature to human advantage. Nevertheless, Christian conservationists had to admit that the evidence was thin, in both Scripture and tradition, for a less domineering, more cooperative model of the human relationship with nature.

Lately there's been a resurgence of interest in what is being called "the green Gospel" (Smith 1997). Smith's article tells of evangelical Christians experiencing a born-again relationship with nature, one that stresses the care of creation as an essential task in the working out of one's own salvation. "For too long," says Peter Illyn, one of the pastors Smith interviewed, "we allowed materialism to let us define domination as taking anything we wanted. Now we are saying, 'There is no scriptural justification whatsoever for that attitude.'"

Not surprisingly, Illyn's creation theology is not always well received within the larger evangelical community. Many Christians do not agree that their tradition is responsible for environmental damage. Many regard environmentalism as the thin edge of a liberal, New Age, neopagan, pantheistic, idolatrous wedge. Moreover, some conservative political leaders who have depended on evangelical Christians to support their agenda accuse the environmental movement generally of being antibusiness, anti-private property, and sinfully socialistic. Still, the green-Gospel movement seems to be gaining adherents, especially in the West.

For many Christians, environmentalism offers a way to affirm the essentially spiritual character of their response to nature without losing touch with the redemptive tradition of orthodox Christianity. The fact that many Christians identify their love of nature as an essential expression of their faith is another piece of evidence of the deep religious wellspring that nourishes environmentalist ideals. So I ask Jenny Holmes: Does valuing creation necessarily mean harvesting of resources is wrong? Is there a place for a spiritual sort of utilitarianism? To put it more bluntly, is there a way to log the Tillamook Forest without offending God?

Holmes gathers her thoughts before she answers. "Christians are not of one mind on this, by any means. Some folks I know are small woodland owners, or work for state forests, and they think more in terms of stewardship, of wise and careful use of the forest's resources. And I think there's a place for that. But it doesn't seem to go far enough. To see the forest as only something useful to humankind is too narrow."

We are quiet for a while, catching our breath as we climb the hill. Then Holmes says, "The Scriptures, in Genesis 2, talk about 'tilling' and 'keeping' the garden. 'Tilling' means reshaping the earth to meet human needs. 'Keeping' means, literally, 'preserving.' So there are two things that have to be kept in balance with each other." She pauses again and fixes me with a direct blue gaze. "We have done too much tilling," she says, "and not enough keeping."

Greatest Permanent Value?

When the Oregon legislature, in 1941, specified that state forest lands were to be managed "for the greatest permanent value . . . to the state," they did not make it clear whether "tilling" or "keeping" was the best way to do that. Given the reigning social values of the day, however, it's likely the legislators regarded timber production as the greatest value to be derived from these lands. That at least has been the position of the Oregon Board of Forestry and the management policy of the Department of Forestry for the past two and a half decades. Now that the trees on the Tillamook have grown big enough to where important—and lasting—decisions must be made, the Board has codified this policy in a formal administrative rule. The new rule also reaffirms another imperative that the policy has stressed all along: that timber production must be balanced with other values.

The Board began drafting the rule in 1997. In January of 1998, after rejecting two earlier draft versions, it approved a rule that defines "greatest permanent value" as "healthy, productive, and sustainable forest ecosystems that over time and across the landscape provide a full range of social, economic, and environmental benefits to the people of Oregon."

The rule directs the State Forester to "maintain these lands as forest lands and actively manage them in a sound environmental manner . . . " (Oregon Administrative Rules 629: 59) while managing also for "properly functioning aquatic habitats," wildlife habitats, "productive" soil and clean air and water, flood and erosion protection, and recreation. A previous draft rule called for "the growing and harvesting of forest tree species as the *leading use* [emphasis mine] for the benefit of the counties and the people of the state of Oregon." Even though that version promised to manage for timber "consistent with protecting, maintaining, and enhancing other forest values," it was withdrawn in November 1997 after opposition from environmental groups. As Geoff Pampush of Oregon Trout told the Oregon Board of Forestry in July, referring to the earlier, rejected draft version, "You may be choosing more narrowly than you have to. It's not clear from the law that timber needs to be first in a hierarchy."

What does the law say? According to a legal and historical review commissioned by the Board (Rice and Souder 1997), it says the Board must manage for the purposes for which the state acquired the land in the first place. And it says the Board must honor the counties' "protected, recognizable interest" in receiving revenue from the lands. In other words, the lands must be managed for timber at some level and in some manner, because the law governing their acquisition (Chapter 530 of the Oregon statutes) says the state may acquire lands that are suitable for the "growing" of "forest crops." And it says that counties have to get some of the money derived from timber harvesting or from any other revenue-producing activity.

But the Board must also manage for those other purposes for which the state may acquire lands under the law. These are water conservation, watershed protection and development, erosion control, recreation, and grazing. The law does not explicitly require that timber be the primary concern. It does not require that the Board maximize or even produce revenues from every acre of Chapter 530 lands. It *does* require that the lands be managed "for the broad goal of obtaining the greatest permanent value to the state."

We stop for a breather, and Vince shares his water bottle with me. I fall into conversation with the man behind me on the narrow trail. His name is Craig, and he is a university administrator. He came out today, he says, because he likes to hike, not because he's an environmentalist. "I'm a realist," he says, traces of his Texas upbringing still clinging to his vowels. "I know people need wood, and I know the reason there's logging is because there's a demand for wood. Logging is going to continue, and so the environmentalists and the timber people are going to have to coexist."

He says he was a little nervous about coming today—afraid he might get suckered into some kind of environmentalist demonstration. "I thought they might want me to chain myself to a tree or something. But these people seem very reasonable." Rick Brown, another National Wildlife Federation staffer who's along on the hike, agrees with this assessment: the Federation, he says, sees itself as a middle-of-the-road conservation group. "We're a pretty centrist organization," says Brown. "We're not trying to shut everything down; we're not the 'lock-it-up-and-walk-away' brand of environmentalists. Certainly there are areas that should be left alone, and these areas I think need to be fairly substantial. Nonetheless, we think appropriate resource management is part of what public lands are about. Our position is—it's a buzzword of late, but we favor the whole concept of sustainability."

Brown, trained in botany and ecology, came to the Federation from a job doing environmental assessments for Forest Service timber sales on the Mount Hood ranger district. The Federation, he says, was glad to acquire his experience working for an agency deeply affected by endangered-species issues. "It was 1987, right in the middle of the owl wars, and they needed somebody who could hit the ground running," he says. "I have done basically forest issues for them ever since." His main interest, however, is in the dry-land pine forests on the east side of the Cascades, which are in many ways in worse shape, with far less attention being paid to them, than the west-side forests, the center of most of the dramatic confrontations over spotted owls and other threatened species.

A Better ESA

Among other items on its agenda, the Federation would like to improve the ponderous workings of the Endangered Species Act. They would like to reform the whole species-recovery process to include more participation from local communities, especially private landowners. The Federation would also like to see more incentives for landowners voluntarily to conserve wildlife habitat, which they say would keep species off the endangered or threatened list in the first place. One such incentive already exists. It's called a Habitat Conservation Plan—an agreement between a nonfederal landowner and the federal government, allowing the landowner to proceed with activities that might harm a listed or sensitive species in the near term, but promise to improve habitat in the long run. The Board of Forestry is now negotiating with the U.S. Fish and Wildlife Service and the National Marine Fisheries Service to get one covering 615,000 acres of state forests in western Oregon.

A Habitat Conservation Plan, as Sybil Ackerman explained to the hikers at Gales Creek, is designed to address a generally acknowledged weakness in the Endangered Species Act—that the law does not do enough about dwindling habitat, the underlying problem in most endangered-species cases. The 1982 reauthorization of the ESA introduced Habitat Conservation Plans to offer private landowners a way to manage without running afoul of the law, and in the process work to improve endangered-species habitat on their lands. The HCP deal is this: The landowner promises to manage the land in specific ways over a specified period of time, with the objective of improving the habitat for the wildlife covered by the plan. In exchange, the landowner gets what's called an incidental-take permit. In the ESA law, the word "take" means, reasonably enough, "harass, harm, pursue, hunt, shoot, wound, kill, trap, capture, or collect . . . . " It is also interpreted to mean changing a habitat in any way that could harm a species.

So an incidental-take permit is in effect a federal guarantee to the landowner: if management activities should cause a "take" in the form of harming an animal or harming a patch of habitat, the government won't sue the landowner under the ESA as long as he or she is complying with the plan—which is, after all, directed at improving the habitat over the long term. Since September of 1996, 197 incidental-take permits have been issued by the U.S. Fish and Wildlife Service, and another 200 HCPs, covering almost 12 million acres, are being negotiated.

The Principle Is Good, But . . .

It would seem that environmentalists would be happy if a state agency agreed to manage forests in a way that would improve wildlife habitat. And, indeed, the National Wildlife Federation and most other groups are in favor of HCPs—in principle. But they argue that these agreements have not been tested over the long term. And they warn of potential unintended consequences of HCPs that could put sensitive species in a worse position than before. The main thing that raises many conservationist eyebrows is a recent clarification on HCPs, known as "no surprises." The intent of this policy, adopted by the Clinton administration in 1994, is to assure landowners that they will not have to modify their management, even if it is later discovered that the habitat needs a different or a more intense kind of treatment than what's spelled out in the HCP. "No surprises" also allows HCPs to cover species that are regarded as sensitive but are not on the endangered or threatened list.

So if the no-surprises policy is followed to the letter, a forest landowner who is operating under an HCP covering Townsend's big-eared bats (let's say) won't have to renegotiate the HCP to incorporate any new science about bat habitat—or any costly new management measures—even if the bat is later listed as threatened. The landowner is shielded from prosecution as long as he or she is managing in good faith under the original agreement. The "no-surprises" provision is supposed to offer a more stable business environment to landowners who want to plan their management and their finances over long periods. Habitat conservation plans are strictly voluntary—landowners don't have to enter into any kind of agreement to improve species habitat if they don't want to. But then the federal government is thrown back on the remedy of taking landowners to court one at a time, trying to recover endangered species one lawsuit at a time.

But environmentalists point to the specter of landowners managing under locked-in Habitat Conservation Plans, impervious to new science and new circumstances, while species like spotted owls and coho salmon continue to slide toward extinction. They don't like the idea of HCPs covering unlisted species. Science, they say, hasn't yet established the habitat conditions that these less-affected but still sensitive species needed. (Indeed, most often it is only when a species is threatened with extinction that its habitat needs become a research priority.) And they don't like the idea of

HCPs being applied to millions of acres of lands when their efficacy at actually recovering wildlife is unproven.

"'No surprises' is an extreme policy to appease private owners and extractive industries," said Diane Valentine of the Oregon Natural Resources Council at the Rockaway Beach endangered-species forum, organized by Sybil Ackerman. "Species are left open to all kinds of nasty surprises down the road." She and others also take a dim view of the long duration of most forest HCPs, fifty or sixty years. The incidental-take permit for western Oregon state forests will have a duration of fifty years if the HCP is adopted as drafted. That length of time is needed, say state forest managers, to allow trees to grow and change into new habitat. But environmentalists say it's too generous a guarantee to the landowner when the fate of a species is at stake.

In the case of the HCP for western Oregon state forests, environmentalists worry that the structure-based management scheme proposed for the Tillamook and Clatsop forests will make it hard for wildlife to thrive, even if the targeted "dynamic balance" of forest structures is achieved as planned. Making animals chase their habitat around on the landscape is too risky. Better, they say, to leave substantial blocks of forest untouched for the spotted owls and marbled murrelets, and for the amphibians, bats, snag-nesting birds, and all the rest. "You don't have to be a scientist to know it makes more sense to err on the side of caution," says Sybil Ackerman.

The Salmon Plan

Most of all, environmentalists worry about salmon. It has been known for a long time that populations of native salmon all over the Pacific Northwest are plummeting. Much of the decline is blamed on human impacts on the environment—farming, livestock grazing, road building, logging, dams, overfishing—although it is probably also influenced by natural ocean and weather cycles (Huntington and Frissell 1997). By the mid-1990s it had become clear that coastal coho species in Oregon were headed for the threatened list. Looking for an alternative to a federal listing, Governor John Kitzhaber called together a host of interested parties, including state and local elected officials, people in land-management agencies and forest products companies, private landowners, and environmentalists.

In 1997 the governor and his group proposed a bold plan: Oregon would nurse coho and steelhead populations back from the brink of extinction without the club of federal enforcement. The Oregon Plan, as it is called, directs state and private landowners to undertake coordinated, voluntary efforts to improve the quality of rivers and the overall health of the watershed in areas where the fish live. Their efforts are to be backed up by stronger state timber harvesting rules and toughened water-quality legislation, and the whole plan is to be monitored regularly by a team of scientists.

The Oregon Plan gained Kitzhaber political points for doing his best to fend off heavy-handed federal control—a hot button in Oregon's independent-progressive political tradition. However, in the summer of 1998, as this book was being finished, a federal magistrate ruled that the coastal coho be listed, and the federal agencies charged with enforcing the Endangered Species Act had no choice but to comply. The coho's listing makes the future of the Oregon Plan uncertain.

State forestry planners had worked with the governor's team to develop strategies that would improve the fish habitat on western Oregon state forests. They wanted to make sure the department's efforts would mesh with those of other stakeholders in the governor's plan. Those strategies are now part of the draft Habitat Conservation Plan for the Tillamook and other western Oregon state forests. However, the forestry department maintains that their HCP is crafted well enough to comply with endangered-species laws on its own, whether the Oregon Plan stands or falls. Says the department's Mike Schnee: "Our recovery strategies should be more than enough to meet state and federal endangered-species law."

Conservation-minded Management

In other words, whatever happens with the Oregon Plan, the Tillamook Forest will be managed so as to encourage the recovery of coho and other sensitive and threatened wildlife. Many environmentalists would prefer that the department drop the notion of structure-based management, and stay on the safe side, reserving large portions of river basins as untouched salmon habitat. One proposal from Oregon Trout calls for setting aside at least half of the Tillamook and Clatsop forest lands, banning any logging at all. Oregon Trout's position is that the Tillamook and Clatsop forests should be "an anchor for salmon recovery" along the northern

Oregon coast. A report commissioned by the group estimates that at the turn of the century Tillamook Bay was the most productive area for salmon on the Oregon coast. Since then populations of steelhead, chum, coho, and chinook have declined to less than one-sixth of their former abundance (Huntington and Frissell 1997). Chum and coho are in particularly bad shape. Chinook, on the other hand, are doing pretty well: some fall chinook runs are almost as healthy as they were at the turn of the century, for reasons not well understood (Huntington and Frissell 1997).

Oregon Trout calls for "conservation-minded management" of all the coastal state forest lands, especially the Tillamook, "the most extensive forested area in the Oregon Coast Range not fragmented by recent timber harvest units" (Huntington and Frissell, 1997). State forestry officials maintain that structure-based management on these forests will be flexible enough to improve habitat for the coho while still permitting a substantial level of timber harvest. Adaptive management—that is, carefully monitoring what happens as a result of management and modifying activities accordingly—is a critical feature of the proposed forest plan. Areas that are or might be habitat for spotted owls, marbled murrelets, and salmon will be managed carefully or left untouched, at least in the near term. In the long run, if structure-based management works, there will be ample older-forest-like areas to serve as habitat for animals that need it.

There are now about thirteen nesting pairs of spotted owls on north-coast state forest land, even though the forests here consist mostly of young, second-growth trees. The proposed HCP would designate four "owl cluster areas" totaling about 40,000 acres of the best available habitat, with corridors connecting them. Within these areas, seventy-acre patches would be left untouched around known nesting sites. The rest of the acreage within the cluster areas could be managed, as long as the objective is to maintain or enhance the existing habitat. The HCP also would protect seventy-acre patches around three owl pairs that are not now nesting within the cluster areas, for as long as the owls are there (Oregon Department of Forestry 1998b, V-12, V-13).

The cluster areas would be managed in this way until other areas of the forest had developed enough of the right kind of structure to replace them—in about fifty years, by the best department estimates. Over the long term, about 103,000 acres, or about twenty percent of the North Coast forest area, would be managed as owl habitat. This would be enough to support twenty-eight pairs of owls, by department estimates. The owl habitat would move around on the landscape as patches of forest move into and out of the various stand structures.

Marbled murrelets, which live at sea but fly inland to nest in trees, are also in residence in the north coastal state forests. Their nests have been spotted in big mistletoe-infested hemlocks near the coast—the mistletoe deforms branches and creates wide, moss-covered platforms for the murrelets to nest on. The draft HCP would protect known and likely murrelet nesting habitat in the coastal spruce-hemlock pockets of the Tillamook and Clatsop over the short term, and it would designate buffers to be managed to accelerate the development of future habitat. Over the long term, as with spotted owls, the habitat could shift across the landscape over time (Oregon Department of Forestry 1998b, V-15).

The HCP is now being revised by forestry department planners after an intense scrutiny and critique by a panel of scientists. Eventually it will need to be approved by the U.S. Fish and Wildlife Service and the National Marine Fisheries Service, and it will then become a legal contract between these agencies and the state of Oregon. Once in place, as part of the Northwest Oregon Forest Plan, the HCP will be reviewed periodically to see whether habitat conditions are developing as planned, and whether the species are using the habitat as expected.

Department officials say the long-term management plan for state forests coupled with the HCP will provide plenty of safeguards for wildlife, both listed and unlisted. "This HCP replaces simple take avoidance with long-term research, monitoring, and adaptive management," says Logan Jones, the forestry department's HCP planning coordinator. "It provides a landscape-level perspective, and it makes it possible for us to carry out our long-range plan. And it's the right thing to do."

What Kind of Forest?

Back at Gales Creek campground, sweaty and pleasantly tired, I chat with another hiker, a woman of perhaps fifty. Her name is Ellen. She was raised in northern California, she tells me, in a family of loggers. "I remember when I was a little girl, my dad took me to see a clear-cut. He seemed to think it was just normal, but to me it looked awful. I said, 'Daddy, why do the loggers do that?' He said, 'Honey, that's just what loggers have to do; they have to cut the trees.' I was only a little girl, but I realized right then that it was wrong. It was plain wrong."

But is it always wrong? I ask her. What if the forest we're talking about is not virgin old growth, but a second-growth forest that has been burned and logged already? What if we're talking about logging it in perhaps the most deliberative manner ever devised, and in a fishbowl big enough so the world can see what happens? Would that make any difference? She gives me a quizzical look: Why should it make any difference? "Not to me," she says.

Not to Sybil Ackerman, either. "If you read the history," she says, "you'll see that the Tillamook was an amazing place. The trees were five feet thick. It was a true ancient forest, a real refuge for wildlife. It succumbed to logging, and then it burned down because of logging. The forest here today is nothing like the forest that was here before. And it is only now beginning to recover. It just doesn't make any sense to say we can now cut it all down and devastate it the way it was before. It just doesn't make any sense."

9

Field Trip: Ric Balfour
Taming the Wild West

Unruly Goings-on

The Tillamook Forest is not a wild forest, but parts of it have a wild feeling—"wild" in the sense of being unmannerly, uncouth, slightly feral. It may have been planted like a garden, but it does not look like one now. Maybe that's because, being young and vigorous, it lacks the stateliness of ancient redwood groves, the senescent languor of 400-year-old Douglas fir forests with trails winding through. Right now the forest is going through an adolescent burst of growth. The young trees are elbowing their way skyward, taking over the landscape the way a gangly fourteen-year-old seems to take over the living room. The Tillamook is not a park, manicured for tourists: there are no trailer hookups or hot showers. This forest draws a wilder crowd. People come here to drink and fight and shoot and tear through the woods on dirt bikes and four-wheelers. Ric Balfour does not condemn people who like to ride and shoot instead of hike or climb, his own favorite modes of recreation. "As a recreation planner, you have to leave that judgmental attitude at home," he says. "It's my job to encourage people to follow the rules. I like to engage them on a friendly basis; that usually works best. And the accent helps."

Ric Balfour is a genial and vigorous New Zealander in his mid-thirties. He has curly red-brown hair and beard, intense blue-green eyes, and a ready grin. He is fit, and looks it. Balfour has the title of Public Use Coordinator for the Tillamook State Forest.[1] Before 1991, the year he was hired, there was no such job. The public use on the forest—and there was a lot of it—had been uncoordinated, and consequently chaotic, for quite a few years before he came. For people who like to play in the woods, the Tillamook amounts to a one-third-million-acre wooded playground just a half-hour's drive from Portland, Oregon's largest city. The population of Portland's metropolitan area is one and one-half million people. Two major highways, U.S. 26 and Oregon 6, head west out of Portland right through the Tillamook. In 1977, the last year for which reliable figures are available, state foresters on the Tillamook counted something like 210,000 visitor-days a year.

The wild visitors are the minority, to be sure. Most people come peaceably to sightsee and picnic, hike and enjoy nature, ride mountain bikes, camp, swim, fish, hunt, and ride ORVs. But peaceable or no, that's a lot of people. It is Balfour's job to see to it that the forest absorbs this crush of visitors without undue damage. That means he has had to tame some of the wilder activities for which the Tillamook has developed a reputation.

Managing Public Use

Today's visitors tend to make more of a dent on the forest than they did in earlier times, before and between the great fires. Then, the main sorts of recreation practiced in the Tillamook country were hunting and fishing. In the mid-1960s, as the young Douglas fir trees began to show their tops over the Himalaya berry and vine maple, the state forestry department put in low-maintenance campgrounds along the Wilson River. These were mainly for the use of hunters and fishermen, but they also attracted families who liked to camp in primitive surroundings. Then came the economic slump of the early 1980s, and state budgets were cut back. The forestry department eliminated campground maintenance and such management of recreation as there had been. Gradually the forest was taken over by a crowd given to drinking, fighting, shooting, vandalism, and indiscriminate off-road driving. There was no routine law enforcement except occasional patrols from county sheriff's deputies, who did not have the wherewithal to suppress every illegal and dangerous activity over miles and miles of bad back-country road, let alone monitor the off-road shenanigans of four-wheel-drivers and motorcyclists, and the dumping of garbage, old car bodies, and worse.

By the end of the 1980s the unruly goings-on in the Tillamook had come to the attention of the state's political leaders. The situation was out of hand. This place, with its proud past and promising future, deserved better. Gail Achterman, a Portland lawyer and Governor Neil Goldschmidt's natural-resources aide, was the one who spearheaded the idea of a recreation plan for the Tillamook. The plan was to include a memorial to Achterman's friend Nancy Ryles, who had recently died of cancer. Ryles had also served in Governor Goldschmidt's administration, and in her younger days in Portland she had led groups of tree-planting schoolchildren out to the Burn.

In 1991, lawmakers passed House Bill 2501, calling for a comprehensive recreation plan "to interpret the history of the forest and to provide for diverse outdoor recreation in the forest" (HB 2501 summary, cited in Oregon Department of Forestry 1992). The "whereas" of the legislation read like this:

> *Whereas the leadership of Governor Earl Snell, State Forester Nels Rogers, and Clatsop County Judge Guy Boyington, and the citizens of Oregon, the forest products industry, labor unions, community groups, local government, state government, schools and universities combined efforts to make the Tillamook State Forest a living **monument to modern forestry**, . . .* (emphasis added)

The plan was "to be consistent with the primary purpose of timber production."

The department went looking for someone to gather public opinion, write a recreation management plan, and submit it to the legislature within a year. Ric Balfour, then finishing up a master's degree in forest recreation management at Oregon State University, was hired in the fall of 1991. He wasn't quite ready to take on a full-time job, but he'd come from New Zealand with a resume full of responsibility in both timber and recreation management on that country's plantation forests. And he knew a good opportunity when he saw it. "If I could have written a job description for myself," he says, flashing a grin, "this would have been it."

The Soft Approach

This day I am a passenger in Balfour's pickup truck, riding along on one of his patrols. We're on a graveled road that hairpins to the east just a mile or so off the highway, when the sound of shooting drifts through the woods. We head in the direction of the sound, a rapid ta-ta-ta-ta-ta that sounds to me like automatic rifle fire. We find the shooters, two men and a boy, up a side road in a clearing. One man wears a khaki field cap and has a rifle slung over his shoulders. The other is bareheaded and carries no firearm. The boy, who looks to be about five, wears rimless, bright-yellow sunglasses. The three of them stand in front of a new-looking red four-wheel-drive pickup truck with monster tires. A target is set up on a stump about thirty feet away. Balfour gets out of the truck and walks over. I watch from the cab, nervous about the guns but wanting to catch the conversation. I roll down the window.

"Hey, how's it going?" asks Balfour in a friendly tone. The men return his greeting civilly. He tells them, "We're asking people to go down to the old quarry if they want to shoot. It's safer down there; the bullets go into the bank instead of through the woods. You look like you're set up pretty safe here, but we prefer people to go down there."

"Okay, no problem," says the bareheaded man. "We'll cruise on down there. Where's it at?" Balfour gives directions, and the men turn and walk toward the pickup truck. "Daddy, why are we leaving?" the boy asks the bareheaded man. "'Cause we can't shoot up here, little buddy. They want us to go somewhere else." The man turns to Balfour and comments on the bullet-ridden condition of most of the signs in the forest. "It's terrible what some people do to those signs," he says.

Balfour departs with a friendly wave of the hand. Back in the truck, he tells me about the time he came across a group of men standing around a couple of pickup trucks with guns arrayed all across the beds. "It looked like there was some clandestine trafficking going on," he says. "I had someone with me, like you today. And she was going, 'Let's get *out* of here!' But I strolled up to them and said, 'Hi, guys, how's it going?'" He grins as he tells this story with a sort of Gomer-Pyle, wide-eyed naivete, mocking himself. "These guys were shooting up the place pretty well, and they were on private land" adjoining the north edge of the Tillamook. "So I told them, 'Y'know, the property owner gets tired of having to clean up people's messes.' I suggested they clean up after themselves, and then I just turned around and walked away. I went back two weeks later, and the place was spotless. So you see, the soft approach works pretty well, most of the time."

Leaving the shooting party, we drive up a steep graveled road to Rogers Camp, just south of the highway near the Coast Range summit. Evidence of dirt bikes is visible in the little half-moons of erosion flaring up from the shoulders of the road. It's audible in the two-stroke whine that keeps drifting in and out of earshot. Rogers

Camp, originally called Owl Camp, was the main staging area for the fireproofing of the Burn. It was also the site where Governor Douglas McKay signed the papers that launched the reforestation effort in 1949, and the site where Governor Tom McCall dedicated the new Tillamook State Forest in 1973.

Today all that is left of Rogers Camp is an old pumphouse, dilapidated and full of bullet holes. Balfour wants to use the pumphouse in a future interpretive display, "if it's still there by the time we get to it." Half a mile later we come to a staging area for the motorcyclists who race through the woods to the south. Not long ago this place was nothing but a big mudhole. Says Balfour: "People used to come in here in their pickup trucks and do doughnuts, and then they go home with the obligatory trophy of mud." Now there's a traffic island, concrete-vault toilets, and a kiosk with a sign politely requesting motorcyclists to drive their vehicles safely and legally.

The Working Forest

Before they could write their recreation plan, Balfour and his team, people from the state forestry and state parks departments, had to find out about the people already "recreating" (in planners' parlance) on the forest. This required a certain shift in the traditional forester mindset, Balfour says. "The public involvement part of it certainly hadn't been something the forestry department had much experience in. Their experience of planning had been to get all the foresters into one room, get information on the timber, and hammer out a harvesting program. That was what a forest plan was about."

In contrast, the recreation plan was deliberately constructed in a more open fashion. Ric and his colleagues at the forestry department did their best to solicit a wide range of opinion. "My idea was that public involvement doesn't just mean having public meetings," Balfour says. "It means that, but it means actively seeking public input. And so I went around to all the different user groups associated with the forest, inviting them to get together with me on the forest." In other words, Balfour made it a point to go out and meet people on their own ground. He rode horses with the horse people and motorcycles with the motorcycle people, hiked with the hikers and driftboated with the steelheaders. "I talked to everybody I could think of," he says, "from the Jolly Jeepers to the Sierra Club."

The motorcyclists were an obstacle at first. They thought they had nothing to gain and everything to lose from what the recreation team was doing. "They'd been overlooked so often in planning processes that they automatically distrusted us," says Balfour. "Fear was a natural reaction. They'd come to the planning meetings en masse, wearing their club colors, and the three people from the Mazamas [hiking] club would be sitting there feeling intimidated. It took me about eight months to convince them that we weren't trying to shut them out."

Public meetings were held throughout 1991-92. "We used a system called listening post," says Balfour, "where you first describe what the meeting is about and present some elements of the planning, and then you invite people to gather round an easel with a blank page." A facilitator elicits people's comments and questions, and a recorder writes these down. There is no debate; the foresters are there to listen to the people. Balfour and his team chose not to solidify certain schemes as Option 1, Option 2, and so forth, because they didn't want to lock in people's thinking prematurely and risk overlooking creative combinations of ideas. "We wanted a more fluid menu system, was what we ended up calling it," says Balfour. "We established a series of different topics and management areas that we needed to address and that had the potential to be funded at some level." The various topics—motorized and nonmotorized recreation, camping, day use, fishing, and several others—were entered on a spreadsheet and blown up into a four-by-eight-foot menu, and people were invited to come up and pencil in their own preferences.

This informality took some getting used to. Not only were the foresters novices at dealing with high levels of public involvement, but some of the interest groups also had a hard time with the concept. "For example, the Sierra Club," says Balfour. "They were used to the federal system [of planning on the National Forests], where you get twenty days to comment on a 500-page, ten-pound document. They couldn't believe we hadn't already made the decisions. They kept asking us, 'Where's the document?' We assured them we didn't have anything written down yet. We had broad objectives, that was all." In the end the Sierra Club did not participate in drafting the recreation plan. The reason, Balfour guesses, is that the Tillamook recreation plan doesn't address either timber or wildlife, two of the Sierra Club's main areas of concern. The public involvement in the recreation plan was so successful,

Balfour says, that a similar model is now being used in drafting the whole Northwest Area long-range forest plan.

Just as the long-range planners are doing now, Balfour and his team made one thing very clear: The Tillamook is a "working forest," meaning a forest in which timber harvest is an essential activity. Therefore, recreation could be accommodated only within that context. Most people seemed to accept this premise, Balfour says—they understood that a hiking trail, for instance, might someday have to be rerouted around a logging operation. Opinion is still far from unanimous, however. Some individuals who came to the planning meetings expressed opposition to logging in principle, and one conservation group is pressing to set aside the Tillamook as a state park.

Confidence

Ric Balfour's personality makes him absolutely perfect for a job like this, juggling many strong opinions in a very public arena. He's positive, energetic, ebullient, persistent, charming. A touch of cockiness is tempered with a disarming sense of humor. He is flexible without being a doormat; firm without being rigid; he listens but doesn't let himself get pulled this way and that. "I feel comfortable with all if it," he says. "I feel I can be the ideas man, and the planner, and the operations guy, and I'd grab onto the end of a jackhammer in a minute." In a twist on the old proverb, his ambition is to be "jack of all trades and master of one"—that is, competent at many things and really good at one thing. "If it doesn't sound too immodest, I'd like to be able to think of myself as a Renaissance individual."

Balfour believes the Tillamook Forest, if properly managed, is big enough to satisfy almost everybody. This is indeed the standard belief under which the Tillamook's managers operate, and just about everyone who works on the Tillamook shares it. "It's not so much a competition between timber and everything else," says Balfour, "it's a matter of how you fit them all in." His confidence is powerfully attractive. I found myself wanting to believe that forest management is nothing more than sound professional judgment, skillful allocation, and sympathetic attentiveness to people's complaints. Listening to Ric Balfour, I didn't want to remember Aldo Leopold's warning about how the complexity of natural systems confounds even the most rational of plans. I didn't want to remember how thoroughly economic and political pressures can overcome even the best intentions of sincere foresters.

After many meetings and countless late nights, Balfour and his team finished the recreation plan within the deadline, and the legislature approved it in January of 1993. Among its many provisions, the plan restricts motorcycles to the forested areas south of the Wilson River Highway. It also calls for rehabilitating the campgrounds and establishing user fees. Two sheriff's deputies have been hired to patrol the forest.

Telling the Story

Balfour and his colleagues also work hard at showcasing the Forest's unique history for visitors. The Tillamook State Forest interpretation plan has identified some fifteen interpretive sites already, including stops at the east and west entrances to the forest. And if all goes well, a Tillamook Forest visitors' center will be open in a few years.

Interpretation and public education, stresses Balfour, are more than nice touches calculated to attract visitors—they are essential in gaining the public's understanding and support of the "working forest" philosophy. Skillful interpretation, in other words, is a preemptive strike against the kind of environmental activism that has shut down much of the logging on federal forests. "Interpretation is what will keep this a working forest," Balfour says. "We do not apologize for timber harvesting. We have enlightened harvesting practices today, and we have strict forest-practice rules in place. If we demonstrate that we're doing a good job on all resource values—recreation, wildlife, watershed protection—then we'll gain back people's trust."

"By Hook or by Crook . . . "

The Gales Creek campground is one of Balfour's first successes. The campground lies at the end of a gravel road that winds down past a stout steel turnpike (locked, on this February day) through a thicket of alders to the creek. From here it's a short hike through the woods to the site of Elmer Lyda's logging operation, where the 1933 fire was supposed to have started. A few years ago the Gales Creek campground was a hangout for off-road drivers and a haven for homeless people. Its picnic tables had been chopped up for firewood, its outhouses tipped over, its creek banks gullied from erosion. Today the campground has sturdy new wooden picnic tables and concrete-vault toilets. It has log barricades to keep vehicles on the road and rock riprap to keep them out of the creek. A campground host is now on duty all summer, and campers are charged a modest fee.

In the middle of what used to be a mudhole is a landscaped island of Oregon grape, salal, and sword fern. The shrubs were dug up and transplanted from the forest nearby by inmates of the South Fork prison camp, a few miles down the highway to the west. South Fork, a minimum-security outpost of the Oregon correctional system, was opened in 1951. Its inmates have felled snags, planted trees, fought fires, built roads, and generally provided low-cost labor for the Tillamook rehabilitation effort ever since.

This landscaping crew worked under Balfour's direction. The men needed some basic training in gardening, he says. "They didn't have much of an idea how to transplant, so they'd just go out into the woods, yank up a bush, carry it back, scoop a hole—" he illustrates all this with his hands— "and plop it in. I said, 'No, no. You've got to keep some soil around the roots.' I told them, 'You need to get some moss and mulch around these plants, keep the roots moist.' I came back later and here was moss scattered all over the ground—but not around the roots. They thought I wanted to pretty the planting bed up. But they understood after another demonstration." He gets along well with the South Fork men. "I don't come across like, 'I'm better than you,' so it's not too long before I'm on good terms with them. They call me 'Kiwi.' Sometimes, when they want to get my goat, they call me 'Aussie.' And I tell them, 'Look, let's get one thing straight: I am *not* an Aussie.'" He grins again, showing that it's all just kidding.

In the dirt next to one of the new picnic tables, Balfour spots a rusty iron railroad spike. "Ah!" he says as he picks it up and examines it. Maybe he'll keep it for a future interpretive display. The spike probably came from the Consolidated Timber Company railroad, which once ran right through here—I can see the suggestion of a level grade in the hill north of the creek. Walking back to the truck, Balfour spies a beer bottle on another picnic table. He strides over, picks it up, and pours out a swirl of stale beer murky with cigarette-butt steepings. He stows the bottle in the recycling bag he always carries in the back of the truck.

Taming the wild Tillamook takes patience, persistence, and persuasiveness, all of which Balfour possesses. He shows me a sign at the head of a trail, a triangle-shaped graphic telling trail users who is to yield to whom (hikers to bicyclists; all to horses; no motorcycles permitted on this trail). "We put that sign up, and it was torn down," he says. "We put it back up and it was shot full of holes. We put a new one up, and it's been here almost a year now." The grin flashes again. "By hook or by crook," he says, "I'm going to get this job done."

Notes

1. Since this chapter was written, Ric Balfour has left the Oregon Department of Forestry, and is now working for the International Mountain Bicycling Association in Colorado.

10

A Walk up Gales Creek Canyon

ON A BRISK OCTOBER DAY, THREE MONTHS AFTER MY HIKE WITH the environmentalists, I visited Gales Creek again. The canyon was a kaleidoscope of scarlet and gold, with splashes of vine maple amid the muted yellow-brown of bigleaf maple and alder, all under a feathery canopy of silver-green needles. It had been raining, and the trail was slippery as I climbed the hill, but a thin sunlight splashed through the green firmament and dappled the duff under my feet. Again I tried to imagine what this place had once looked like: two blackened hillsides meeting at an acute angle, a silver thread of stream seaming them together, smoke curling from heaps of pale ash, black snags poking up into the September drizzle. And now here it is, utterly transformed. How can this be? What's the story here?

As I started on this journey through the Tillamook's past and present, I knew the story of this forest was going to be more complicated than it looked, and so it has turned out. The story of Gales Creek Canyon, like the story of the Tillamook itself, depends on who's doing the telling. For some people, it's a story of Man triumphing over one of Nature's dirtiest tricks. For others, it's a story of Nature persevering despite all the abuse Man can heap upon her. Both stories offer the same evidence; the crucial difference is the focus. What is figure and what is ground? Who are the main characters, and who are the supernumeraries? It depends. What we see when we walk out into the Tillamook depends on the stories we tell ourselves about reality.

I want us to keep this point in mind as we evaluate our original hypothesis, which is, that the existence of this forest, uniquely conceived and created, represents a synthesis between the frontier ethic and the arcadian vision—that it forges the beginnings of a third story that borrows from both of these stories, but somehow reaches beyond either one. We now need to test this hypothesis. Can the "working forest" really work?

To begin the discussion, we need to refer again to the dichotomy I proposed in Chapter 3—keeping in mind its disclaimers and limitations. The point of the dichotomy is to stress the very different ways in which the arcadian and the frontier worldviews frame reality. Can the "working forest" work? It would be helpful if everybody agreed on how to go about testing such a proposition, if there were a disinterested source of Truth to which we could appeal for the "right" way to proceed. But there is none. We have only stories. The frontier worldview and the arcadian worldview each offers its own stories, its own claims to truth, its own assumptions that filter every fact, every definition, every piece of evidence, every sequence of logic, every conclusion.

This does not mean these worldviews and the stories they tell us have no bearing on reality. If that were true, they would be of no use to us. Although they are not themselves reality, they disclose reality by revealing limited, grounded, situated, particular truths. The question now is how to take the particular truths about the Tillamook that are disclosed by the arcadian worldview and the frontier worldview, and talk about what they add up to. Then we need to see whether this new synthesis, if there is one, can help us decide what to do next.

What Would a Synthesis Look Like?

If there could be a coming-together of the frontier and arcadian worldviews, a synthesis, what would it look like? To help us answer this question, I would like to offer an outline of the main tenets of these worldviews, the bedrock assumptions to which people refer every new piece of knowledge. These assumptions are tacit and sometimes even unconscious, and that is partly why they have such power to shape thought and feeling. I may believe passionately that thinning a young Douglas fir stand will leave the forest in a "better" condition than before, but I may not stop to realize that I must be deriving this opinion from notions of what makes a forest "good" and how humans ought to be involved in the process of making forests good.

This outline will necessarily be a gross oversimplification; a worldview, even more than a story, is always more subtle and nuanced than a bare outline can show. Nevertheless, examining the main assumptions of these two worldviews will, I hope, reveal the incompleteness and inadequacy of each one.

The frontier worldview says:

• Nature is fundamentally "other" from humans.
• Nature is a set of potentialities waiting for humans to actualize them.
• Nature is a machine with predictable laws.
• Human manipulation of nature is necessary and right.
• Nature is robust and will bounce back from our impacts.
• Science yields the truth about our relationship with nature and also tools to carry out the manipulation.
• Nature's function is to nurture our bodies—our material selves.

The arcadian story says:

• Nature and humans are fundamentally the same—we are all life forms in the same biotic environment.
• Nature's purpose is to be itself, perfectly actualized on its own terms and needing no improvement from humans.
• Nature is a living thing with whom we are in relationship, whether we know it or not.
• Human manipulation of nature is a necessary evil at best.
• Nature is characterized by fragile and delicate balances and is easily upset.
• Nature itself yields the truth about our relationship with it— nature's processes are to be taken as moral instruction.
• Nature's function is to nurture our souls—our aesthetic and moral selves.

I have tried to show through the preceding chapters that each of these worldviews offers an incomplete, flawed, and finally unsatisfactory framework for expressing the complexity of the Tillamook story. Now let's look at what happens when we put them together. We get a much more complex, organic, open-ended, flexible, and ambiguous framework.

A synthesis might say:

• Nature is neither coexistent with humans nor wholly "other." We are a part of nature but also separate from nature. Our human consciousness enables us to see points in our being where we seem to intersect with nature, and points where we do not seem to intersect.
• Nature has no purpose; it exists on its own inscrutable terms.

- Nature is neither a living being nor a machine, but a community of living and nonliving elements and processes.
- Human manipulation of nature is inevitable, but we do not control nature.
- Nature is a complicated matrix of dynamic and stable processes; it is both robust and fragile.
- Our ideas of about nature are cultural inventions that disclose a limited truth about our place in the world. We have the opportunity to create a working truth in conversation with the rest of the community.
- Nature can nurture our bodies *and* our souls.

A synthesis of these two worldviews offers fewer answers and poses more questions. It has less narrative and more dialogue; less command and more conversation. Because it is ambiguous, it does not function as a cultural guide quite so efficiently as do the first two stories. It doesn't give us answers so much as offer a different way of seeing—a way that might fulfill Aldo Leopold's prophetic vision of "the land ethic." In his classic 1949 essay of the same name, Leopold writes, "A land ethic . . . cannot prevent the alteration, management, and use" of natural resources, "but it does affirm their right to continued existence, and, at least in spots, their continued existence in a natural state." A land ethic, he says, "changes the role of *Homo sapiens* from conqueror of the land-community to plain member and citizen of it" (Leopold 1970). For humans to embrace their role as citizens of a land community, they must begin to see the relationship between themselves and the land in a new way. In looking for guidance on how to frame a synthesis, we could do worse than Aldo Leopold. Trained as a game manager, his outlook at first firmly utilitarian, Leopold over the course of his life came to a more complex, inclusive, and paradoxical understanding of the relationship between humans and nature.

The several writers I've read who have proposed a dichotomy of thought similar to mine don't agree on precisely where to locate Leopold within it. I think that says a lot. Paul Hirt seems to put him, tentatively, in the frontier camp (to use my terminology, not Hirt's). In his 1939 essay "A Biotic View of the Land," Leopold cautions his colleagues in the forestry profession against intensive, high-yield manipulations of the forest, but he does not advocate a no-use policy. Instead, drawing on the then-infant science of ecology, he suggests that foresters ought to regard forests as "communities of living, interdependent organisms" (Hirt 1994, 42) and be accordingly more cautious about trying to grow only "good" species and eliminate "bad" ones. In the same essay Leopold argued that the less "violent" the manipulation of the ecosystem, the greater the likelihood that it would remain functional and, in Hirt's summary, "continue to offer utility value" (42-43). Worster likewise puts Leopold among the utilitarians: "For all his disenchantment [with the utilitarian bent of the forestry profession], he never broke away altogether from the economic view of nature. In many ways his land ethic was merely a more enlightened, long-range prudence: a surer means to an infinite expansion of material wealth . . . " (Worster 1977, 289).

Bob Taylor, on the other hand, seems to locate Leopold closer to the heart of the arcadian tradition. "He criticized the practice of conquering wilderness land solely for the purpose of converting it to economic use," says Taylor (1992, 55), "and he incisively noted that 'a stump was our symbol of progress.'" Leopold's *A Sand County Almanac,* Taylor says, was "the precursor to much of the environmental literature from the 1960s and 1970s that aimed to reform and perhaps even replace what were thought of as the ethical weaknesses of conventional progressive conservationism" (55).

The point here is that Leopold does not fit neatly into either camp. He sees nature neither as a dead thing, a commodity for human exploitation, nor as a mystical entity to which humans can only bring degradation. Donald Worster observes that Leopold used both mechanistic and organic metaphors to describe his ideas—in one essay talking about the wisdom of "keeping every cog and wheel" as "the first precaution of intelligent tinkering," and in another talking about the land as "a single organism." Worster takes this to be a contradiction, a flaw in Leopold's philosophy. Leopold's "vacillation between root metaphors" means, says Worster, that he did not succeed in resolving the tensions and ambiguities between the two opposing sets of values:

> It might be maintained that Leopold was attempting to reconcile these rivals, at long last, in a new conservation synthesis; his readers will have to assess for themselves how successful this reconcilitation was (Worster 1977, 289-90).

This reader assesses Leopold more kindly than Worster seems to do, for I sense that he embraces the fundamental moral imperatives of both worldviews, and brings them together in his concept of *community,* which advocates for an ethical treatment of land that does not leave human needs behind. Leopold's idea of community implies that an ethic that ignores human welfare for the sake of the land, or ignores the land's welfare for the sake of humans, is no ethic at all, for it fails on both the moral and the practical level. "When we see land as a community to which we belong," Leopold wrote in *A Sand County Almanac,* published the year after he died, "we may begin to use it with love and respect. There is no other way for land to survive the impact of mechanized man, nor for us to reap from it the esthetic harvest it is capable, under science, of contributing to culture" (Leopold [1949] 1970, viii).

How to achieve a land ethic? First of all, "quit thinking about decent land-use as solely an economic problem," says Leopold. "Examine each question in terms of what is ethically and esthetically right, as well as what is economically expedient." Not *either-or,* but *both-and:* Economics, ethics, and aesthetics are interwoven dimensions of the human relationship with the natural world, and they cannot be separated. Leopold goes on to say, in perhaps his most famous quotation: "A thing is right when it tends to preserve the integrity, stability, and beauty of the biotic community. It is wrong when it tends otherwise" (224-25).

Leopold represents the stirrings of an ecological conscience that elevates the land to a community of which we humans are a part—an essential part, but no more important than any other part in light of the integrity of the community. His idea of a land community also extends and enriches the idea of human community. It invites a new way of thinking not only about the land but about ourselves, and about one another. And that begins to answer the question, Why? Why is it important to bring these stories together? Why is it important to tell the Tillamook's story in a more complex, ambiguous, open-ended way?

On the most practical level, it is important because it will help us imagine a range of actions beyond the two extremes of *log-it-off* and *lock-it-up.* We in the Northwest have witnessed in painful detail the ongoing battles in the federal forest arena, a war going on so long that it has become "part of an Oregon political tradition" (Liberty 1997). It is a war between factions informed by incomplete and flawed versions of reality. The constant conflict eventually produces a siege mentality, combat fatigue, ill will between neighbors, and procedural gridlock. Telling a different story might reveal a different set of choices.

For another thing, the exhausting conflict distracts all parties from an immediate and very real threat to forests, and that is conversion to other uses. When is a forest not a forest? When it's a housing development. Today there are 2.3 million people in the Willamette basin—seventy percent of all Oregonians live here. By 2040, if we keep growing at our current rate, there will be another 1.5 million, according to figures from the conservation group 1000 Friends of Oregon. That is the equivalent of adding a city the size of Portland and another the size of Salem (Liberty 1997). Oregon's population growth and ensuing development is gobbling up farmland and forest land at an alarming rate. Not only are cities expanding, but rural land is being rezoned for residential and commercial use, and more people are moving out to live on ten or twenty acres of formerly undeveloped forest or farmland.

Between 1970-74 and 1982, according to Forest Service surveys, 63,000 acres of prime nonfederal forest land were lost to other uses. Urban growth ate up 45,000 acres of forest land during the same period. Figures from another source show that in the following decade, 30,400 acres of mostly prime forest land in the Willamette and lower Columbia basins were converted to urban and rural development. Oregon's farsighted growth-planning and land-use framework has put the brakes on this process to some degree, but no land-use system in a free-enterprise economy can stop growth or change. If Oregonians continue to consume forest land at the same per-capita rate until 2040, we will have lost 175,000 acres of our best forest land to development (Liberty 1997). That's an area half the size of the Tillamook Forest. Our constant wrangling over timber management blinds us to this greater threat. A new story might help us look to our forests for both bodily and spiritual sustenance. It could teach us to cherish them both more realistically and more fiercely, rather than sitting by as market forces turn them into housing developments or ranchettes or strip malls.

Perhaps an even more important reason to integrate these two worldviews is that a new story can help us integrate fragmented dimensions of ourselves. The frontier and the arcadian worldviews suffer from a onesidedness about human nature: the one focuses exclusively on material concerns; the other exclusively on aesthetic and spiritual concerns. But just as we are more than the sum of our body's appetites, we are also more than the sum of our soul's yearnings. The frontier vision masks one essential human dimension; the arcadian vision masks the other. This matter-spirit split has a long tradition in western thought, and it tends to pop up in all the discussions about the place of humans in nature. Here is an opportunity to reframe the question, to come to terms with the duality and paradox of our own being, and to acknowledge that we are both material and spiritual creatures—not that we have a material "side" and a spiritual "side," but that our material and spiritual selves are as thoroughly interwoven as a river is with its banks.

Does the "Working Forest" Really Work?

Does the future envisioned for the Tillamook by its managers help us tell a new story? I am going to argue that it does, if the intentions of structure-based management are honestly carried out, and if certain attitudes are adopted by those who are concerned with the future of the Tillamook—its managers, the people who live nearby, and those people who are challenging the state's management plans.

Now, when I say "certain attitudes," I can hear some readers thinking, "Oh, sure, if only people would just be nice and cooperate. Right. Well, maybe in a perfect world." This is not what I mean. The world does not have to be perfect in order for us to create a new story about the Tillamook and act upon that story. People don't have to be any politer or more ethical or more unselfish than they really are. They do have be willing, for the sake of their own long-term best interest, to delve into their assumptions, haul them out and scrutinize them, and maybe discard a few.

Tools are available to help us do this. In the past few years social scientists and communications experts have developed a set of discussion strategies directed at fostering a more civil discourse in disputes over natural resources. Known collectively as "multiparty collaboration" or "collaborative learning" (Daniels and Walker 1997), these strategies are being used to create a forum for solving disputes that is very different from the conventional public-participation exercise offered by land-management agencies as the sole way for people to air their concerns.

In conventional public participation, ". . . the agency is assumed to make decisions and the publics can provide comment," say Gregg Walker and Steven Daniels in a paper about collaboration—or rather, the lack of it—at President Clinton's 1993 Forest Conference.

In reality, public participation is often structured as an internal/ external, us versus them, zero-sum conflict situation. In that context, strategies of both the agency and the publics more likely become competitive rather than collaborative, centered around the distributive allocation of a fairly fixed set of resources (Walker and Daniels 1996, 80).

In contrast, multiparty collaboration, or collaborative learning, involves interdependent groups working together to affect the outcome of an issue in which they share an interest. "It is based on joint learning and fact finding; information is not used in a competitively strategic manner. Collaboration encourages exploration of underlying value differences and recognizes the potential for joint values to emerge" (Walker and Daniels, 81). It stresses "principled negotiation" to keep the focus on shared interests rather than on separate positions (Fisher and Ury 1991).

Collaboration does not mean everything is on the table. It does not mean people have to negotiate their interests away for the sake of harmony. And it does not mean an unstructured, anything-goes, do-your-own-thing atmosphere. If anything, the discussion in a collaborative learning context is far more structured than it is in a conventional public meeting. Daniels and Walker describe a nine-step, iterative framework for discourse (1997, 84) that allows participants not only to learn about the complexities of the natural resource issues at hand but to acquire "communication competence" by practicing skills such as listening, questioning and clarification, feedback, dialogue, and collaborative argument.

Collaboration enables participants to learn from one another. It lets them be honest with themselves and others about what their real interests are. It extends the power to change the situation from one entity—the agency—to the whole complement of parties, and to their negotiation relationship. By participating together, disputants maintain ownership in reaching an agreement. As a result, people who come in with strong opinions often find they are able to modify a formerly rock-ribbed stance when the collaboration produces some better way to get what they really want. In other words, in a collaborative setting, participants come to the table with one set of convictions—one worldview—and leave with the beginnings of another. Three conditions must be met, says another team, if any natural-resource debate is to succeed (Shindler and Cramer 1997). First, the discussion must be *informed*—parties must strive for an understanding of the complexities of the issue. Second, it must be *deliberative*—"public discourse should proceed in such a way that there are real opportunities for mutual learning and reflective thinking." Finally, it must be *discursive*—it must encourage full interaction among a wide range of stakeholders and interests.

People can learn to approach natural resource disputes in this informed, deliberative, discursive, collaborative way. But it takes work, and it takes courage. It demands a critical examination of one's own stories, and that is not easy. Exchanging a simple story for a more open-ended one demands that we give up certainty; it demands that we find new ways of seeing, knowing, and being. The obstacles lie in the comfortable old ways, in what people "know" about forests and human nature, what they "know"' about how to be a good forester and how to be a good environmentalist.

New Ways of Knowing

When we learn anything new, we go through a mostly unconscious process of measuring the new information against our worldview to see where it fits and how we are to make sense of it. If you and I learn a new piece of information and our worldviews are different, then I am referring the new data to one set of stories and you are referring it to another. We may use the same words to talk about our new discovery, and we may think we are communicating perfectly. But the words we assume to be transparent carry hidden baggages of meaning.

Consider, for example, the notion of "adaptive management," a key provision of structure-based management. The Tillamook's foresters pledge to monitor closely the effects of their management on the forest's plants, animals, soils, and riparian areas, and alter their management activities whenever necessary. Environmentalists agree that adaptive management is a good idea. But in order to monitor effectively, you have to know what you're looking for, says Nancy Langston in *Forest Dreams, Forest Nightmares* (1995):

> Monitoring is never entirely objective, for it requires an implicit definition of what is healthy and what is not. Before people can decide if an action harms the land, they have to start out with an idea of what harm means. And that is where cultural conflicts are sharpest. People have always monitored, but we have changed our ideas of what are good and bad effects (286).

Structure-based management's adaptive-management provision begs the question that foresters will know when a given management strategy crosses a threshold of harm. But they may not always know. Forests are influenced by a host of abiotic and biotic factors—climate, geology, soil, slope, vegetation, and cumulative natural and human disturbances—interlacing in complicated ways. In a real forest, it is difficult to discern the effect of any particular factor at any given time and place. And because forests live longer than people, the effects of any change in its patterns of life may not be immediately apparent. There is indeed a large body of knowledge on the effects of various disturbance patterns on various forest types, but none of the research has been going on long enough for managers to predict with certainty how these effects will play out over a hundred or two hundred years. Much is known about how forests function, but much is still unknown, and much is scientifically debatable.

The point here is not that adaptive management is wrong or useless, but that as a set of strategies it is not as straightforward as it seems. The idea of adaptive management refers tacitly to the frontier worldview's assumption, "nature is a machine," and to the corollary assumptions that whatever exists can be understood (Langston 1995), and that for every problem there is a solution. Within the context of the Tillamook's management, these may well be reasonable assumptions. They may well represent those limited, situated truths we talked about earlier. But they need to be brought out into the light and examined.

Having said that, I think we are very fortunate in this age to be able to see the workings of the Tillamook Forest in light of science— one of the most robust, complex, and credible stories the human race has ever developed. It is only because science has given us a wide platform of common understanding, a broad enough basis of consensus about how the world works, that we can even begin the conversation about forests. Thanks to science, and ecology in particular, we can describe a forest's functioning and weigh the effects of various human actions. Science can't offer certainty, but it can offer a fair degree of predictability. Without it, adaptive management would be meaningless, but with it, scientists can gradually refine their learning over time, not only in quantity of information gathered but in precision of information-gathering tools.

And not only scientists. Adaptive management should be more than just a step in a management sequence. It should be an ongoing conversation in which information circulates freely about the Tillamook's management activities, the observable outcomes of these activities on the forest, the developing scientific knowledge about forests, and the needs and interests of the people whose lives are affected by what happens on the Tillamook. For the idea of adaptive management to become meaningful in the new Tillamook story, managers will have to monitor with a respectful attention to processes whose full ramifications are unclear. They will need to be willing to change their minds in light of new information, and willing to invite interested nonscientists to accompany them on their journey of discovery.

For their part, the environmental community will have to accept that the mere observation that forests are complicated doesn't amount to a trump card obviating any kind of management. After a 1996 talk by silviculturist Chad Oliver on some of the principles of structure-based management, a member of the audience asked this question: How can we even dare try to manage a system like a forest, which is "not only more complex than we think but more complex than we *can* think?" Interactions within systems, Oliver agreed, become exponentially complicated as the components become more numerous, with the result that *"everything* is more complex than we can think." A systems approach, the kind of thinking that underlies structure-based management, is an improvement over linear thinking, he said, but it's not perfect. Nevertheless, "we have to be careful not to fall into the steady-state trap" by assuming that doing nothing will keep things as they are.

It is not enough, in other words, to observe that forests are complex and then simply throw up the hands. That is too easy. In fact we know quite a lot about forests, more than we've ever known, and far more than people knew when the heavy logging of half a century ago was going on. These forests are now our responsibility, and we must deal with them. Pleading ignorance does not let us off the hook. "[One] still has to manage [the forest]; there is no neutral position possible . . . " (Langston 1995). We may manage well, or we may manage poorly, we may manage by neglect or omission, but manage we must.

As a further example of a seemingly straightforward idea that carries a weight of implicit assumption, many foresters have argued that the Douglas fir forests of the Coast Range are "robust," able to bounce back from disturbances. Empirically this seems reasonable. The region's wet climate and mild temperatures make it one of the best tree-growing environments in the world (Waring and Franklin

1979, cited in Tappeiner et al., in press). What's more, the natural history of these forests is a history of repeated pounding with catastrophic disturbances—massive fires, mostly, but also windstorms and landslides. It seems safe enough to infer that if the forest can withstand big assaults, it ought to be able to withstand smaller, incremental disturbances like thinning or patch-cutting of trees or even large-scale clear-cutting.

It may seem safe, but it may be wrong. These smaller disturbances, in the aggregate and over time, could well have an effect on the patterns of life in these forests that the bigger fires and storms never had. A clear-cut may look in some ways like the aftermath of a forest fire, but clear-cutting does not have the same ecological effects as fire. The same type of disturbance may have different effects depending on the composition of the forest at the time it hits. A wildfire in a mature forest stand will produce a pattern of regrowth different from that which comes in after a wildfire in a younger, managed stand. Even the same disturbance in the same type of forest can have different effects across the disturbed area, or different effects from one year to the next. If a fire occurs after a good seed year for alder, the burned area will likely be dominated by alder if it is left alone. If the fire hits the same stand following a good Douglas fir seed year, Douglas fir has a better chance of dominating.

The long-term effects of these differences are not clear, and they cannot be predicted with absolute reliability—a forest is not a machine. But there will be effects. The forest of the future will inevitably be different from the presettlement forest of the past. Moreover, human impacts on the forest do not replace nature's impacts—they add to them (Langston 1995). The fact that nature sometimes appears to wreak havoc on an ecosystem in no way justifies additional damage from human activities. Here again we have an assumption—nature's robustness—that refers to the frontier worldview.

In the case of the Tillamook, the forest may well be robust enough to withstand a fairly high human impact without permanent harm to its basic processes. But it may not be so easy to determine where the critical thresholds of these processes are. How much disturbance can a stream take before it ceases to be healthy fish habitat? Are some kinds of disturbances better than others? Is it possible to mitigate all, some, or any of them? Is it wise to mitigate every disturbance? Could some disturbances be "bad" now but "good" in the long run?

The science exists to answer questions like these. For example, recent research is showing that some of the woody debris and gravel that makes for good fish habitat in a coastal river may have come not from the immediate streambank but from landslides that tumbled from steep headwalls (Reeves et al. 1995, cited in Tappeiner et al., in press). Such slides may destroy habitat in the short term, but they probably create habitat over the long term as the debris and gravel settle. Thus landslides, which the public generally considers "bad" for the forest ecosystem, may in fact be one of the essential catastrophic disturbances that make the coastal forest what it is.

Finally, let us look at the notion of "saving" the forest—the purpose for which the hikers were invited by the National Wildlife Federation to gather at Gales Creek. The word "save" is a rich storehouse of emotional connotation. "Save" means rescue, spare from harm, deliver from punishment, preserve, guard against loss, keep in health and well-being, set aside for a high purpose, redeem, sanctify. The object of the action of saving is very often a living thing, a person or a personality. As applied by the environmental community to forests, the word refers strongly to the arcadian worldview, to notions of nature as a living thing perfectly actualized without any help from humans and also as a fragile and delicate being that needs our protection.

Leaving aside the inherent contradiction between these two assumptions, the first problem with this tacit reference, in the case of the Tillamook, is that it is factually incorrect. The forest now on the ground got started with a lot of help from humans. The second problem is that it isn't clear at all that preserving the Tillamook from logging is the best way to "save" it. That position implies that logging a forest is tantamount to destroying it—an assumption that goes unchallenged in much environmentalist rhetoric. What should we be saving forests *from?* As we have seen, the pressure of development is an immediate threat to the continued existence of some forests. Profitable logging, for all its past excesses, is one hedge against the assault of development pressures. The state's foresters have a statutory obligation to manage the Tillamook and other state forests so as to keep them in a forested condition. This would be difficult if there were no money to pay for it.

And what should we be saving forests *for?* Some environmentalists argue that tourism dollars can replace timber dollars. One study found that Tillamook Bay fisheries generated $6.2 million in personal income in 1994 (Oregon Trout 1997). Obviously there's a difference between $6.2 million and the $10 million estimated yearly timber revenue from the Tillamook State Forest starting in the next few years. But leaving that aside, advocating nothing but recreation on the Tillamook reinforces the arcadian idea that forests have nothing to do with our material selves and our material needs—even though recreation has distinct material impacts on the forest environment, a reality that is sometimes overlooked. This is as one-sided as advocating nothing but logging.

More practically, reserving forests off-limits to logging tends to drive logging to other, perhaps more fragile environments—to shift it "someplace else, and no place is really someplace else" (Langston 1975, 283). As more land is withdrawn from timber production, other forest landowners are tempted to try to squeeze more timber from what land is left. The Sierra Club has proposed turning the Tillamook into a state park. Oregon has a reputation for beautiful, well-maintained state parks, but in the last few years, for a variety of reasons, the state's parks budget has suffered heavy cuts in general-fund support. User fees have spiked, and still the parks are understaffed and suffering from lack of maintenance. For a while it looked as if some parks would have to be closed, even sold off. That threat was averted for the time being, but the issue may come up again.

Aldo Leopold, whom I am holding up as a model for a new way of thinking, did not embrace the conservationist agenda wholesale. Conservationists, he thought, lacked critical judgment and a capacity for self-examination—"two prominent aspects of his own evolution," says the historian Stephen Fox: '"We face a future marked by a growing public zeal for conservation,' [Leopold] told a National Wildlife Federation meeting in 1937, 'but a zeal so uncritical—so devoid of discrimination—that any nostrum is likely to be gulped up with a shout'" (Fox, 247).

Perhaps Oregonians would be willing to tax themselves to support a 364,000-acre state park. (Currently Oregon has 92,000 acres of state parks). This is a legitimate question for debate, but it needs to be teased apart from its tacit assumptions and examined on its merits. Here again is an opportunity for a conversation in light of a synthesis between the frontier and arcadian worldviews, informed by a fuller idea of the place of humans in nature, what we need from nature, and the consequences of our choices. On the other hand, those who advocate heavy logging on the Tillamook, in the belief that all a community needs to be prosperous is plenty of timber, should take a hard look at the record. That notion is an example of "folk economics," says the economist Tom Power, and it is incomplete and misleading. Raw-material supply has only a tenuous relationship to community welfare in a resource-dominated economy. Extractive economies tend to follow a boom-and-bust cycle—a pattern so drearily familiar in the Northwest that "it would seem prudent for any community to avoid becoming a timber town" (Power 1996, 137). Market forces are a much stronger influence than log supply. In boom times, plenty of logs usually means plenty of work (not always—logs are not necessarily processed locally), but when markets take a dive, plenty of raw material doesn't solve the problem, and can make things worse.

Ultimately, says Power, it's better for a town to diversify and to focus on building up other, less tangible but economically important community endowments like a solid physical infrastructure, good schools, knowledgeable people, an entrepreneurial spirit—and a pleasant-looking landscape. Dependency on a single extractive industry tends to work against this kind of economic development, he says. This is not to say that logging can't be a vital part of a diversified economy. But it shouldn't be the only game in town.

New Ways of Being

Another potential obstacle to a new Tillamook story lies in the professional culture of those who will be managing the forest. As we have seen, the idea of scientific management has its roots in the frontier story, although I think we have also seen that it departs from that story in significant ways. Still, what environmentalists most want to know about structure-based management is, will it really be a better way to manage forests, or will it be merely a kinder, gentler version of production-driven timber management? The intention is good; will the actions match the words?

David Clary, in his critique *Timber and the Forest Service* (1986), paints a picture of a professional cadre of federal foresters who were so thoroughly indoctrinated with one big idea—the need to avert a timber famine—that they failed to notice that their priorities for National Forests were departing more and more from those of the American public they were supposed to be serving. I have already mentioned Paul Hirt's harsher appraisal of the Forest Service's "cult of cornucopia" by which heavy logging continued to be blessed in the face of mounting evidence that it was both unsustainable and environmentally damaging. Further, Hirt says, the agency kept its institutional blinders in place by marginalizing environmental activists, treating them as just one more interest group wanting a piece of the pie instead of as a prophetic voice challenging the whole scientific-management paradigm (Hirt, 228).

Nancy Langston poignantly describes the confusion and denial of Forest Service managers in the Blue Mountains when it became increasingly obvious, as she says, that their management practices were unraveling the ecosystem. "Each time, when faced with complexity, foresters eventually denied it and retreated into their certainty. In their minds they partly acknowledged this complexity and partly denied it, just as the same forester could simultaneously have both a knowledge of ecology's interconnections and a faith in his own ability to design a more efficient forest. Foresters were not, as many environmentalists claim, greedy or stupid. Like everyone else, they needed to hold onto a story that made their lives make sense" (Langston 1995, 298).

Stories tend to be self-reinforcing. The methods and tools foresters know best tend to become the terms within which the problems are framed. An old adage says, "If the only tool you have is a hammer, everything looks like a nail to you." Clear-cutting and replanting in west-side Douglas fir forests solved the problem of poor reforestation in the 1940s and '50s; therefore, reforestation became the main problem to be solved, and then, by extension, the main management goal—because the tools and techniques were available to do it. It also was more than coincidence that clear-cutting became the silvicultural method of choice in these forests at a time when demand for wood was heavy and prices were high.

The alternative management strategies posed by structure-based management are not all new. Various types of uneven-aged management were going on in Oregon forests in the 1930s, but at the time there was little research or technical support to back these efforts up (Tappeiner et al., in press). The advent of clear-cut silviculture coincided with the burgeoning of a forestry research machine largely focused on even-aged, clear-cut methods. "If the development of both [even- and uneven-aged] systems had proceeded simultaneously and with the same emphasis on developing the supporting technology," says one silviculturist, "a more diverse range of timber management options might have been developed for the forests of coastal Oregon" (Tappeiner et al., in press).

The difficulty of reforestation is an objection still thrown up almost automatically by some foresters whenever anyone proposes doing something other than clear-cutting and replanting Douglas fir in Oregon's west-side forests. This is not to say that reforestation is a trivial issue, or that its difficulty is a specious objection: it *is* hard to get Douglas fir seedlings growing under a canopy of bigger trees. But it can be done, if the manager is willing to trade off some growth and yield and pay close attention to light levels and vegetation cover. The difficulty of getting Douglas fir to grow under a canopy is a biological fact, but it does not have to drive the silvicultural decision. Some management objectives may be more important than easy reforestation of a valuable timber species. A new idea may be worth the risk that reforestation will be difficult or will demand special tools or techniques.

The point of all this is that once a constellation of values is fixed in a person's mind, it is not easily dislodged—something most of us have experienced (painfully) when a new fact or insight challenged a certainty in our lives. Foresters have traditionally been and are in many ways still steeped in a technically oriented, quantitatively rigorous professional culture that has until very recently been centered around maximizing timber production. Can they turn to embrace the complexity and uncertainty of managing for a variety of goals and tradeoffs? Can they alter a reward system that for many years has tied professional advancement to timber yield? Are they open to conversation with citizens holding passionately opposing views?

All the Oregon Department of Forestry people I talked to are sincere in their intentions to make structure-based management work. They see it as the best hope for our society to integrate all the uses and values of forests in one place. I have a lot of sympathy with this view, and that is why I wanted to examine it closely in this book. But for structure-based management to fulfill its promise, foresters will have to think and act in ways that go against the professional grain.

Everything I have seen so far indicates that the Tillamook's foresters are willing to do that. That they chose structure-based management in the first place is a telling example. SBM is derived from New Forestry ideas about forests as biological systems first and foremost, and those ideas are in keeping with Aldo Leopold's ethic of preserving the biological integrity of the land. If it is carried out as planned, SBM will not eliminate economic considerations, but it will not let them drive the decision process, either. Another good sign is the forestry department's willingness to let the public and the scientific community take part in the planning. They seem to be offering not just a token "public comment period" on plans already set, not just a perfunctory and selective sweep of the scientific literature, but a real opportunity to let scientists and lay people help shape the future of the Tillamook, within the constraints of the law, in a collaborative fashion.

For its part, the environmental community is offering mostly well-informed responses to the state's draft plans. To support its proposal to reserve large areas of the Tillamook and Clatsop State Forests for salmon habitat, for example, the conservation group Oregon Trout commissioned a detailed report from two fisheries biologists. The report outlined the history of the decline of salmon in the Coast Range, inventoried the watersheds, and developed a scheme to rate the conservation priority for each watershed. It also advanced four alternative proposals detailing various levels and kinds of protection (Huntington and Frissell 1997). Most other environmental groups have weighed in with accurate facts and careful arguments. Such thoroughness indicates that members of the environmental community, like the Tillamook's foresters, are paying attention to the information from the land and not only to the stories inside their heads.

A Conversation

I have used the word "conversation" throughout this discussion to show what I think is an essential element of a synthesis between the frontier and arcadian worldviews. It may seem to some readers that I am using it in a fanciful way, to refer to a discourse that includes nonhuman and even nonliving participants—the wildlife that live on the forest, the plant communities, the streams, the geological processes, and the web of interactions among them. Yet all these things and processes have something to tell us, something to show us. "There are ways of living on the land that pay attention to the land, and ways that do not," says Nancy Langston. "The land is full of information." Embarking on a conversation with the land will enable us to pay attention to this information, attend to it with respect and humility. Coho and salamanders can't talk to us, but they can communicate with us in (among other things) fluctuations in their population numbers. Becoming fluent in the language of the landscape means learning to listen to such signals.

But I also mean "conversation" in a literal sense. The story of forest management in the past decades has very often been the story of command and control: experts tell the forest what to do, and then they tell the people that it is all for their own good. The information flowed one way. In the past couple of decades, with expanded opportunities for the public to influence forest management, the information has begun to flow two ways. What I would like to see is information flowing many ways, links of discourse among many differing positions. My simplistic outline of the frontier and arcadian worldviews captured some of the major unspoken assumptions of the two, but in real life there are many worldviews, many nuances of thought and opinion and feeling, not only among professional foresters and members of the environmental community, but among ordinary citizens like you and me. A respectful conversation probing these opinions, eliciting their unspoken assumptions, and seeking ways to pull our ideals and interests together, would go a long way toward creating a new Tillamook story. I think the evidence shows that such a conversation is beginning to happen on the Tillamook.

I would like to make one final observation. This whole process is risky, for the outcome of a conversation is not always consensus, or even the dynamic equilibrium between differing positions that makes compromise possible. Sometimes the outcome is grudging accommodation; sometimes it is a breakdown of communication; sometimes it is war. Many environmentalists are willing to accept some level of timber harvest, which says they're subscribing to a worldview that's not purely arcadian, one that takes human material needs into account. But some reject the idea of any timber harvest on the Tillamook at all. Some foresters are eager to try the whole range of structure-based management tools. Others think the rush to alternative silvicultural methods on public lands is not only scientifically unsound but a shameful caving-in to political pressure.

Is it risky to start a conversation among people with such different views? You bet it is. It's always a risk to engage yourself in another person's story, and it's always a risk to be honest about your own story. You run the risk of being wrong, or getting hurt, or getting too mad to keep talking, or making the other person too mad to keep talking. You run the risk of breaking the relationship, leaving it even worse than it was before. Yet the potential rewards are great. Many of us have experienced that mysterious energy that sometimes emerges in a group of people who, for the sake of an important task, are willing to confront, discuss, and work through their differences. The result is a supple flow of wisdom that blends bits of knowledge into a shared story and weaves fragments of human ego into a larger community. Being in this flow makes you feel part of something bigger than yourself, yet more *yourself* than you ever did working alone.

This synergy doesn't always happen, of course. More often than not, there is mere accommodation, followed by a parting of the ways and a shrug, *oh well, you can't expect too much, people are human after all*. And sometimes there is conflict and breakdown and gridlock and alienation. But sometimes this mysterious flow does happen, and when it does, it is a powerful and wonderful thing. In my experience, it happens most often when people come into the encounter willing to work, willing to suffer, and willing to be changed. They have to be willing to work at learning, at understanding, and at overcoming their biases. They have to be willing to suffer the discomfort of rethinking their own stories and the pain of confrontation and sometimes-harsh words. And they have to be willing to be changed into wiser, subtler, gentler, and humbler members of a community.

If the community of the Tillamook can bring these commitments to the task of finding a more humane and workable forestry, then we might just have the beginnings of a new story, not only for the forest, but for ourselves.

Epilogue to the Second Edition

I T HAS BEEN FIVE YEARS SINCE *THE TILLAMOOK* WAS FIRST PUBLISHED, and the story needs a bit of updating. By now the reader knows the main framework: The state's forests are to be managed under the structure-based management plan. The Oregon Board of Forestry (the appointed citizen body that oversees the state's forest policy) has adopted the plan, and the Tillamook's managers are carrying it out.

Recently the plan has been challenged by two organized efforts representing (as I've called them in this book) the frontier and the arcadian points of view. The venue for the first was the Oregon legislature. Oregon's current poor economy has caused tax revenue to plunge, and that has sent legislators and local governments scrambling for dollars. A Republican representative introduced a bill in the spring of 2003 that would have had the effect of designating timber as the primary value of state forests.

The bill was intended in part as an economic stimulus to county governments. The reader will remember that timber revenues from the Tillamook and Clatsop state forests flow into county coffers under a deal that was struck back in 1939, when a law was passed that made it possible for the state to undertake the reforestation of the vast Tillamook Burn. The fifteen counties where the burned forests once stood ceded these lands to the state, and in return they were promised a substantial share of the revenues when the new trees grew big enough to harvest.

The 2003 bill had the support of many, but not all, players in the timber business. It passed the Oregon House of Representatives easily, but ran into a deadlock in the Senate Rules Committee, whose membership was evenly divided along party lines.

Legislators who backed the timber-first idea took another run at their goal. In a process known as "gut and stuff," they modified a loosely related Senate bill that had come before the House. They amended the bill to require that the Tillamook and Clatsop state forests be managed for the maximum output projected under a timber-yield model developed for these forests by a scientist at Oregon State University. That bill also passed the House with a good-sized majority.

All this was happening as the legislature was winding up a long and contentious effort to balance the state's budget. Before the the House had passed the second bill, the Senate had ended its session and senators were on their way home. Missing its chance for Senate ratification, the bill died.

Had either of these bills become law, the management of the Tillamook and Clatsop state forests would have changed to resemble that of an industrial tree farm. According to an Oregon Department of Forestry analysis, the first bill, if it had passed, would have increased timber yield by 75 percent and brought in another $28.7 million annually to counties and other local taxing districts. Of course, such projections must make guesses about factors impossible to predict with certainty, such as future timber prices, which have a lot to do with how much revenue is derived under any kind of management. Prices can vary widely, as anyone who grew up in a boom-and-bust timber town can tell you. At the moment prices are in a slump, and it is not clear how much a flood of public timber into a depressed market would help local governments.

Nevertheless, the timber-first idea is not likely to go away. An industry trade group that supported the bills contends that the state's structure-based management plan is too stingy with the cut and too costly in its operations. They say state forest-practice rules (which everyone who cuts timber has to follow) provide enough protection for the environment, and reserves aren't necessary.

Also in the summer of 2003, a coalition of environmental groups and tourist-focused businesses in northwestern Oregon filed an initiative petition with the Secretary of State's office. If the proponents of this plan can collect enough signatures, the measure will be on the ballot in November 2004. Their proposal calls for reserving half of the land in the Tillamook and Clatsop state forests from logging, except for some thinning to increase the forest's structural complexity in those areas. Proponents of this idea say it would produce some timber revenue, although not as much as the current structure-based management plan. They are opposed to the current plan because, they say, it would harm habitat for threatened and sensitive wildlife and erode other values of the forest that are hard to measure in dollars: the capacity of forested watersheds to purify water and absorb atmospheric carbon dioxide ("ecosystem services" in policy-wonk-speak), as well as the aesthetic and spiritual meanings and values that forests hold for people.

Meanwhile, the Board of Forestry and the Oregon Department of Forestry hold to the validity and the popular support of their structure-based management plan, which they regard as a complementary third way between industrial-style management on private lands and reserve-centered management on federal lands. They say that neither the timber-first idea nor the 50-percent-reserves idea represents the wishes of most people for state forests. All sides, they say, were fairly represented in the planning process; the groups opposed to the plan had their chance.

There is a mildly aggrieved tone in some of these foresters' voices as they speak of the opposition to structure-based management; how can anybody object to a "win-win" proposal like this? They are believers. Give us a chance to make this thing work, they say, and we will prove that the Tillamook and the rest of Oregon's northwestern forests, the finest tree-growing lands on God's green earth, will provide the people with all the blessings of the forest, forever. Let's allow the forest to grow into its array of structures, from young to old, from simple to complex. Let's give it time.

But there may be no time. The timber-first idea came close to becoming law this year, and it's likely to emerge again in some form in the next legislative session. Hoping to avoid this likelihood, the Tillamook's managers are calculating ways to increase the cut as much as they can while keeping to the principles of structure-based management. They'd rather bend their own rules than have their whole management program mandated by law. They realize that structure-based management is a philosophical middle way, distinct from the objectives of both the timber industry and the environmental community. They have few allies and many critics. Theirs is a lonely path.

❧

THAT'S THE STORY UP TO THIS POINT. I can't tell you what the outcome will be, but I do have some closing thoughts on what seems to be happening in Oregon's forests and outside of them.

First, the state's commitment to structure-based management places these forests in the middle of the spectrum between the intensively managed, production-focused forests of the wood-products industry, and the passively managed federal forests, where ecosystem considerations have (at least for now) superseded economic ones. Both these types of forests can be "sustainable" *if* they are managed to maintain the land's productive capacity while producing the intended benefit—whether wood products or wildlife habitat or ecosystem services or spiritual and aesthetic values. But neither of these ownerships, private or federal, is *trying* to systematically sustain a full range of forest benefits, from economic to social to ecological, on their lands. The state forests have moved into that role. In so doing, they have broadened and enriched the diversity of forests across Oregon's landscape.

There is a great concern for "biodiversity" in forest management nowadays. An ecosystem that contains many kinds of living things is assumed to be healthier, more robust, and more sustainable than one that contains few kinds. If this principle applies to a forested landscape, then one might infer that it is good to have some production forests, some reserve forests, and some forests devoted to multiple values. One size does not fit all. From a diversity perspective, having three kinds of forests seems a safer bet than having only two.

Second, the state's managers see their approach as a means to consensus on forest management questions beyond the borders of state forests, which amount to just 3 percent of Oregon's forested land. Structure-based management, they say, can satisfy at least some competing interests, and its goals are big enough to enable people with different convictions to work together. If it can help Oregonians forge a consensus in a small arena, maybe it can produce lessons useful in a larger one—say, the federal forests, where ill will and procedural gridlock have reigned for more a decade.

Five years ago, when I wrote this book, the Tillamook's managers were holding public forums in which they invited citizens to engage the concepts and the fine points of structure-based management, challenge them, pick them apart, hash them out. Now that the public hearings are over (although people are welcome to air their concerns at Board of Forestry meetings, which are always open to the public), and the management plan is for now in place, and the interested parties seem to be moving away from collaboration and into more-conventional roles of partisanship. For this reason, I see more at stake than how many board feet of timber per year the Tillamook should produce, or how long a stand of trees should be left to grow there. Right now seems a critical moment, not only for what happens in Oregon's state forests, but for what happens to the ideal of management based on consensus.

When I started this book, my hypothesis was that the Tillamook's story represented the beginnings of a synthesis between the arcadian and the frontier points of view. "Here," I wrote, hopefully, "we finally have a chance to form a truly stable, sustainable, and humane relationship with our forests."

That seemed a reasonable hope five years ago. Today I am not so sure. The next few years will tell, and I will be watching.

Gail Wells
September 2003

References

Ackerman, Sybil. Personal interview. September 9, 1997.

Anderson, Chris, and Lex Runciman, eds. 1995. *A forest of voices: Reading and writing the environment.* Mountain View, CA: Mayfield.

Arnold, Mel. 1942. "Arsenal out of ashes—Tillamook Burn salvage." *Sunday Oregonian Magazine,* October 4, 1942:5.

Balfour, Ric. Personal interviews. September 1, 1994 and February 24, 1995.

Beh, John L. 1951. *The Tillamook burn: A survey of a problem area* (unpublished senior thesis). On file at Oregon State University library.

Beuter, John H. 1994. *Legacy and Promise: Oregon's forests and wood products industry.* Report for the Oregon Business Council and the Oregon Forest Resources Institute.

The Bible. 1977. The new Oxford annotated study Bible, revised standard version. New York: Oxford University Press.

Brooks, David J., and Gordon E. Grant. 1992. *New perspectives in forest management: Background, science issues, and research agenda.* Research paper PNW-RP-456, USDA Forest Service. Corvallis, OR: Pacific Northwest Research Station.

Caufield, Catherine. 1990. "The ancient forest." *The New Yorker,* May 14, 1990:46-84.

Cheek, Kristin Aldred. 1996. *Community well-being and forest service policy: re-examining the sustained yield unit.* M.S. thesis, Oregon State University College of Forestry. Copy in possession of the author.

Clary, David A. 1986. *Timber and the forest service.* Lawrence: University Press of Kansas.

Cox, Thomas R. 1974. Mills and markets: *A history of the Pacific coast lumber industry to 1900.* Seattle and London: University of Washington Press.

Cox, Thomas R., Robert S. Maxwell, Phillip Drennon Thomas, and Joseph J. Malone. 1985. *This well-wooded land.* Lincoln and London: University of Nebraska Press.

Cronon, William. 1992. "A place for stories: Nature, history, and narrative." *Journal of American History,* March 1992:1347-1376.

Daniels, Steven E., and Gregg B. Walker. 1997. "Collaborative learning: Improving public deliberation in ecosystem-based management." *Environmental Impact Assessment Review* 16:71-102.

Fick, Larry, and George Martin. 1992. *The Tillamook Burn: Rehabilitation and reforestation.* Forest Grove: Oregon Department of Forestry.

Fick, Larry, and George Martin. 1993. Personal interview. Sept. 8, 1993.

Fisher, R., and W. Ury. 1983. *Getting to yes: Negotiating agreement without giving in.* New York: Penguin Books.

Force, Jo Ellen, Gary E. Machlis, Lianjun Zhang, and Anne Kearney. 1993. "The relationship between timber production, local historical events, and community social change: A quantitative case study." *Forest Science* 39:722-742. Cited in Cheek, 1996.

Fox, Stephen. 1981. *John Muir and his legacy: The American conservation movement.* Boston and Toronto: Little, Brown and Co.

"From Ruin to Rejuvenation" (videocassette). Salem, OR:

Association of Oregon Counties, 1978.
Gale, Richard P., and Sheila M. Cordray. 1991. "What should forests sustain? Eight answers." *Journal of Forestry* 89(5):31-36.
Gale, Richard. 1995. Personal interview. April 17, 1995.
Gober, Patricia. 1993. "Americans on the move." *Population Bulletin* 48(3):2-28.
Greeley, W.B. 1951. *Forests and Men*. Garden City, N.Y.: Doubleday & Co.
Guldin, James M. 1996. "The role of uneven-aged silviculture in the context of ecosystem management." *Western Journal of Applied Forestry* 11(1):4-12.
Hayes, John. 1998. *An independent scientific review of Oregon Department of Forestry's proposed western Oregon state forests habitat conservation plan*. Report prepared for the Oregon Department of Forestry, July 27, 1998. Copy in possession of the author.
Haynes, Richard W., Darius M. Adams, and John R. Mills. 1995. *The 1993 RPA timber assessment update*. USDA Forest Service General Technical Report RM-259. Portland, OR: Pacific Northwest Research Station.
Hirt, Paul. 1994. *A conspiracy of optimism: Management of the national forests since World War Two*. Lincoln and London: University of Nebraska Press.
Holbrook, Stewart. 1941. "The terrible Tillamook fire." *Sunday Oregonian,* August 24, 1941:1-7.
Huntington, Charles W., and Christopher A. Frissell. 1997. *Aquatic conservation and salmon recovery in the north coast basin of Oregon: A crucial role for the Tillamook and Clatsop state forests*. Report prepared for Oregon Trout. Portland: Oregon Trout.
Johnson, Elizabeth A. 1992. *She who is: the mystery of God in feminist theological discourse*. New York: The Crossroad Publishing Company.
Labhart, Mark. 1994. Personal interview. August 24, 1994.
Langston, Nancy. 1995. *Forest dreams, forest nightmares: The paradox of old growth in the inland West*. Seattle: University of Washington Press.
Leopold, Aldo. [1949] 1970. *A Sand County almanac, and sketches here and there*. London, Oxford, and New York: Oxford University Press.
Levesque, Paul. 1985. *A chronicle of the Tillamook County forest trust lands, Volumes 1 and 2*. Tillamook: Paul Levesque and Tillamook County.
Levesque, Paul. 1994. Personal interview. August 17, 1994.
Liberty, Robert. 1997. "The future of Eden's hedge: The forests of the Willamette Valley basin in the twenty-first century." Speech given at the Oregon State University College of Forestry, Oct. 23, 1997, as first in the 1997 Starker Lectures series. Published version in press.
Limerick, Patricia Nelson. 1987. *The legacy of conquest: The unbroken past of the American West*. New York: Norton.
Long, James. 1993. "Of grants and greed." *The Oregonian,* May 23, 1993, 1f.
Lucia, Ellis. 1975. *The big woods: Logging and lumbering from bull teams to helicopters in the Pacific Northwest*. Garden City, N.Y.: Doubleday & Co.
Lucia, Ellis. 1983. *Tillamook burn country: A pictorial history*. Caldwell, ID: The Caxton Printers, Ltd.
Lyon, Thomas, ed. 1989. *This incomperable lande: A book of*

American nature writing. New York: Penguin Books.

Maser, Chris. 1988. *The redesigned forest*. San Pedro, CA: R. & E. Miles.

Mason, David T. 1927. "Sustained yield and American forest problems." *Journal of Forestry* 25:890-894. Cited in Cheek, 1996.

McKibben, Bill. "An explosion of green." *The Atlantic Monthly*, April 1995:61-83.

Meinig, D.W. 1993. *The shaping of America: A geographical perspective on 500 years of history. Volume 2: Continental America 1800-1967*. New Haven and London: Yale University Press.

Merchant, Carolyn. [1980] 1990. *The death of nature: Women, ecology, and the scientific revolution*. San Francisco: Harper.

Munger, T.T. 1941. "They discuss the 'maturity selection' system." *Journal of Forestry* 39: 297-303.

Nash, Roderick. 1983. "A wilderness condition." From *Wilderness and the American mind*. New Haven: Yale University Press. Reprinted in Chris Anderson and Lex Runciman, eds. 1995. *A forest of voices: Reading and writing the environment*. Mountain View, CA: Mayfield, 410-427.

Office of the Attorney General. 1997. *Oregon Board of Forestry forest lands: an historical overview of the establishment of state forest lands*. Unpublished report; copy in possession of the author.

Office of the Secretary of State. 1994. *Oregon blue book, 1993-94*. Secretary of State, Salem, OR.

Oliver, Chadwick D. 1992. "A landscape approach: Achieving and maintaining biodiversity and economic productivity." *Journal of Forestry* 90:9, September 1992.

Oregon Administrative Rules, 629:35.

Oregon Department of Forestry. 1984. *Long range timber management plan, Northwest Oregon area state forests*. Tillamook: Oregon Department of Forestry, Northwest Oregon Area.

Oregon Department of Forestry and Oregon Department of Parks and Recreation. 1992. *Tillamook state forest: Comprehensive recreation management plan*. Salem: Oregon Department of Forestry and Oregon Department of Parks and Recreation.

Oregon Department of Forestry. 1993. *Tillamook burn to Tillamook state forest*. Salem: Oregon Department of Forestry.

Oregon Department of Forestry. 1998a. *Northwest Oregon state forests management plan*: Draft. April 1998. Salem: Oregon Department of Forestry.

Oregon Department of Forestry. 1998b. *Western Oregon state forests habitat conservation plan*. Draft. April 1998. Salem: Oregon Department of Forestry.

Oregon Employment Department. 1993. *Regional Economic Profile, Region 1*. Portland: Oregon Employment Department.

Oregon Employment Department. 1996. *Regional Economic Profile, Region 1*. Portland: Oregon Employment Department.

Oregon Employment Department. 1996. *Regional Economic Profile, Region 1 Update, December 1996*. Portland: Oregon Employment Department.

Oregon Trout. 1997. "Native salmon and Oregon's Northwest state forests." Information sheet no. 1. Unpublished report. Portland: Oregon Trout.

Perlin, John. 1991. *A forest journey: The role of wood in the development of civilization.* Cambridge, MA, and London: Harvard University Press.

Petersen, Jim. 1994. "Voices in the forest: An interview with Bob Zybach." *Evergreen*, March-April 1994.

Pinchot, Gifford. 1910. *The fight for conservation.* New York: Doubleday, Page and Co. Cited in Taylor (1992).

Plassmann, Thomas, O.F.M., and Joseph Vann, O.F.M. 1954. *Lives of saints, with excerpts from their writings.* New York: John J. Crawley & Co.

Power, Thomas Michael. 1996. *Lost landscapes and failed economies: The search for a sense of place.* Washington D.C. and Covelo, CA: Island Press.

Priaulx, Arthur W. "Big Tillamook Burn again may be green." *Sunday Oregonian Magazine*, March 31, 1946.

Pryne, Eric. "The good side of forest fires." *The Seattle Times*, August 9, 1994.

Puter, Stephen. 1908. *Looters of the public domain.* Cited in Levesque 1985, 1:48.

Pyne, Stephen. 1982. *Fire in America: A cultural history of wildland and rural fire.* Princeton: Princeton University Press.

Quammen, David. "Dirty word, clean place." *Writer's Northwest*, Spring 1992:1-3.

Reeves, G.H., L.E. Benda, K.M. Burnett, P.A. Bisson, and J.R. Sedell. 1995. "A disturbance-based ecosystem approach to maintaining and restoring freshwater habitats of evolutionarily significant units of anadromous salmonids in the Pacific Northwest." American Fisheries Society Symposium 17:334-349.

Rice, Teresa A., and Jon A. Souder. 1997. *Managing Oregon's Chapter 530 lands.* Report to the Oregon Board of Forestry. Salem: Oregon Department of Forestry.

Richen, Clarence. 1994. Personal interview. June 9, 1994.

Robbins, William G. 1988. *Hard times in paradise: Coos Bay, Oregon, 1850-1986.* Seattle and London: University of Washington Press.

Robbins, William G. 1989. "Western history: A dialectic on the modern condition." *Western Historical Quarterly* 20:429-49.

Romano, Benjamin. 2003. "Everyone wants a piece of the Clatsop and Tillamook State Forests" and subsequent articles in a series. The Daily Astorian, July 11, 14, 15, 16, and 17. On the web at http://www.dailyastorian.info/main.asp?SectionID=58. Last accessed August 9, 2003.

Roosevelt, Theodore. 1908. Opening address to conference of state governors called to address the topic of conservation. Copy in possession of the author.

"Salvage logging bill passes in House." *The Oregonian*, March 17, 1995.

Schallau, Con. 1989. "Sustained yield versus community stability: An unfortunate wedding?" *Journal of Forestry*, September 1989.

Schwantes, Carlos A. 1989. *The Pacific Northwest: An interpretive history.* University of Nebraska Press, Lincoln and London.

"Scientists advise against proposed dead timber cut." Medford *Mail Tribune*, March 9, 1995.

"Senate panel approves environmental exemptions for some logging." *Sunday Oregonian*, March 26, 1995.

"Seven key elements." *Forest Log* (a publication of the Oregon Department of Forestry), July-August 1994:6-7.

Shindler, Bruce, and Lori Cramer. 1997. "Changing public values: Consequences for Pacific Northwest forestry." Essay prepared for Forests and Society—Implementing Sustainability, interdisciplinary workshop, Oregon State University, 5-6 December, 1997.

Slotkin, Richard. 1985. *The fatal environment: The myth of the frontier in the age of industrialization, 1800-1890.* New York: Atheneum.

Smith, David M. 1986. *The practice of silviculture, 8th ed.* New York: John Wiley & Sons.

Smith, Jeffery. 1997. "Evangelical Christians preach a green Gospel." *High Country News* 29:8, April 28, 1997.

Society of American Foresters. 1993. *Task force report on sustaining long-term forest health and productivity.* Bethesda, MD: Society of American Foresters.

Spies, Thomas, David Hibbs, Janet Ohmann, Gordon Reeves, Rob Pabst, Fred Swanson, Cathy Whitlock, Julia Jones, Beverly C. Wemple, Laurie Parendes, and Barbara Schrader. In press. "The ecological basis of forest ecosystem management in the Oregon Coast Range." Chapter 3 in *Forest and Stream Management in the Oregon Coast Range.*

Stafford, William. 1962. *Traveling through the dark.* New York: Harper & Row.

Stegner, Wallace. 1992. *Where the bluebird sings to the lemonade springs: Living and writing in the West.* New York: Random House.

Tappeiner, John C. II, David Hibbs, and William H. Emmingham.

In press. "Silviculture of Coast Range forests." Chapter 7 in *Forest and stream management in the Oregon Coast Range.*

Taylor, Bob Pepperman. 1992. *Our limits transgressed: Enviromental political thought in America.* Lawrence: University Press of Kansas.

Tillamook Pioneer Association. 1972. *Tillamook Memories: Places we love come back to us as sweet music.* Tillamook Pioneer Association.

Torres, Lou. 1992. "Tillamook State Forest begins returning long-range investment." *Forest Log 1992 Annual Report.* Salem: Oregon Department of Forestry.

Walker, Gregg B., and Steven E. Daniels. 1996. "The Clinton administration, the Northwest Forest Conference, and managing conflict: When talk and structure collide." *Society & Natural Resources* 9:77-91.

Walstad, John D. 1992. "History of the development, use, and management of forest resources." In *Reforestation practices in southwestern Oregon and northern California*, ed. Stephen D. Hobbs, Steven D. Tesch, Peyton W. Owston, Ronald E. Stewart, John C. Tappeiner III, and Gail E. Wells: 26-46. Corvallis, OR: Oregon State University Forest Research Laboratory.

Waring, Richard H., and J.E. Franklin. 1979. "Evergreen forests of the Pacific Northwest." *Science* 204:1380-6.

Webster's New World dictionary of the American language, 2nd College Edition. 1974. David B. Guralnik, editor. Cleveland and New York: William Collins & World Publishing Co., Inc.

White, Richard. 1991. *"It's your misfortune and none of my own:" A history of the American West.*

Norman, OK, and London:
University of Oklahoma Press.
Worster, Donald. [1977] 1994.
*Nature's economy: A history of
ecological ideas.* 2nd ed. Studies
in Environment and History.
Cambridge, New York, and
Melbourne: Cambridge
University Press.

Index

Achterman, Gail, 145, 146
Ackerman, Sybil, 125-31, 137, 139, 143
Acquisition Act of 1939, 123
acquisition laws governing state forest lands, 71, 121, 135
active management, 71, 75, 86, 87, 135
Adam, Mike, 107
adaptive management, 90, 91, 141, 142, 163, 164, 165
administrative rule for state forest lands, 71, 134, 135
alder, 2, 3, 83, 89, 93, 97, 105, 151, 154, 166
amendment to Oregon constitution, 14, 20, 60, 62, 123
ancient forest, 2, 58, 143, 144
arcadian worldview. See worldview, arcadian
Astoria, OR, 29, 64, 99

Balfour, Ric, 144, 145, 146, 147, 148, 149, 150, 151, 152, 153
Bay City, OR, 29
Benton County, 61
biodiversity, 77, 78, 82, 94, 95, 178
Blodgett, D.A., 28
Blodgett, John W., 32, 63
Board of Forestry. See Oregon Board of Forestry
bond issue, to finance reforestation, 14, 59, 60, 61, 62, 123
Boyington, Guy, 14, 146
Brown, Rick, 136
Bull Run reserve, 115
Bureau of Land Management, 94, 101

CCC. See Civilian Conservation Corps

campgrounds, 121, 145, 151: Gales Creek, 125, 126, 127, 129, 130, 131, 137, 143, 151, 152; Jones Creek, 73
canopy, forest, 2, 54, 95, 97, 101
capital, role in development of NW lumber industry, 27, 28, 31, 32, 34, 37, 42, 117
Carlton, OR, 64
cedar, 2, 8, 57, 112, 132: western red, 7, 32, 97, 102
Chan, Sam, 101
Chapter 530 law, 71, 135
Cheek, Kristin Aldred, 116, 117, 118
Christian: influences on philosophy of resource use, 132, 133, 134; upbringing of John Muir, 48
Civilian Conservation Corps, 8, 9
Clatsop County, 15, 101, 123
Clatsop State Forest, 172, 175, 176
Clary, David, 169
clear-cutting, 1, 50, 51, 65, 75, 80, 91, 98, 102, 103, 104, 105, 126, 143, 166, 170
Clements, Frederic, 110
climax, in forest succession, 3, 4, 110
closed-single-canopy stands, 79, 80, 82
Coast Range, 14, 36, 43, 56, 70, 79, 96, 102, 141, 147, 165, 172
Common School lands, 121
community: ecological, 110, 157; forest, 2, 56; human, 159, 173, 174; land-, 157, 159
community welfare, 116, 117, 118, 124, 169
conifers, 2, 59, 75, 76, 86, 97, 102, 110
conservation, 47, 48, 50, 52, 54, 55, 113, 118,

119, 120, 121: of forests, 34, 46, 34, 46, 119, 120, 172; of natural resources, 47, 113, 121, 135, 140, 141; organizations, 72, 118, 127, 130, 136, 138, 150, 160, 168, 172; synthesis, 158
conservation philosophy, 103, 133: as contrasted with preservationism, 48, 50, 52, 54, 55. See also environmentalism, Progressive conservationism
Consolidated Timber Co., 63, 64, 152
Coos Bay, OR, 1
Coos County, 120
counties, state partnership with, 14, 21, 71, 72, 78, 91, 122, 123, 135, 175
Cox, Thomas, 27, 36, 53
Cronon, William, 4, 5, 42

dairying, 19, 35
Daniels, Steven, 161, 162
Depression, 14, 19, 57
disturbances, ecological, 58, 77, 79, 86, 88, 95, 106, 107, 164, 165, 166, 167
diversity: biological, 77, 78, 82, 94, 95, 98, 102; of forest structures, 77, 79, 95, 97, 106
Donation Land Act, 25
Douglas County, 120
Douglas fir, 2, 3, 4, 7, 8, 15, 16, 19, 32, 56, 57, 60, 63, 69, 70, 74, 80, 82, 89, 93, 94, 95, 96, 97, 98, 101, 102, 103, 131, 144, 145, 155, 165, 166, 170, 171
Drinnon, Richard, 41
Dwyer, Judge William, 96, 100

Earth Day, 1, 47, 49
ecology, science of, 4, 87, 136, 157, 164: deep ecology, 52

ecosystem, forest, 60, 64, 71, 76, 96, 107, 109, 125, 134, 158, 166, 167, 170
Ecosystem Workforce, 99, 105, 106
Elliott, Francis, 120, 121, 122
Elliott State Forest, 121
Elsie, OR, 19
Emmingham, Bill, 94, 97, 98, 102, 104, 106
endangered species, 78, 82, 126, 128, 136, 137, 138, 139. *See also* wildlife, threatened
Endangered Species Act, 89, 127, 129, 137, 140
environmentalism, 2, 43, 47, 49, 50, 51, 52, 53, 54, 55, 64, 65, 66, 72, 74, 86, 88, 90, 107, 132, 133, 134, 136, 158, 163
environmental organizations and activists, 52, 64, 65, 72, 74, 86, 88, 90, 125, 127, 128, 129, 133, 135, 138, 139, 140, 151, 152, 154, 163, 165, 167, 168, 170, 172, 173, 176
erosion, soil, 70, 71, 104, 115, 135, 147
Eugene, OR, 61
European-Americans, 22, 38, 41, 45, 56, 57, 114
European forests, 98

federal forests, 86, 89, 96, 99, 100, 101, 104, 116, 118, 119, 124, 151, 159, 178
federal government, 13, 21, 25, 27, 124, 127, 137, 138, 140
ferns, 2, 16, 21, 70, 75, 89, 132, 152
fir, grand, 97
fire: as a management tool, 57; forest, 3, 24, 56, 57, 58, 60, 64, 95, 96, 102, 103, 104, 105, 110, 120, 166; protection measures against, 22, 61, 119,

120, 121; roads, 13. *See also* Tillamook, fires
firebreaks, 8, 9, 10, 14, 15, 47
firefighting crews, 8, 9, 10,13, 15, 47, 152
fires, 10, 57, 64, 120. *See also* Tillamook, fires
floods, 102, 103, 104
flood protection, 71, 135
foreclosures, 14, 122
forest, 1-6, 15, 19, 21, 32, 33, 46, 47, 50, 51, 53, 54, 60, 62, 64, 65, 67, 68, 74, 76-80, 82, 83, 87, 88, 89, 93, 95-98, 100, 105-27, 130, 131, 134-39, 143, 152, 160, 161, 163-73: definition of, 2, 44; federal reserves, 45, 115, 116; human relationship with, 6; management of, 38, 50, 65- 68, 78, 86, 87, 91, 92, 94, 103, 108, 111, 116, 119, 121, 126, 127, 130, 132, 134, 135, 138-42, 150, 157, 160, 161, 163-66, 169, 170, 171, 173; Tillamook, before the Burn, 7, 11, 13, 23, 56, 57, 58, 60, 132. *See also* old-growth forest, second-growth forests, Tillamook State Forest
Forest Ecosystem Management Assessment Team, 96
forest products industry, 50, 139
Forest Service (USDA), 13, 46, 67, 72, 89, 94, 96, 100, 103, 104, 116, 117, 118, 119, 124, 136, 160, 169, 170
forest structure: layered, 75, 79, 80, 82, 95; older, 65, 74, 75, 79, 80, 82, 89, 90, 95, 96, 101, 141
forestry: 1945 special committee, 21; practice of, 1, 6, 38, 39, 47, 50, 51, 66-69, 72, 77, 89, 92, 94, 95, 98, 99, 104-

6, 108, 109, 116, 119, 121-24, 146, 157, 158, 174; research, 76, 170
Fox, Stephen, 46, 54, 55, 168
Franklin, Jerry, 76, 108
frontier, 21, 22, 24, 25, 29, 35, 53, 37, 41-43, 45, 46, 47, 53, 60: as story theme, 5, 37, 44, 47, 39; definition of, 37; in historical analysis, 39, 40; promise of, 28; values of, 22, 23, 29, 34, 37, 51, 65, 66. *See also* worldview, frontier

Gales Creek, OR, 7, 8, 13, 19, 60
Garibaldi, OR, 29
Glenwood, OR, 19
Goldschmidt, Gov. Neil, 145, 146
Gomez, Doug, 107

Habitat Conservation Plan, 82, 83, 87, 88, 90, 91, 127, 129, 130, 137, 138, 139, 140, 141, 142
habitat, wildlife, 54, 57, 65, 67, 71, 74, 76, 77, 78, 82, 86-89, 95, 96, 99, 100, 101, 108, 128, 135, 137, 166, 167, 172
Hammond's flycatcher, 107
Hayes, John, 87, 108
Headlight, 28, 32, 36
helicopter: logging and management with, 70, 71, 76; used in seeding Burn, 2, 15, 20
hemlock, 2, 3, 7, 56, 82, 97, 102, 142
Hillsboro, OR, 64
Hirt, Paul, 40, 50, 67, 118, 119, 124, 157, 158, 169
Hobsonville, 29, 30
hoedads, 16, 59
Holbrook, Stewart, 58, 63
Holloway, Ross, 86, 91
Holmes, Jenny, 130, 132, 134

Homestead Act, 25, 26
homesteaders, 25, 26, 29
House Bill 2501, 146
huckleberry, 57, 89, 132

Indians, 19, 22, 24, 29, 39, 57, 130. *See also* Native Americans
intensive forest management, 67, 103, 111, 119, 157
Isaac, Leo, 103

Jefferson, Thomas, 25, 40, 53
Jewell, OR, 19
Jones Creek Park, 73

Kilchis River, 19

Labhart, Mark, 69-78, 90, 92, 93, 96
land ethic, 157, 158, 159
land grants, 26
landslides, 104, 166, 167
Lane County, OR, 56, 61
Langston, Nancy, 163, 170, 172
Leopold, Aldo, 48, 50, 68, 150, 157, 158, 159, 168, 171
Lewis and Clark journals, 19, 23
logging, 21, 38, 50, 51, 58, 60, 64, 67, 69, 79, 82, 86, 96, 97, 102-7, 112, 119-21, 136, 139, 140, 143, 150, 151, 165, 167, 168, 169: historical, 112-14; as a pioneer enterprise, 34; camps, 8, 9, 10, 64; companies, 7, 9, 31; innovations in technology, 33; with helicopters, 70, 71; railroads, 33, 63; with tractors, 74
Lucia, Ellis, 28, 33, 34, 58, 60, 63. 64
lumber, 1, 26, 27, 29, 30, 31, 53, 54, 62, 122
lumbering, 22, 26-37, 53, 58. *See also* forest products industry
Lyda, Elmer, 60, 151

Maas, Kathy, 101
Manifest Destiny, 22
maple, 89, 93: bigleaf, 2, 3, 97, 154; vine, 2, 3, 4, 89, 145, 154
marbled murrelet, 74, 83, 87, 88, 127, 139, 141, 142
Mason, David T., 116
maturity selection, 103
McCall, Gov. Tom, 17, 18, 148
McKay, Gov. Douglas, 14, 17, 18, 148
McKibben, Bill, 48, 50, 52
McMinnville, OR, 64
Meinig, Donald, 22, 41, 42
Miami River, 19
mills, wood-products, 1, 8, 11, 25, 27, 29, 30, 31, 32, 33, 36, 37, 53, 54, 64, 99, 100, 101, 105, 112, 116, 117, 120
mining, 32, 37, 38
Mining Act of 1872, 26
Mist, OR, 19
monitoring, 90, 91, 107, 140, 141, 142, 163, 165
monoculture, 94
Montesano, WA, tree farm, 59
Mount Hood National Forest, 115
Muir, John 47, 48, 49, 52, 54
multiple use of forests, 119, 121
Multiple Use-Sustained Yield Act of 1960, 118
Multnomah County, 61
myth: in interpreting frontier history, 37-43, 60; qualities in Tillamook story, 63, 65, 66

National Forests, 89, 96, 101, 115, 116, 118, 119, 124, 149, 169
National Marine Fisheries Service, 88, 127, 137, 142

National Wildlife Federation, 125, 126, 129, 136, 138, 167, 168
Native Americans, 23, 57, 68
natural regeneration, 102, 103
natural resources, 21, 34, 40, 46, 51, 109, 120, 123: use of, 22, 32, 34-36, 40, 157; conflicts about, 6, 78, 161-63
nature, 4, 38, 46-53, 60, 66, 68, 145, 154, 156-158, 164, 166, 167: human relationship with, 22, 34, 37, 45, 46, 67, 132, 133, 156, 157, 161, 168; mythical qualities of, 22, 40, 47; steady-state and dynamic views of, 4, 107
Nehalem, OR 19
New Forestry, 76, 77, 104, 108, 171
northern spotted owl, 74, 83, 87, 89, 95, 96, 100, 106, 107, 127, 136, 138, 139, 141, 142
Northwest Forest Plan (federal), 86, 94
Northwest Oregon State Forest Management Plan, 65, 67, 68, 75, 78, 79, 83, 86, 88-91, 96, 101, 126, 127, 130, 141, 142, 150, 161, 172

old-growth forest, 2, 65, 74, 77, 103, 104, 100, 126
Oliver, Chadwick, 77, 165
Oregon Board of Forestry, 71, 72, 83, 88, 125, 127, 129, 130, 134, 135, 137, 175, 177, 179
Oregon Conservation Commission, 120, 121
Oregon Department of Forestry, 13, 18, 65, 67, 69, 73, 75, 78, 82, 83,

86, 87, 88, 89, 90, 91, 93, 101, 126, 127, 129, 130, 134, 140, 141, 142, 145, 146, 148, 153, 171, 176, 177
Oregon legislature, 175
Oregon Plan, 140
Oregon State University, 60, 87, 94, 95, 98, 108, 146, 176
Oregon Trout, 125, 135, 140, 141, 172
Oregonian, 1, 31, 31, 58
Organic Act of 1897, 116
overstory, 75, 97, 101, 102
Owl Camp, 14, 17, 148

partial cutting, 65, 82, 86, 103, 104
Paulus, Fred, 62
Perlin, John, 112, 113
Perry, Dave, 60, 64, 95
Phellinus root rot, 89, 107
Pinchot, Gifford, 46, 48, 54, 72, 116, 117
plantations, forest, 13, 65, 78, 80, 89, 95, 96, 97, 98, 102, 119, 146
planting of trees, 7, 12, 13, 15, 16, 20, 59, 65, 77, 82, 95, 113, 114, 119, 144, 146, 152. *See also* reforestation
Portland, OR, 1, 12, 16, 19, 34, 36, 59, 61, 64, 116, 126, 129, 131, 145, 160
Power, Thomas, 36, 118, 124, 168, 169
preservation of forests, 113, 115, 126, 134
Priaulx, Arthur, 58, 59
progress as an ideal, 39, 40, 47, 53
Progressive: political movement, 46, 120; ideals, 47, 116, 123; conservationism, 46, 50, 52, 66, 78, 158
Public Interest Committee, 88, 130

railroads, 32, 34, 114, 115: companies and land grants, 26, 27; into Tillamook County, 24, 34, 36, 43; logging. 19, 33, 63, 152
recreation, 65, 71, 72, 73, 78, 88, 144-46, 149-51, 168: plan for Tillamook State Forest, 73, 146, 148-50
reforestation, 62, 105, 113, 114, 120, 121, 123, 170, 171: bond issue to finance, 17, 59, 60; methods, technology, 13, 102, 103, 104; of the Tillamook Burn, 13, 14, 15, 17, 20, 38, 44, 47, 58, 59, 60, 62, 64, 66, 93, 94, 103, 148. *See also* planting of trees, seeding of Burn lands
regeneration: stand type, 79, 80, 82. *See also* natural regeneration, planting of trees
riparian areas, 76, 82, 83, 86, 88, 90, 91, 163
roads: early wagon, 24; forest, 13, 15, 20, 63, 70, 73, 104, 139, 145, 146, 147, 151, 152
Robbins, William, 41
Rockaway Beach, 127, 139
Rogers Camp, 17, 147, 148
Rogers, Nelson S., 13, 14, 146
Roosevelt, Franklin, 62
Roosevelt, Theodore, 115, 116, 120, 123, 124

salmon, 66, 76, 82, 86, 172: chinook, 82, 141; chum, 82, 141; coho, 82, 138, 139, 140, 141, 172
salvage logging, 11, 14, 16,19, 51, 63, 64, 65, 76, 123
San Francisco, 28, 29, 30, 31

Schallau, Con, 117
Schnee, Mike, 75, 76, 77, 79, 87, 90, 91, 140
Schwantes, Carlos, 34, 43
Seaside, OR, 64
second-growth forests, 2, 98, 131, 141, 143
seeding of Burn lands, 15, 16, 20, 21, 106
selective cutting, 103
settlers: in the New World, 45, 115; in Tillamook country, 22-25, 30, 34, 56, 57; in the West, 23, 25-27, 40
severance tax, 59, 61, 62, 123
Sierra Club, 74, 125, 148, 149, 168
silviculture, 47, 65, 74, 77, 87, 95, 98, 102, 103, 106, 170
Siuslaw National Forest, 96, 99, 101
Slotkin, Richard, 40, 42
Smith, Joseph, 29, 30, 31, 37
snags, forest, 11, 13, 17, 20, 21, 58, 74, 75, 79, 80, 86, 89, 90, 95, 106, 107, 139, 152, 154
Snell, Gov. Earl, 12, 13, 21, 61, 62, 146
soil erosion. *See* erosion, soil
South Fork prison camp, 16, 152
spruce, 7, 24, 29, 56, 57, 82, 97, 98, 142
state ownership of forest lands, 13, 62, 122, 123
stewardship ethic of land use, 47, 51, 116, 122, 134
structure-based management, 65, 67, 75-80, 87-92, 96, 126, 127, 139-41, 161-65, 169, 170, 171, 173, 175, 176, 177, 178
succession, ecological, 110, 111
sustainability of forest use, 68, 91, 93, 105,

109, 110, 111, 114, 116, 123, 124, 134, 136
sustained yield, 34, 116, 117, 118, 119, 124
Suzuki, Nobuya 108
synthesis of worldviews 154-58, 168, 172

taxes: on timber land, 11, 13, 59, 61, 62, 120, 121, 123; to reforest Burn, 21, 62
Taylor, Bob Pepperman, 50, 52, 55, 158
technology, 42, 66, 102, 105, 119, 170: as part of frontier worldview, 37, 45, 47; Native American, 57
thinning, 65, 69, 70, 73-75, 80, 86, 95-97, 99, 101, 102, 106-8, 155, 166
Thomas, Jack Ward, 100
Tillamook: country, 10, 16, 43, 56, 57, 65, 145; fires, 1, 2, 7-12, 19, 20, 27, 56-58, 60, 63-65, 76, 80, 93, 95, 106, 131, 145, 151; legend, 58, 60, 64, 68; reforestation, 13, 14, 15, 17, 20, 38, 44, 47, 58-60, 62, 64, 66, 93, 94, 103, 148
Tillamook, OR, 35, 36, 64, 90, 93, 94, 99
Tillamook Bay, 23, 33, 80, 141
Tillamook Burn, 1- 3, 13, 14, 37, 38, 44, 45, 47, 57-60, 62, 65, 66, 102, 103, 105, 123, 125, 126, 175
Tillamook County, 14, 21, 33, 57, 61, 64, 100, 101, 122, 123: early landowners in, 32, 63; early population of, 58
Tillamook State Forest, 1, 2, 5, 6, 15, 17, 38, 44, 50, 53, 59, 65-68, 72-76, 79, 89-97, 99, 105, 106, 110, 111, 125, 127,

130, 134, 139-46, 148-55, 160, 161, 163-69, 171-76: harvest from, 70, 72, 73, 78, 80, 82, 88, 91, 125, 126, 134, 135, 140, 141, 146, 150, 151, 173; management plan for, 89; recreation plan for, 73, 146, 148-50; visitor's center, 93, 151
timber, 1, 20, 22, 23, 25-27, 31-36, 44, 57, 58, 62, 65, 67, 72, 76, 96, 100, 101, 104, 105, 108, 129, 134, 148, 149, 160, 168-71: losses from fires, 11, 12, 20, 93: revenues 14, 21, 63, 73, 78, 91, 126, 167
timber industry, 14, 26, 45, 50, 51, 59, 61-63, 65, 67, 88, 92, 94, 100, 136
Timber and Stone Act, 26
timber-dependent communities, 78, 116, 117, 124
Timber, OR, 19
Trask Basin prototype plan, 80, 82
Trask River, 19, 76
Turner, Frederick Jackson, 39, 40, 41

U.S. Fish and Wildlife Service, 88, 127, 137, 142
University of Washington, 76, 77
understory: in forest, 75, 82, 89; stand type, 79, 80, 82
utilitarianism, 46, 48, 52, 53, 157, 158

vegetation control, 65
Vernonia, OR, 19

Walker, Gregg, 161, 162
Washington County, 14
Weeks, Jennifer 107
West, the American, 22, 25-29, 32, 36, 38, 40-45, 54, 115, 116, 117

Weyerhaeuser Co., 59, 63
White, Richard, 22, 25, 29, 32, 36, 40, 54
wildlife, threatened, 78, 82, 83, 87-89, 100, 128, 136, 137-40
Wilson River, 16, 19, 73, 145: Highway, 59, 69, 151
woody debris, 76, 86, 90, 101, 166
worldview, 38, 39, 43, 44, 50, 51, 69, 155, 157, 158, 160, 162, 163, 168, 172, 173: arcadian, 5, 39, 47-50, 52-54, 60, 109, 154-56, 158, 160, 167, 168, 172, 173, 179; frontier, 38, 39, 43, 45, 46, 49-51, 65, 66, 154-57, 160, 164, 166, 168, 169, 172, 173, 179. *See also* synthesis of worldviews
World War II, 20, 53, 63, 105
Worster, Donald, 47, 48, 49, 50, 110, 158

Yamhill County, 14, 21
Yamhill *Reporter,* 23, 28, 36

Other titles in the
Culture and Environment in the Pacific West series

Series Editor: WilliamL. Lang

Empty Nets: Indians, Dams, and the Columbia River
by Roberta Ulrich

Frigid Embrace: Politics, Economics, and Environment in Alaska
by Stephen Haycox

The Great Northwest: The Search for Regional Identity
edited by William G. Robbins

Planning a New West: The Columbia River Gorge National Scenic Area
edited by Carl Abbott, Sy Adler, and Margery Post Abbott

About the Author

Gail Wells is an independent writer, editor, and communications consultant. She lives and works in a renovated nineteenth-century country schoolhouse on three acres near Monmouth, Oregon, that has been in her family for three generations. She is at work on a book of essays about making a family place one's own. She is also the coauthor, with Dawn Anzinger, of *Lewis and Clark Meet Oregon's Forests: Lessons from Dynamic Nature* (Oregon Forest Resources Institute, 2001). She and her husband John have two grown children.